# DEALING WITH
# disruptive students
## IN THE CLASSROOM

Jerry Olsen & Paul Cooper

THE TIMES EDUCATIONAL SUPPLEMENT

KOGAN
PAGE

*For our children*

First published in 2001

Kogan Page Limited
120 Pentonville Road
London
N1 9JN
UK

Stylus Publishing Inc.
22883 Quicksilver Drive
Sterling
VA 20166-2012
USA

The views expressed in this book are those of the authors and are not necessarily the same as those of *The Times Educational Supplement*.

**British Library Cataloguing in Publication Data**

A CIP record for this book is available from the British Library.

ISBN 0 7494 3132 6

Typeset by D & N Publishing, Marlborough, Wiltshire
Printed and bound in Great Britain by Biddles Ltd, Guildford and King's Lynn

# Contents

# Preface

The bookshop browser who picks up this volume with a view to buying it will not need to be told that disruptive behaviour in schools is a complex problem. A major intention of the book is to help the reader to engage with this complexity in positive and effective ways. Having said this we do not claim that this book contains all the answers to all the questions about all the behavioural problems that teachers encounter in their daily practice. No such book exists, nor could exist. What this book offers is an opportunity for readers to reflect on some familiar and some less familiar ways of thinking about and approaching such problems. In particular we hope that readers will see the value of using well established behaviourist approaches within a systems framework. Our key message is that teachers can influence and shape student behaviour most effectively when management techniques are employed with careful reference to the social and institutional contexts that impinge on behaviour. Put simply, we believe that positive behaviour can be facilitated by the practice of cooperation rather than coercion. We see this task in terms of the need to create the conditions that give students *access* to positive behaviour, rather than seeing behavioural norms as things to be imposed on students. In this sense it is not the behavioural techniques alone that change students' behaviour, rather it is the manner in which these techniques are developed, agreed to and applied that make up the core of the approach presented.

The specific interventions described in this book have been selected largely on the basis of the first hand experience of one of the authors (Olsen). In addition examples are provided from published sources. As such they are presented as examples of what worked in particular situations with particular people at a particular time. This is not to say that they will always work in other situations. What we think will work, by and large, is the thinking that underpins the analysis of problem situations and the endeavour to actively involve relevant stakeholders in the generation of solutions. Ultimately, this is a book about how to encourage students to choose to behave in positive, pro-social and pro-school ways.

*Jerry Olsen, University of Canberra, Australia*
*Paul Cooper, University of Leicester, England*
*April, 2001*

# Acknowledgements

This book was first conceived at the University of Cambridge School of Education in the spring of 1999. Paul was on the staff there and acted as Jerry's host during his study leave from the University of Canberra. The book emerged from a shared and long standing interest in the application of systems theory to social, emotional and behavioural problems in schools. We'd both like to thank our mutual friend and colleague Dr Jim Mitchell (retired from the University of Canberra) for bringing us together.

Susan Trost worked tirelessly, researching elements of the book, reading through drafts, and offering suggestions. We are especially grateful.

Particular thanks are due to Pam Fairhurst, Julie Bethwaite (Cumbria LEA), Lynne Blount and Val Scott (Essex LEA) for their constructive contribution to the development of the evaluation strategies described in Chapter 10.

Thanks are also due to Peggy Nunn, in Cambridge, for her efficient and always good-humoured secretarial support, and to Jonathan Simpson at Kogan Page. The anonymous reviewer whose thoughtful and constructive comments helped clarify and extend some of our thinking also deserves our appreciation and thanks.

Thank you to Peter Olsen for his talented drawings and to Alan Nicol for his skilled work on figures. Thanks also to Sandi Plummer, Tony Shaddock, Ken Howell, Scott Henggeler, Robert Tauber, Vern Jones, Scott Dolquist, Ann Loftus, George Huitker, Careen Leslie, Dylan Mordyke, and Anna Olsen for helpful discussion, and to Rebecca Frantz and Joan Livermore for generous support. We are grateful to all these people.

The book includes contributions from the following, to whom we are also grateful: Phillip Hopkins, who currently teaches in the School of Teacher Education at the University of Canberra; Ann Owner, who manages the education services of the Australian War Memorial in Canberra; and Mick McManus, who is Principal Lecturer in the School of Education, Leeds Metropolitan University, for kind permission to reproduce the extract from his work that appears on page 19.

Rosanne, Catherine, and Emily Cooper, as always, were, throughout the long process of writing this book, more tolerant and supportive than they had to be of disruptions to family life.

Finally, we'd like to thank the curator of the Freud Museum in Hampstead for a memorable and diverting morning's visit.

# 1
# Dealing with change effectively

## Problem behaviour and the problem of change

It was late one black autumn night, and there was a drunk on his hands and knees rummaging in the dead leaves beneath a street light. After a while a woman came by and stopped. Although aware of the woman's presence the drunk ignored her, and, not unlike a pig searching for truffles, continued to prod and probe in the disc of light beneath the lamp.

After watching the drunk for some time, the woman asked, innocently, 'Have you lost something?'

'Quiche,' slurred the drunk without looking up. 'I've losht my quiche.'

'The poor man must be starving, to be searching for food in such a filthy place!' thought the woman. But after watching the drunk scraping tracks through the leaves for another minute or so the woman understood. 'Keys!' she said out loud. Then she added, with an air of triumph, 'You've lost your keys!'

'Thash what I shed,' said the drunk, still continuing with his search. 'I losht my quiche.'

Wanting to be helpful, the woman tried to re-engage the drunk. 'So you dropped your keys somewhere under this streetlight!'

For the first time since the woman's arrival the drunk stopped his foraging and fixed her with the unsteady gaze from one bloodshot eye. He was becoming irritated by this unwelcome and inquisitive stranger. 'Although it is none of your bishnish, for your info-mayshun, I losht my key-sh over there!' With that the drunk raised an unsteady hand and, swaying on the rickety tripod of his knees and one arm, pointed to the other side of the street, which was in complete darkness.

As the drunk resumed his search, the woman pondered the situation, but failing to make sense out of it asked, 'But if you lost your keys over there, why are you looking for them over here?'

The drunk now looked up from his search, annoyed by the stupidity of this question. This time both bleary eyes were directed at the woman, as the drunk said condescendingly, but with surprising clarity: 'I am searching over here because the light is better over here. Nobody could find anything over there in the dark, because it is too dark to find anything over there!' Now it was his turn to feel triumphant. 'So if you don't mind, I cannot waste any more time answering your childish questions. I still have to find my quiche.' Then, as he once again plunged snout first into the illuminated pile of dead leaves, the drunk mumbled to himself, 'and after that I've got find my damn car!'

This old joke illustrates a lot about human behaviour. Like all good jokes it points to some kind of basic truth that most people instantly recognize. On the one hand we sympathize with the woman's compassionate and logical approach, on the other hand we see something undeniably human in the drunk's behaviour. Most of us know exactly what it feels like to be engaged in a totally irrational pursuit and to be resentful of the intrusions of others, however well meaning and even potentially helpful these might be. Of course, at the time when we are engaged in the irrational behaviour we do not see it as irrational. When we are looking for our keys where the light is, rather than where we lost them, we are doing it for what seems to us, at the time, a very good reason. In fact the more some interfering busybody tries to tell us how irrational our behaviour is, the more we want to show them that it is they who are wrong. In order to do this we put more effort into our irrational pursuit. In return the busybody will sometimes put more effort into their mission of telling us that we are wrong. And so on...

At the heart of this situation is the problem of change. Somebody deviates from the pattern of behaviour that is expected, and some one else decides that this is unacceptable and must be stopped. The change to the normal pattern of things has to be irradicated or reversed and circumstances restored to how they were before the change took place. Sometimes this is a very straightforward process, and the perpetrator of the unwanted behaviour responds to the demand to stop what they are doing. This happens everyday in classrooms and families all over the world: the child begins to make a loud and irritating noise, the parent/teacher says, 'Stop doing that!'; the child stops. In other cases, however, the child doesn't stop, and the more the parent/teacher demands silence the louder and more irritating the noise becomes.

At the heart of this book is a simple argument: If the approach adopted by the school doesn't work, change it to an approach that does work, preferably one that is supported by research evidence.

Of course, in the case of the drunk, there would be no joke if he simply accepted the young woman's logic, and adjusted his search strategy accordingly. And, by and large, it has to be said that most employees do not get the sack, most families do not fall victim to estrangement or divorce, and most students do not find themselves excluded from school. It is surprising, perhaps, the extent to which human beings accept and submit to the behavioural demands and limits that other people assert. On the other hand it is cooperation of this kind that keeps social interaction in general positive and productive. It is the guiding principle of this book that we can understand and exploit the processes by which people gain each other's cooperation, even in circumstances where an individual appears to be bent on being, at all costs, uncooperative.

## Emotional and behavioural difficulties (EBDs) and antisocial behaviour in schools

Schools and classrooms are excellent places for learning about this to-ing and fro-ing of control, consent, cooperation and resistance in social and interpersonal relations. In many classrooms much of the time the emphasis is on consent and cooperation, with most students and teachers working harmoniously toward common goals. Sometimes, however, things go wrong, and when things go wrong teachers and students sometimes adopt one or other of the roles of the drunk and the woman in the story that opened this chapter. In this section we explore the range and nature of some of the problems that teachers in schools may experience.

It is estimated that in England, at the time of writing, between 10 per cent and 20 per cent of school students in the 4 to 16 age range experience emotional and behavioural difficulties (EBDs) to a degree that causes significant impairment to their social and educational development (Young Minds, 1999). The problems that fall under the heading of EBDs include, among others: depression, phobias and conduct disorder. The prevalence of these problems increases to its peak in the adolescent years. It is difficult to make national comparisons, because of differences in classification systems, but current evidence would suggest that in the United States similar levels of problems exist (Walker, Colvin and Ramsey, 1995). In practice, of course, it is often difficult to separate the emotional problems from the conduct problems.

In addition to these severe behavioural problems is a range of more minor, but, to teachers and their classes, often equally disruptive patterns of unwanted behaviour, which might be termed 'routine indiscipline'. The British government published one of the most comprehensive surveys of this problem ever undertaken (DES, 1989), and revealed the following key problems as being most commonly cited by teachers in primary and secondary schools in England and Wales:

- talking out of turn;
- calculated idleness and work avoidance;
- students who hindered other students in their work;
- students who were not punctual;
- students who made unnecessary non-verbal noises.

The authors of the report concluded that, in contrast to the more deep-seated problems referred to earlier, these routine acts of indiscipline were largely the product of contextual factors in the classroom or school situation. The major remedies for these problems were seen as residing in the need for improved school effectiveness, through the development of carefully targeted, clear and comprehensive whole-school policies, and the improvement of teachers' classroom management skills.

An important thing to bear in mind here is that in the school and classroom context it is sometimes difficult to draw a clear-cut distinction between emotional and behavioural difficulties and routine indiscipline. The methods by which the school and teacher create an environment that promotes the positive engagement of students from both of these groups are often identical.

A unifying feature of all EBDs, whether they are seen as reflecting underlying disturbance or as routine indiscipline, is that they are disturbing to schools, teachers and others who come into contact with the child who appears be at the centre of these problems, in that they undermine, subvert or detract from the formal educational functions of schools. The array of behavioural manifestations that might fall under the heading of EBDs is enormous and, at times, seemingly paradoxical. Students' emotional difficulties may manifest themselves in terms of extreme withdrawal from social involvement, leading to social isolation within school, and possibly truancy or school refusal. At another level, the student with emotional difficulties may simply be preoccupied with emotional concerns to the extent that this interferes with the learning process. Students with emotional difficulties may be involved in bullying, either as victims or perpetrators. They may be violent towards others, or, in some cases, be self-harming. Children with such difficulties may also engage in attention-seeking behaviours, which can involve activities that attract the positive or negative attention of others. The energy that is devoted to such behaviour is often at the expense of 'legitimate' classroom behaviour, and consequently tends to attract the negative attention of teachers, in the form of reprimands and punishments. To the attention-seeking child, however, negative attention is a desirable alternative to no attention at all.

As already noted, the most commonly cited forms of behavioural disturbance in classrooms take the form of unauthorized student talk, the hindrance of other pupils from working and other forms of behaviour that interfere with teaching and learning such as the use of verbal and non-verbal interventions, as well as forms of student behaviour that directly challenge the authority of the teacher (from straightforward 'cheek' to verbal abuse, and, in rare cases, physical assault) (DES, 1989; Wheldall, 1987). Other sometimes extremely severe problems include: hyperactivity, bullying, problem sexual behaviour and damage to property. Less disturbing (in the sense of disruptive) but evidently 'disturbed' behaviours include extreme inattentiveness, socially withdrawn behaviour, and phobic and obsessive patterns of behaviour (Blau and Gullotta, 1996). Of related concern is a group of problems that whether or not they are enacted in the school environment are often related, directly or indirectly, to dysfunctional conduct or under-performance in school. This group includes delinquency and substance abuse.

The form of behaviour most disruptive to schools, families and communities is what might be termed 'antisocial' behaviour. This is behaviour that is characterized by rule infringement, hostility to others, defiance of authority and aggression towards others (Walker, Colvin and Ramsey, 1995). Patterson, Reid and Dishion (1992), in their study of antisocial boys, defined antisocial behaviour in terms of 'coercion'. This empirically derived definition proposes that a core feature of antisocial behaviour is a range of behavioural events, experienced by others as socially aversive, that are characterized by the application, by an individual, of physical or psychological force in order to achieve desired ends.

# The development of serious behavioural problems

Patterson, Reid and Dishion (1992) identified nine variables that they found to be consistently associated with the development of delinquency and antisocial behaviour in boys. These are:

- social disadvantage;
- ineffective parental discipline;
- lack of parental supervision;
- parental use of physical punishment;
- parental rejection;
- peer rejection;

- membership of deviant peer group;
- academic failure;
- low self-esteem.

These variables are incorporated in a four-stage model, which describes the sequence of events commonly leading to what Patterson, Reid and Dishion term 'the career antisocial adult'. The stages are:

1. **Basic training**: this is the pre-school phase in which the child is 'trained' in coercive behaviour in the home setting. Parents and family members are often the unwitting trainers, who provide models and reinforcement for coercive behaviours through their daily interactions with their children.

2. **The social environment reacts**: behaviours which were, for the child, functional in the home situation are challenged when he enters school. The child becomes increasingly unmanageable as the antisocial behaviours escalate. This leads to conflict and rejection by parents, peers and the school.

3. **Deviant peers and polishing antisocial skills**: the experience of rejection leads to emotional problems, and as the child enters early adolescence he is drawn to a deviant peer group in which his skills of coercion are further reinforced and developed.

4. **The career antisocial adult**: this stage is characterized by the social marginalization of the adult. He will experience disruption in his personal relationships; will have difficulty securing and sustaining employment. He will be at greater risk than non-antisocial adults of mental health problems, substance abuse and imprisonment.

There are obvious limitations to this model. First, it deals exclusively with males. Second, it deals solely with long-term antisocial behaviour. Third, it focuses entirely on social and psychological issues, with no reference to individual predisposing factors, such as the biological dimension. This said, the model illustrates the interactive and cumulative nature of the way in which emotional and behavioural problems often develop. Put another way, the model illustrates the way in which a perceived problem (eg a child's non-compliant behaviour) is met with an attempted solution (eg direct opposition), which in turn leads to the exacerbation of the original problem (eg increased intensity of non-compliant behaviour), which in turn has further negative consequences (eg peer rejection) and so on. At the heart of this book is the conviction that it is only when we can begin to understand the complexity of such interactions that we can begin to intervene effectively in order to change a negative impetus into a positive impetus.

# The biopsychosocial perspective

The biopsychosocial approach draws on insights gained from research in genetics and cognitive neuroscience, and seeks to utilize understanding of the ways in which individual biology might interact with social and psychological factors. This paradigm is associated with sociobiology (Wilson, 1975), evolutionary psychology, and evolutionary psychiatry (Stevens and Price, 1996), each of which stresses the biological and evolutionary foundations of human behaviour.

The phenomena of attention deficit/hyperactivity disorder and Asperger's syndrome are examples of problems which may fall under the umbrella of EBDs and are believed to have biological bases. It is not necessary to elaborate in detail on the nature of these medically defined conditions. It is important, however, to stress two things about them: they affect a significant proportion of the school population, with a prevalence rate of 3–5 per cent for AD/HD, and 1:300 for Asperger's Syndrome; and they provide sources of disquiet for academics and professionals socialized into the psychosocial perspective and the rejection of the medical model.

The crucial aspect of the biopsychosocial approach is that it is interactional. It is not the same as the traditional medical model, which is often portrayed in terms of crude biological determinism. For example, a biopsychosocial approach does *not* suggest that a child born with a particular biological tendency is doomed to a particular pattern of life and behaviour. Rather the biopsychosocial approach highlights potential risk factors that can be averted by intervention (Frith, 1992). This is a developmentally informed approach which often stresses early intervention. Biopsychosocial interventions always place a heavy emphasis on psychological, social and educational factors, with biomedical intervention being only seen as an adjunct to these.

There are, of course, some well-grounded concerns about what is sometimes seen as a return to a biological perspective. Fears of a resurgence of eugenics are sometimes expressed (Rose, 1997, Slee, 1998). These fears, however, are based on a conflation of scientific and historical-political factors. Positive perspectives on the biopsychosocial approach stress that for it to work properly, the approach depends on effective interdisciplinary cooperation (Cooper, 1996). The challenge for the biopsychosocial approach (as it is for any other approach) is for it to be implemented in a responsible and professional way, and with the focus being firmly placed on the need to serve the best interests of the apparently problematic individual in his or her social context. This means that solutions may be sought to problems at the level of the individual, at the level of the individual's social and physical environment, or, at the level of the interaction between the individual and their environment.

# Behavioural, cognitive, and systemic interventions

Much of the outcomes evidence on the effectiveness of interventions used with children who display emotional and behavioural difficulties, aside from chemical interventions, falls into three broad schools of thought – Behavioural, Cognitive, and Systemic. Each of the three schools contains a variety of interventions. To better understand what the literature says about outcome studies, we give below a simple problem behaviour as an illustration, a brief definition of each of the three schools, and an example of an intervention for this problem drawn from each of the three schools.

Behavioural theorists (eg Wheldall, 1987) believe that the most effective way to help children with problem behaviours is to *teach the child new behaviours*, reinforce the child when he or she behaves appropriately, and withdraw the reinforcement, or punish the child, when he or she behaves inappropriately. A side benefit of directly changing the child's behaviour is that the child's *perceptions* might change, for example, the child's self-esteem may improve.

Cognitive theorists, like Seligman (1990), also believe that children displaying behavioural and emotional difficulties need to be taught new skills, but they teach different skills. To change a child's inappropriate behaviours, Cognitive theorists believe that one *changes the child's perceptions*. By changing beliefs, teaching the child to think or perceive differently, one can change a child's behaviour. In some ways, then, cognitive interventions work in the opposite direction to behavioural interventions.

Systems theorists (eg Cooper and Upton, 1991) believe that children displaying behavioural and emotional difficulties are a product of the *interactions*, the links between the child and people in his or her world. One should study these links between people even more than study the people's behaviour or attitudes, and study the pattern, the life of the behaviour problem, because problems can take on a life of their own. An intervention for a child displaying a behavioural difficulty could involve changing the way adults respond, interact, and communicate around the problem. To help the child, a mediator might change the structure and pattern of interactions between stakeholders, especially between parents, the teacher, and the principal. In its pure form a mediator might not teach the child anything, and this is an essential difference between systemic thinking and the other two schools, behavioural and cognitive, both of which involve teaching the students new skills.

## Example of interventions

PROBLEM: At school, Ruth hits children who tease her

For a behavioural approach one might analyse what happens around the hitting, just before the behaviour, the 'antecedent', and just after the behaviour, the 'consequence' (A-B-C analysis):

1. Antecedent – Children tease Ruth.
2. Behaviour – Ruth hits children.
3. Consequence – Ruth is sent to 'time-out'.

A behavioural analysis of this sequence might lead us to believe that children teasing Ruth cue her hitting, but that 'time-out' as a consequence has no deterrent effect on her hitting, otherwise Ruth would stop. An intervention could include the following changes to the antecedents and consequences of the problem behaviour:

1. Antecedent – Teasing children are not allowed to play near Ruth.
2. Behaviour – The teacher watches for times when Ruth plays cooperatively and does not hit.
3. Consequence – Ruth gets a point on a points-card for every playtime that passes when she does not hit, and these points are later exchanged for time on the computer.

A cognitive approach might include a different analysis of hitting, an A-B-C-D-E analysis around Ruth's sequence of thinking:

1. Adversity – The other kids tease me.
2. Belief – That means the kids must hate me.
3. Consequence – That hurts my feelings, so I hit them.

A possible cognitive intervention would aim to break the sequence at the belief stage by teaching Ruth to argue with, to 'dispute', her faulty perceptions:

4. Disputation – Just because they tease me doesn't mean they hate me; they tease lots of kids.
5. Energization – I still feel a little sad, but they don't make me angry any more.

So, by changing her perceptions, Ruth stops her feelings from being hurt, and changes her hitting behaviour.

A systemic analysis might point to problems in the interactions between Ruth's mother and the school. Perhaps Ruth's mother is in a coalition with Ruth against parents of other children, and against the school, and the barriers between adults have solidified the parents and staff into warring camps. The interactions have formed into a Victim-Persecutor-Rescuer triangle, and this has blocked communication between the important adults in Ruth's life. Ruth's mother sees her child as a victim, and she is driven to protect her daughter from the teasing children at school, and from teachers who won't stop the harassment. She urges Ruth to stick up for herself whenever children tease her.

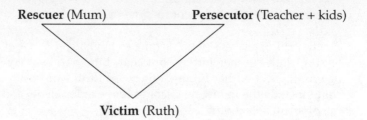

**Rescuer** (Mum)                    **Persecutor** (Teacher + kids)

**Victim** (Ruth)

A possible systemic intervention could involve a mediator who looks for strengths in the various systems – home/school/peers – and helps the parents and staff find common ground, for example, that teasing and hitting are circular, the anger is feeding a bi-directional escalating beast – teasing begets hitting; hitting begets teasing; teasing begets hitting, and so on. Parents and staff both agree that such behaviours need to be dealt with in the school. The mediator uses these common standards of parents and staff as strengths between the home and school systems to assemble an agreed-upon policy against verbal and physical bullying in the school. This builds a cooperative alliance between the adults in Ruth's life, stops the escalating tit-for-tat payback between children, and between adults, and stops Ruth's hitting.

On their own, each of these interventions would have drawbacks. Behavioural and cognitive interventions give only short-term change, systemic approaches in isolation seldom have the power to work. As we discuss below, the most effective interventions for students who display emotional and behavioural difficulties combine techniques drawn from all three schools – behavioural, cognitive, and systemic, as well as chemical, educational and other forms of intervention that are shown in the research literature to work.

## Evidence for the effectiveness of interventions

The first thing to note here is that, in practice, intervention with EBDs is rarely an evidence-based practice (Walker, Colvin and Ramsey, 1995). Popular texts which deal with approaches to behaviour management tend to offer descriptive accounts of approaches and their theoretical underpinnings, with only limited reference to their measured effectiveness. Intervention strategies, therefore, tend to be chosen for ideological and other reasons, rather than for their evaluated effectiveness.

This leads us immediately to a central claim that has been made for the behavioural paradigm: that it offers educational researchers: [an] extremely effective methodology to evaluate the effectiveness of change and innovation, irrespective of its theoretical origins, providing that there is commitment to conceptual rigour coupled with a reluctance to talk about 'benefits which cannot be measured' (Wheldall, 1987: 13). Wheldall goes on to caution (somewhat trenchantly):

---

If they [ie educational researchers] do want to talk about unmeasurable benefits they may as well save themselves the trouble of carrying out research in the first place, and to discuss them *ex post facto*, when the evidence has not gone your way, is quite simply dishonest.

---

This scathing rebuke for the perceived woolly mindedness of some educational research is well placed and provides us with a firm basis on which to proceed with a comparative analysis of the effectiveness of different approaches to dealing with social, emotional and behavioural difficulties.

In setting out on this quest there are two major characteristics of effective interventions that we will seek to assess. The first of these is generalizability. This describes the extent to which the behavioural changes attributed to a particular intervention are sustained in settings other than the one in which the change is secured. The second characteristic of effectiveness is maintenance. This refers to the extent to which the changes are sustained over time (Stokes and Baer, 1977).

## The effectiveness of behavioural and cognitive behavioural approaches

The behavioural and cognitive behavioural approaches continue to be dominant approaches for dealing with antisocial and other emotional and behavioural problems throughout the world. Early ethical concerns about its over-reliance on punishment have been resolved, with modern behavioural approaches being focused on the reinforcement of positive behaviour (Wheldall, 1987) and cognitive training in self-management (Yell, Drasgow, and Rosalski, 1999), though the legacy of this negative approach is still to be found in the practice of some teachers (Yell, Drasgow, and Rosalski, 1999).

Walker, Colvin and Ramsey (1995) describe and evaluate a series of behavioural interventions aimed at reducing 'negative-aggressive behaviour among elementary school-age boys'. The interventions employed were: adult praise, token reinforcement and cost contingency (ie the loss of previously awarded points as a form of punishment). Two groups of six students were studied, and assigned to two different experimental conditions one after the other, each for three months. The difference between the two experimental conditions related to the combinations in which the interventions were applied. Outcomes of the study indicated that the use of social praise alone was extremely ineffective in promoting pro-social behaviour and reducing negative behaviour. By contrast the combination of social praise, tokens, and cost contingency was found to be highly effective in achieving positive change in the experimental setting. However, generalization and maintenance effects were reported to be poor. Follow-up studies carried out one month after the children were returned to the settings from which they had been referred found the improvements maintained, but after six months levels of negative behaviour had returned to baseline levels.

The pattern of high efficacy in the immediate situation where the intervention is applied, but generally poor maintenance and generalization of positive effects is characteristic of behavioural and cognitive behavioural approaches. Kazdin (1998), in a rigorous review of the effectiveness of different psychological 'treatments' for children with conduct disorder, found that the best evidence for cognitive-behavioural approaches in randomized clinical trials involved problem-solving skills training. The findings of a number of studies indicated that this clinic-based intervention approach significantly reduced aggressive and antisocial behaviour in the home, at school, and in the community, but these improvements were only maintained for a maximum of one year after treatment ended, and usually, one assumes, much less.

Researchers found more powerful effects when they taught parent management skills to the parents of antisocial children and adolescents. This involves a therapist working with the parents of an antisocial child, but often without the therapist having direct contact with the child. The therapy sessions involve training the parents in constructive ways of viewing behaviour, and in the techniques of behaviour management, including reinforcement strategies and the manipulation of antecedents and consequences. As the parents' mastery increases they are encouraged to address wider problems, including such things as their child's educational difficulties and or/his or her school behavioural problems. The best effects of this approach are reported in terms of the normalization of children's behaviour (ie when compared to their age peers) in family, school and community settings. Furthermore, follow-up studies have found long-term gains of one to three years, whilst two studies are cited which claim 10–14 year maintenance (Kazdin, 1998). Other evidence for efficacy of parent training is found in the work of Patterson, Reid and Dishion (1992) and a model described by Reid (in press).

The evidence reviewed here indicates that if the aim of intervention is to produce generalized positive outcomes that are maintained over time then it is necessary to move beyond focusing on the child's surface behaviour alone and to give detailed consideration to a wider range of social and psychological factors. In particular, this involves giving attention to individuals' cognitive processes and social relationships. These findings resonate powerfully with Patterson, Reid and Dishion's (1992) coercion model, and indicate the possibility that students' antisocial and aggressive behaviour is learned, and that this learning can be undone and replaced by new learning if interventions are targeted on changing the way in which the child goes about achieving their goals. One way of doing this seems to involve direct intervention in their thinking and problem-solving processes, though this approach will not give the long-term change of other approaches. The most promising approach, however, seems to involve intervening directly in the processes which are posited to be key influences in the generation of the undesirable behaviour in the first place: that is the interaction between the child and his or her family. This brings us neatly to a consideration of systemic approaches.

# The effectiveness of systemic approaches

Henggeler and Borduin (1990) describe a 'multisystemic model' of intervention. This differs from other systemic family therapy models in that it employs non-linear systemic approaches alongside more conventional approaches. This means that the multisystemic approach, whilst recognizing the interactional and relational aspects of childhood behavioural problems, also involves an appreciation of the personal and individual developmental factors. So, the multisystemic approach will, when appropriate, employ conventional behavioural and cognitive interventions that are unambiguously directed at changing the individual's behaviour. A particular feature of the approach is that it is community based, with the therapeutic team going into the neighbourhoods, schools and families of difficult teenagers, and being available to provide support when and where it is needed. The approach also demands a cooperative relationship to be developed between members of the therapy team and individuals in the target community (Henggeler, 1999).

Existing systemic approaches, they claim, have at least three weaknesses: 1) they fail to sufficiently consider the role of individual characteristics of the child, or systems outside the core family, like the school, peers, grandparents, etc; 2) they tend to ignore the child development research; 3) they ignore 'linear-reductionist' approaches, like behaviourism, and even consider the approaches inherently 'bad' (Henggeler and Borduin, 1990).

Evidence for the success of this model is impressive. Henggeler and Borduin (1990) cite nine separate studies undertaken between 1986 and 1996 that indicate that the multisystemic approach is effective in reducing the aversive behaviours and increasing the prosocial behaviours of, traditionally, the most difficult client group, that is, serious, often chronic juvenile offenders, including those convicted of sexual and other violent crimes and substance-abusing and – dependent individuals. These studies report that the improvements observed were maintained for periods of up to three years.

Henggeler and Borduin (1990) provide detailed accounts of three studies which illustrate the efficacy of the multisystemic approach. The first study involves 79 African American, mostly male, adolescent repeat offenders from working-class backgrounds. These offenders each received, on average, 20 hours of multisystemic therapy. The outcome of this group was compared with that for a group of 22 adolescents with similar characteristics, and a control group of 44 adolescents exhibiting no problems. On the basis of pre- and post-treatment assessments of the adolescent and their parents, and an assessment battery including a personality inventory, behaviour rating scales, self-report and observational measures of family relations, it was concluded that the multisystemic intervention resulted in a statistically significant decrease in conduct problems, anxious withdrawn behaviours, immature behaviour and level of association with delinquent peers.

Specific improvements included statistically significant decreases in conduct problems, repeat offending, anxious withdrawn behaviours, immature behaviour, drug and substance abuse, and level of association with delinquent peers. On the positive side improvements were observed and reported in family relations, parent–child interactions, improved peer relations and increased school attendance.

# Combining models

In many respects what is new about the approach developed throughout this book is the combining of behavioural, cognitive, systemic and other approaches, a proposition that may seem patently obvious, but is seldom used as a basis for practice. Over the years these different schools of thought have sometimes been portrayed as being in conflict with one another. Accusations of reductionism have been levelled at behavioural theorists, whilst systems approaches have been criticized for the lack of hard evidence about their efficacy. As we have seen, the multisystemic model (Swenson et al, 1998) has produced some of the most impressive evidence of effectiveness so far available. Interestingly, this apparently successful approach to helping youths at risk can be measured, and combines those approaches that have at least some empirical support, including behavioural (Munger, 1993), cognitive behavioural (Kendall and Brasswell, 1993), and the structural and strategic systems approaches of Minuchin (1974) and Haley (1987). It is our view that this evidence base provides a powerful endorsement for the approaches we outline in this book. We recognize also, however, that we are by no means the first to recommend a systems framework in relation to emotional and behavioural difficulties in schools. We are aware of the debt that some of our thinking owes to the earlier work of writers such as Amatea (1988), Brown (1986), Okun (1984), Williams and Weeks (1984), Campion (1985), Provis (1994), and Dowling and Osborne (1995). Acknowledgement of this is provided in earlier publications (Cooper, Smith and Upton, 1994; Cooper and Upton, 1991; Olsen, 1989a, b; Olsen and Nathan, 1987). It is hoped that the readers will see the ways in which the present book complements and extends this existing work.

# 2

# Teaching, learning and disruptive behaviour

In this chapter we examine some important features of the school situation and how these may relate to issues of disruptive behaviour. In particular we will focus on the ways in which teachers and students influence one another in the classroom, and how knowledge of these patterns of influence might help in the prevention and management of disruptive behaviour. Before doing this, however, we will briefly address some common but unhelpful ways of thinking about disruption that can undermine the teacher's ability to deal effectively with problem behaviour.

## Myths about teaching and disruptive behaviour

There are some common myths about disruptive behaviour in the classroom. As with most myths they are each based on a grain of truth, but the myth-making process has distorted and subverted that truth and turned it into nonsense.

### 'Good teachers don't have discipline problems'

This is the myth that is promoted by that staffroom bore whose response to other people's complaints about classroom behaviour problems is to say 'I don't have discipline problems', or (with reference to the child with whom you have difficulty) 'he is no trouble in my lessons.' The effect of this myth is to encourage secrecy and shame to be attached to behavioural problems, so that they remain hidden from outside scrutiny. This myth can also lead to a tendency to pathologize and reject children who present difficulties rather than to engage in efforts to address problems constructively. Ironically, therefore, this view can be associated with student exclusion and draconian selection processes that some schools employ.

The problem with this myth is that it is based on a wholly erroneous view of the nature of teaching and learning as a static process, whereby the teacher transmits and the student receives. Teaching (good teaching, that is) is essentially a process of exchange and negotiation, in which the teacher constantly creates, delivers and modifies learning situations in response to developing knowledge of the nature and characteristics of individual students. The teaching and learning process, like human relationships, involves the coming together of individuals with all their idiosyncratic differences and differing agendas, expectations, desires and intentions. This means that sooner or later a conflict of intentions and interests is inevitable. There is bound to come a point, even in the classroom of the most effective and charismatic teacher, when this conflict leads to a breakdown (or potential breakdown) of the pattern of co-operation.

## 'Teachers are born and not made'

This is another powerful myth. It is encapsulated in the view that skilled teaching is a consequence of a certain personality type. From this viewpoint good teaching is often coupled with the idea of personal charisma. This is a seductive view. It is clearly the case that charismatic individuals, by definition, are attractive and popular with others. It is also the case that charismatic people are able to exert influence over others. These characteristics are of obvious value to the teacher. On their own, however, they do not make for a good teacher, any more than they make for a good politician or other leader. There are qualities of thought and reflection, which are not necessarily visible to the observer, that are essential to effective teaching, as well as qualities of empathy and a willingness to listen to others that are essential to effective teaching.

The dangers of the 'charismatic' view can be illustrated by an experience had by one of the authors during a research project. The author had observed a very popular and charismatic teacher deliver an English lesson to a group of 11-year-olds on the subject of the similarities and differences between plays and novels. The lesson had been apparently very successful. The teacher had made an exposition and engaged the class in a carefully orchestrated question and answer session, before giving them some written work. He had employed group work also. The atmosphere in the classroom was purposeful, productive and lively, and the students maintained a high level of on-task behaviour throughout, whilst clearly enjoying interaction with the teacher. At the end of the lesson both teacher and students felt that the lesson had gone well, and that it represented a good example of an effective teacher promoting effective learning. The teacher felt that he had 'got across' the key differences between novels and plays, and the students felt that they had completed the lesson tasks appropriately, and were pleased with the support that the teacher had given them. In particular many of the students referred to the kindliness and humour of the teacher and the warmth and pleasantness of his personality. What also emerged, however, from these conversations was the bafflement among some students as to what the lesson had actually been about. One of the students, for example, was puzzled because he did not know what 'a novel' actually was. It is important to stress that these students were not complaining. Rather, they gave the impression that the fact that they had not understood the content of the lesson was a minor flaw in what had been a generally enjoyable experience. That is, they had gained satisfaction from passing an hour in the company of a likeable adult, and for them the curricular content was subordinate to this pleasure.

In the case of this teacher, he detected the gap in the students' knowledge in a subsequent lesson and dealt with it. The point illustrated by this story, however, is that the charismatic, personally engaging person is not necessarily an effective teacher. In fact such personality traits can have the potential to mask ineffective teaching.

## 'You've either got it or you haven't got it'

Another variant of the 'teachers are born and not made' myth is that 'you've either got the ability to be a good teacher or you haven't'. In this myth good teachers are sometimes portrayed as 'the hit squad', 'the cavalry', or 'the super-teacher/head' who are called in to sort out the problems of lesser mortals. The arrival of the saviour may even be greeted by the unfortunate recipient(s) of the service with the words: 'thank goodness you've arrived!' The implications of this myth are that there is a cadre of 'good teachers' somewhere out there, and that this group can be contrasted with those less-good and bad teachers. The problem with this view is that it portrays teaching ability as a fixed quality of the individual. It fails to take into account the complex nature of teaching and ways in which the characteristics of the individual teacher interact with the teaching environment. An individual teacher's performance in a particular setting will inevitably be influenced by a range of factors, to the extent that the same teacher may be successful on one occasion but unsuccessful the next.

This point is illustrated by a story told by Mick McManus about the time when he was deputy head teacher in a special school for children with behavioural and learning difficulties (McManus, 1994). He describes the story as 'painfully embarrassing'. The following are his own words:

## Mick McManus's story

In 1985 I left my post in a school for secondary age students with moderate learning difficulties and behavioural problems and began a three-year second-ment to research behavioural problems and exclusion from school. I had worked in the school for five years, and although the students were extreme-ly difficult, I seldom found myself under pressure. I put it down to experience (I had previously run a unit for excluded students on my own), expertise (I thought I had the necessary teaching skills), and understanding (degrees in psy-chology and sociology).

The secondment came to an end but not before the manuscript of my book on how to cope with troublesome students had been delivered to the pub-lisher (McManus, 1989). Returning to school, full of ideas, I found I couldn't control my classes. All my skills and expertise had no effect. The students I had known had left, and none of those in the school remembered me. Although I had written a book about surviving in such situations, I couldn't survive myself. I began to consider throwing in the job altogether. My book lists 50 classroom management skills, but they couldn't have seemed more irrelevant.

What had happened? In taking a detached approach to the problems of teaching difficult children, I had forgotten about the need for the personal qualities of resilience, patience, optimism and indestructibility. I had been suc-cessful before, not just because of my skills, but because I had convinced the students I was dependable – that no matter what happened, or however they behaved, I would still be working with them in the morning. Establishing that level of trust takes time. Things improved a little after the first term, and by the end of the year I was more or less back on the stable footing I had enjoyed before I left.

(McManus, 1994: 60–61)

So, what is Mick saying here? His key words are 'resilience, patience, opti-mism and indestructibility'. On the face of it these words might be inter-preted as personality characteristics, and thus supportive of our second myth. This is not so, however. Mick's point is that although there are impor-tant skills to be learned that will help the teacher to be successful in coping with disruptive and difficult students, skills alone are not enough. Those skills have to be practised over time. They do not necessarily produce instant results. They may even fail disastrously when they are first tried. Success depends on the ability to apply the intervention that is appropriate to the context. By context we mean, among other things, the history of the relationship that exists between the teacher and the student, group or class and the way that interacts with the current situation. Mick McManus's story illustrates this powerfully. Influence in the classroom is not just a one-way process.

# Teaching as a 'craft'

The complex 'craft knowledge' of teaching (Tom, 1984) involves highly specialized understandings (Brown and McIntyre, 1993; Cooper and McIntyre, 1996) which are built up over time and largely through experience. Like other areas of skilled performance (such as the arts, sport, scientific research, carpentry, and architecture) experienced practitioners can often be distinguished from novices by their level of competence and explicit knowledge about what they are doing. There is other knowledge, however, that may be fresher in the mind of the novice than in that of the experienced practitioner, because the knowledge is so internalized by the experienced practitioner and such an integral part of his or her daily practice, that it is no longer a subject of conscious reflection. It doesn't need to be reflected on. The value of this automaticity is that it enables the skilled teacher to act quickly and sure-footedly in the busy classroom situation, whilst having their mind free to concentrate on other issues. In these (ideal) circumstances management of the classroom situation may appear to be effortless and incidental to the subject content of the lesson. Research has shown that teachers make many, probably hundreds of, decisions in the course of a teaching day, which are based on an appraisal of the conditions in which they are operating and the relationship of the conditions with tasks they want students to perform (Cooper and McIntyre, 1996; Brown and McIntyre, 1993). Similarly, they will be able to tell at a glance whether or not the majority of students in the class are engaged in the desired state of activity, and will know when and how to intervene in order to adjust and maintain this state (ibid). Although this craft process is necessarily partly unconscious at the time of execution – if it were not it would be mentally exhausting – it can be brought to the surface and made available to teacher reflection when required, as research studies show (eg Clandinin, 1986; Brown and McIntyre, 1993; Cooper and McIntyre, 1996).

# Bi-directionality in the classroom and the relationship between behaviour and learning

Of course, the flow of influence in the classroom is not just one way, though maybe we sometimes wish it were, rather it is 'bi-directional' (Shavelson *et al*, 1986). Teachers bring influence to bear on students, and students bring influence to bear on teachers. This view is fully consistent with current conceptualizations of the nature of teaching and learning as 'transactional' processes (Bruner, 1987). According to this view the teacher's task is to provide a structure, like a builder's scaffold, for the learner. The effectiveness of this scaffolding process depends on the extent to which the teacher has gained accurate insight into the level of understanding and current educational capacity of the learner (Bruner and Haste, 1987). The crucial issue here is that fundamentally the individual child has two levels of learning capacity, the first is the capacity that can be achieved by the child alone, and the second is the capacity that can be achieved by the child with the aid of a more competent helper (eg teacher). This second level of capacity has been termed the zone of proximal development (ZPD) (Reiber and Carton, 1987).

Both access to the ZPD, and the effective educational manipulation of it, are dependent on social processes. Teachers and learners have to be able to interact purposefully with one another, and be willing to share their personal ways of seeing the world. Teachers and learners must not only be able to tell each other what they know and can do, but also what they do not know and cannot (at the moment) do. Effective teaching and learning, therefore, is dependent on the age-old human qualities of honesty and trust (Cooper and McIntyre, 1996).

Teachers' craft knowledge has been shown to be concerned, in part, with the know-how of working in the ZPD (ibid). Students also, have been shown to possess their own 'craft knowledge', which involves strategies and techniques for exploiting the 'scaffolding' provided by the teacher. And just as a further aspect of teachers' craft knowledge involves strategies and techniques for managing the behaviour and misbehaviour of students, so students possess an equivalent set of skills for managing their teachers.

# Power in the classroom

As we enter the 21st century, world changes are creating a new set of challenges for us all. Not least are the confusions and insecurities created by the collapse of old certainties. Along with the constant threat of economic recession, the past 50 years have seen the gradual dissolution of some key anchors of stability, such as the family, life-long employment and the value of education. People of all generations see themselves as vulnerable and, in many respects, alone and facing an uncertain future. Teachers feel persecuted from above by what they see as the increasingly unreasonable demands of cash-strapped governments and bureaucrats who fail to take account of the realities of teaching (Garner, 1999). As teachers are squeezed by policies and dictates that constrain their ability to cater for the needs of children, who are also exposed to social and personal stressors, it is not surprising that the disruptive behaviour of some students seems to be on the increase. It is an interesting coincidence, for example, that the moves towards an increasingly centralized education system in England and Wales, with the imposition of a national curriculum, a system of national testing and a system of teacher evaluation which is widely perceived by teachers to be narrow and arbitrary, has been accompanied by a massive increase in student exclusion from school (Parsons, 1999; Hayden, 1997).

One head teacher's response to this situation was to take a stand and declare her intention to 'take back ownership' of her school. 'From that moment,' she stated, we were going to do what the children needed, not what other people were trying to impose on us or emotionally blackmail us into accepting'. In the face of feelings of powerlessness, this head and her colleagues set out to take power back.

We might compare this teacher's indignation and determination with that of Tom, who was a student in a residential school for boys with emotional and behavioural difficulties at the time (Cooper, 1993: 59):

---

I was messing around in my old school – like in lessons. I'd just start playing around and that in lessons. They was trying to make out that I was worse than I was. Half of the time, I was just shouting things out; talking, standing up – things like that. Just walking around like. They'd tell you to 'get out' for a little reason, and I'd say, 'I ain't getting out!' And there'd start an argument, with me and a member of staff... Them just dragging me out. They was trying to make out I was worse than I was.

---

Here we have another example of an attempt to challenge the power of others and to take power back. This should not be surprising, as power can be thought of as a basic human need (Glasser, 1986). In the classroom, or any group situation for that matter, power is sometimes the focus of a struggle. Whether this is the case or not, the distribution of power is a key factor in the regulation of the classroom situation.

Discussions of classroom discipline have often treated the exercise of power as a misguided behaviour (eg Dreikurs, Grunwald and Pepper, 1982). Nevertheless, most of the questions teachers ask about classroom discipline are about power – 'How do I get him to stop yelling out?', 'What if he ignores me and keeps banging the chair?', 'How can I get him to behave when his parents can't even control him?'. The inference is 'How can I get the power to help him behave so he doesn't hurt himself or others?'. Teachers don't like to ask directly about power, but they would like more of it in the classroom. Similarly, students who are described as being disruptive often account for their negative behaviour in terms of retaliation against teachers' illegitimate use of power, and their own belief in their right to assert their own power (eg Rosser and Harré, 1976; Tattum, 1982; Cooper, 1993).

# Types of power

We can think of power as having five different bases (French and Raven, 1960):

1. Coercive power – based on threat of punishment. Teachers and students can frighten and humiliate each other.
2. Reward power – based on the use of rewards. Teachers and students can reward each other through the use of praise and the showing of approval.
3. Legitimate power – based on social position that is identified with a specific realm of authority. We commonly associate this more with teachers than with students, in that teachers by virtue of their adult status, and their very role as teachers are often seen as having authority and legitimate power. There are circumstances, however, where students may exert legitimate power in the classroom, through their status within the student peer group, or through their status within the formal hierarchy of the school (eg as a prefect, member of a prestigious school team, head boy or head girl), or by virtue of the social status of their family of origin.
4. Referent power – based on personal liking and respect. This can apply equally to teachers and students.
5. Expert power – based on the possession of special knowledge that is respected and valued by others. This can be based on respect for the teacher's pedagogical skills and subject knowledge, or the student's particular skills and high performance in a subject area.

These five bases of power can be divided into two groups (Tauber, 1986: 1) Coercive, reward, and legitimate power are position powers. Individuals wield these powers by virtue of their social position, for example as teacher, or as a leading member of the formal or informal student hierarchy; and 2) referent power and expert power are personal powers. Individuals wield these powers as a result of their perceived personal qualities and skills.

## Position powers
Coercive, reward and legitimate powers are important and certainly play a significant role in classroom interaction for both teachers and students. But

position powers also have drawbacks. Coercive, reward, and legitimate power bases can be deceptively attractive because they can produce results in the short term. A quick threat, a promise of reward, or a reprimand, may calm the storm for a moment. As when the teacher says: 'Liam, stop that right now or you can stand outside,' or, when Liam says to the teacher: 'If you let us watch a video this lesson, we will do the written work for homework.'

The problem with position powers, however, is that they can become self-defeating. The threat that is never carried out loses its power, and the threat that is carried out loses its mystique, demanding a more fearsome threat the next time to produce the same result. Similarly, promises and rewards really have to be valued by the person at whom they are aimed, leading to demands for increasingly elaborate and extravagant rewards. And if promises and rewards are not delivered they create an even worse situation than existed before they were introduced. In these circumstances teachers and students may come to resent each other because of the way in which position powers can be seen to be so openly manipulative. Furthermore, 'legitimate power' really only works where there is a genuine consensus of values. It is more often the case that one person's legitimate power is another person's illegitimate power, as when the teacher says to Liam: 'You may the boss among your mates in the playground, but in my classroom, I'm the boss and you do as you are told,' and Liam thinks to himself: 'My dad's right when he says that teachers don't know what they're doing. They're fools. Those who can, do; those who can't, teach!'

### Personal powers

Referent power, which is based on individuals' identification with and respect for others, is probably the most potent of the five social bases (Tauber, 1995). Teachers who wield referent power get from their students feelings of personal affection, loyalty and admiration. Students have a reciprocal identification and a shared identity with the teacher; a perceived similarity of goals and interests, and a desire to model themselves on him or her. Students want to behave in a way that merits the teacher's respect. Referent power flows from the quality of interactions between the teacher and students.

Students who exude referent power make it easy for teachers to reciprocate. Unfortunately, disruptive students often do not display such power to teachers. In fact they will tend to present in quite the opposite way. As we noted in the opening chapter of this book, it is not uncommon for disruptive students to present with a coercive style (Patterson, Reid and Dishion, 1992). However, given the way in which referent power can set in motion a reciprocal pattern, it seems that a key skill for teachers to learn might be how to develop referent power in the classroom.

Teachers also need to understand and enhance their expert power, as students commonly respect teachers with expert power for their competence and good judgement (Cooper and McIntyre, 1996; Tauber, 1995). They want access to the valuable knowledge, information, or skills that these teachers have. Because of the teachers' experience and abilities, they know what they are talking about and, therefore, they wield power.

We have all seen it. The student, who is oppositional and defiant in the classroom, but who becomes a compliant learner in the motor vehicle workshop under the tutelage of an expert mechanic. Community experts can help enormously with students. For example, during the time one of the authors and his colleagues worked with students who were suspended or expelled from local schools in Australia, he approached the local professional basketball team to teach basketball skills to the students. By aligning themselves with the power of others, these teachers enhanced their own power.

Tauber (1995) noted that referent and expert powers are often misunderstood. He reports a study in which students were noted to behave badly for certain teachers, whilst they behaved well for others, particularly a technology teacher. The teachers who experienced the negative attitudes and behaviours of the students tended to think that these other teachers wielded more coercive, reward, and legitimate power. But Tauber's research showed this was not the case. Children behaved better for certain teachers because these teachers held relevant knowledge and skills that were respected or desired by the students. The students embraced the goals and interests of these adults, and saw these mechanics, sports-people, musicians, etc as the people they hoped to become.

A British study conducted by one of the present authors (Cooper, 1993) sheds interesting light on the connections between these different aspects of referent power, and their impact on students' self-image, behaviour and prosocial attitudes. The study focused on boys who were students in two residential schools for adolescents with emotional and behavioural difficulties. A key feature of both schools was the involvement of the boys in practical, domestic and maintenance activities around their school premises. This extended to boys being given responsibility for the care and maintenance of prescribed areas of their schools, such as bedrooms and a 'club hut'. In turn, these activities were associated with the boys' involvement in the decision-making processes of their schools, through group meetings and systems of 'shared responsibility'.

According to the boys' own accounts, these activities contributed significantly to improvements in their images of self. They learnt, primarily, that they were worthy of trust and could handle responsibility. For many of these boys it was a new experience to be acknowledged by adults as having these qualities. This sense of being valued for what they could do, rather than being constantly vilified for what they had difficulty doing (eg in terms of their social behaviour and academic competence) provided a basis for improvement on a range of fronts. In particular, they tended to develop a sense of pride in their competences and achievements and thus in their environment. This sense of pride often extended further into a sense of commitment to their schools as communities, and to their fellow students and the staff who worked with them. In a significant proportion of cases this commitment was extended to the classroom and their academic work.

Central to these developments, however, was each boy's sense of being valued as an individual in the context of a community. These boys were valued for the contribution they made to the community. This was based on the important idea that everyone has a contribution to make, whether it be mechanical skills, building skills, doing the laundry or making tea. In both schools senior students were often involved in the care-taking of visitors. Students who had been excluded from mainstream schools, and described as 'antisocial', 'vicious' and 'completely out of control', would often find themselves being described by visitors (such as educational psychologists, placement officers, interview candidates, and visiting teachers) as 'charming', 'helpful' and 'very pleasant'. Ironically, this sometimes worked against the school, in that visitors would go away with the impression that the schools did not cater for 'difficult' students!

## The legitimate uses of power

Lewis (1991) suggests that teachers use the five bases of power to achieve three specific goals: the control, management, and influence of students. Whether we like it or not the teacher's job involves all of these functions. Whenever the teacher thinks that it is necessary for a student or group to do something that they don't necessarily want to do, the teacher has to be able to exert control. Whether it is to comply with health and safety regulations in a fire drill, in a lab or on a field trip, or to maintain 'examination conditions' in a formal test, the teacher has to have strategies that will usually lead to student compliance with the rules. Teachers will also need to be able to manage pupil behaviour, in the sense of shaping and guiding the students' behaviour in certain ways, so that, for example, students develop particular habits of working. Management differs from control in the sense that it is less directive, and relies on the ability to facilitate the internalization of rules and procedures, rather than simple compliance with the teacher's instructions. 'Influence' is an even more subtle concept, whereby student thought and behaviour is guided by the teacher in unobtrusive ways, so that the student experiences the acceptance of the guidance as a matter of choice.

Lewis's study of teachers suggests that these goals are often connected with the power bases in specific ways:

- teachers use rewards and coercion in order to exert control;
- they use legitimate power in order to manage students;
- and they use referent or expert power in order to influence students.

Theoretically this is all nicely cut and dried, when the reality clearly is not, as Mick McManus told us at the beginning of the chapter. And yet when teachers and students are asked about the characteristics of effective teaching, they invariably refer to a range of qualities that can be summarized in terms of teacher firmness, fairness, care for students and the ability to be interesting (eg Tattum, 1982; Cooper, 1993; Keys and Ferandes, 1993; Charlton, 1996), all of which can be mapped onto the goals of control, management and influence. On the other hand, there is also a large body of evidence (some of which appears in the texts already cited) which shows that teachers sometimes provoke disruptive behaviour by being 'too strict' (overly controlling); 'too soft' (not controlling enough); by being not friendly enough, and by being too friendly; by being not clever enough and by being too clever.

The crucial point here is to do with balance and context. It is easy to make the mistake of thinking that effective teaching is really all about teachers controlling students, *or* managing students, *or* influencing students, and that, therefore, only certain forms of power are legitimate or appropriate for the classroom situation. As we have already noted, however, the forms of power we are concerned with constitute parts of the social toolbox that we all (including our students in schools and universities) carry with us throughout life. It is a feature of the human imperative to wish to assert ourselves; to get our own way, and to make an impression on people we meet. However, severe social impairments proceed from having only limited access to these tools, as was illustrated in the last chapter when we discussed the relationship between antisocial behaviour and a coercive social style (Patterson, Reid and Dishion, 1992). Similarly, individuals whose only channel is referent power, may well find themselves bewildered when their talents and expertise alone are insufficient to produce the influence they believe they deserve. Therefore, it is the job of the teacher to harness *all* of these drives in the service of their professional commitment. Precisely how this should be done will vary from context to context.

Mick McManus, for example, showed us that the ability to 'control' and 'manage' is diminished in the absence of 'influence'. This rare account shows how such referent power often has to be built up over time. The following example, which is based on a personal account of one of the authors (Olsen, 1997a), further illustrates the need for balance across the different powers.

# Mr Faulkner

Although Mr Faulkner was stern and didn't smile much, the children in his Year Four primary class had a grudging respect for him. The year was 1957.

The classroom was organized to build on knowledge, day by day, and he didn't tolerate those who deviated from this sense of direction. The students didn't drift, and Mr F didn't spend time managing disruptive children. The parents supported him (Legitimate Power); students respected him; they valued what he taught them (Expert Power), and the class worked well as a unit (Referent Power).

Mr Faulkner's behaviour management system was non-verbal and it allowed him to continue his lessons while he communicated non-verbally to disruptive students that they should 'get back on task'. Six desks were placed in each of five rows. Each row was a team and students were regularly mixed up into different teams. Along the top of the blackboard (and they were black in those days) he listed the five rows and, during the day, at unannounced times, he put a chalk mark under whichever row was working hardest, or was quietest, or got their books put away quickest during the transition between one lesson and the next. This was a group incentive (Reward Power).

| Row 1 | Row 2 | Row 3 | Row 4 | Row 5 |
| --- | --- | --- | --- | --- |
| III | II | IIII | IIIII | I |

So, what happened when someone in one of the row-teams caused trouble? What happened if a boy deliberately put his books away slowly to lose points for his team members and get back at someone? Mr Faulkner had another simple strategy, a non-verbal system that didn't waste valuable teaching time. He wrote the person's name on the upper left-hand corner of the board. There was no discussion, because Mr Faulkner assumed that the students were aware of what they had done wrong. (If they weren't immediately aware this was a signal for them to examine their behaviour.) Each further infringement earned a cross after the name. Each cross meant a very long 10 minutes after school with him (Coercive Power).

Mr Faulkner's system worked quietly and effectively and has some similarities to the assertive discipline approach proposed by Canter (1976). But, would it work in the 21st century?

The point is, of course, that some of the things that Mr Faulkner could have taken for granted in 1957 are less certain for teachers in the year 2000. Mr Faulkner could rely on legitimate power for example. In the more stable world of the 1950s the role of teacher carried with it authority and respect. This respect was not confined to the school, but was reinforced in the community by the majority of students' parents. Also, the value of education was less in dispute than today and easier to demonstrate. The difficulty of sustaining legitimate power makes the display of referent and expert powers less easy.

We cannot turn the clock back to 1957, even if we wanted to. What we can do, however, is look at ways in which teachers can promote harmony and order in the classrooms of today. There is every reason for modern teachers to strive with confidence for what Mr Faulkner achieved almost half a century ago. If they are to be successful in this it will help for them to give careful consideration to how power operates in classrooms, and how teacher power and student power can be harnessed in cooperative ways. This is the task of the rest of this book.

# 3

# The power–caring balance: sources of biological power

This chapter looks at some basic biological needs in children and adults, needs we should try to satisfy. Teachers who understand these needs and learn to use them can develop particular sources of power in their classrooms. Much of the theory we use in the power–caring balance in Figure 3.1 comes from studies in behavioural ecology, for example, Lea (1984), Krebs and Davies (1981), de Waal (1982, 1989), and discussions by Olsen (1989, 1993). Studying the ecological basis of some human behaviours can help us see patterns and understand motivations that would otherwise seem illogical and baffling.

As a primary school teacher in South Australia one of the authors (Olsen) can remember some good times, and more than a few hard times with the Year Six children placed in his charge, and remembers some incidents because they didn't make sense at the time. On one occasion the whole class was on a field naturalist trip down near the mangrove swamps at Port Augusta. Two boys, Peter and Liam, who were normally disruptive, were being normal – poking classmates, teasing classmates, hitting classmates, and showing their considerable lack of interest in everything the teacher and the rest of the class did that morning. As the group moved through the mangroves, the class ran into one of those tidal rivulets, about 3 metres across, that runs into the sea from the red sandhills. The class couldn't cross.

They milled around for a time then, suddenly, Peter and Liam, the boys who usually caused the class so much trouble, changed. They focused on the problem of crossing the rivulet, and they discussed the welfare of the class. Peter and Liam took charge, they organized for the class to build a bridge from driftwood beached on the shore and lying around in the mangroves, and showed great concern that each of their class members crossed safely. When Peter and Liam changed, the group dynamics changed, the class functioned as a unit with a cause, and at the same time the teacher was pleased but a little confused, about the sudden change in these two boys with such a colourful history of low-level and high-level harm. One couldn't help but relate it to things drawn from animal studies. A change in circumstances in a squabbling group, or between squabbling neighbours, meant that former enemies, or irresponsible juveniles, suddenly dispensed with their antagonistic or immature behaviour and combined forces to thwart some danger. Was this the case with Peter and Liam?

Many years later, as a school counsellor in Canberra working with troubled students in schools, there were similar incidents. One Year Six boy, who had violently attacked a teacher with a chair, and some of his classmates with his fists, was with the counsellor in his office when an excited child came rushing in and screamed that a young boy had shut his finger in a large sliding door. The counsellor, with the student who had been attacking people for the previous month, ran to help the trapped child. When the 'troubled' boy noticed that the child's finger had actually been severed, and that the other students were standing around staring in horror uncertain what to do, he organized them. He calmly sent for a container of ice for the severed finger, and told the other students, and staff, that if they rushed, doctors might be able to reattach it.

These dramatic changes in children often felt as though we had tapped some natural, and powerful drive to care for, protect, and nurture others: drives that hadn't been tapped before.

The biological needs outlined by Glasser (1993) are:

- to have play and have fun;
- to be free and make choices;
- to exercise power and influence;
- to belong and love others;
- to survive.

Here we have considered some other theories, including principles from behavioural ecology, and made some changes to Glasser's hierarchy of needs. We would add to Glasser's construct – status, reciprocal co-operation, and caring, because these are important biological needs in social animals (Figure 3.1). Glasser's bottom two needs, survival, and belong and love others, are from Maslow's hierarchy (Maslow, 1970) and accepted by most educators. We have placed 'love others' into caring. Be free and make choices can be included under individual power (to control your own life). The need for fun and play can be incorporated into all five needs. For example, many businessmen and women strive in the corporate world to win individual power and status and influence over their competitors. For them, it's fun. Most sports that involve scoring points also involve the systematic gaining of status, and one can 'belong' to a team, and cooperate with team members. Much about

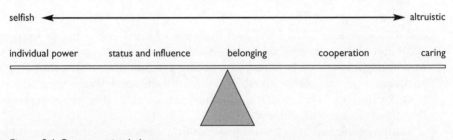

Figure 3.1 Power–caring balance

belonging is belonging to a group, and cooperative motivation is heavily influenced by the goals of the group. Finally, one can use play as a form of affection and caring.

These five needs are placed on an individual power–caring balance with the behaviour style of these needs moving from selfish to altruistic (Figure 3.1).

Behavioural ecologists contrast 'selfish' behaviour with 'altruistic' behaviour (Krebs and Davies, 1981). A definition of an 'immature' child could be 'a child who thinks only of himself, never of others'. He doesn't cooperate or care for others; he is selfish not altruistic. 'Immature' children also tend to act on short-term goals instead of long-term goals, so these are included in the balance. That is, they operate on the left-hand side of the power–caring balance. These children may be stuck in a cycle competing with other children and adults around 'individual power' and 'status and influence' because their natural capacity for 'reciprocal cooperation' and 'caring' has never been tapped. Aggressive children often seem to be on a sort of 'payback' system. They see themselves as having been harmed by the misdeeds of others, or about to be harmed, and they need to respond measure for measure to keep things 'fair'. It's 'me', or perhaps 'us' (their family, their peer group) against 'them' (everybody else). They don't trust teachers to stick up for them, so they fight their battles for themselves.

If those children who harm themselves and others are often imbalanced to the left, we need to give them alternative forms of individual power and status and influence on the left side of the continuum. But we also need to help them move to the right side of the continuum and meet their needs for belonging, reciprocal cooperation and caring. We need to aim them towards more long-term goals and balance their interactions with people so they have individual power, and status and influence in the way they belong to the group, but also they belong by reciprocal cooperation and caring.

# Future and social concern statements

We teachers use some statements with misbehaving children that keep the teacher and child to the left-hand side of the power – caring balance and focus the child and ourselves on short-term goals. 'Do as I say' is speaking from a basis of individual power and status and influence, and children can resent the inference of 'Do as I say'. However, if we use future and social concern statements – 'You'll have to leave if you continue to disrupt the class. It's not fair to those preparing for the test', we are operating from a basis of power, reciprocal cooperation and caring for others, and we aim towards long-term goals. This makes our requests more balanced and less resented by students.

# Elements of the power–caring balance

Let's look at the five needs in the power–caring balance drawing from behavioural ecologists (de Waal, 1982, 1989, Krebs and Davies, 1981) as well as psychologists and educators such as Lea (1984), Epston (1988), Coopersmith (1967), Adler (1932), Johnson *et al* (1984), Glasser (1986), Sherif (1956), Dreikurs, Grunwald and Pepper (1982), and Balson (1987).

1. Individual power – the individual may be stronger or more highly motivated than his competitors.
2. Status and influence – the individual may have high rank or significance amongst his peers, for example, he may have special alliances, skills or an essential role in the group that makes him influential.
3. Belonging – the individual will strive to belong to a group so he can survive, be cared for, and fulfil his need to have power, status, and to cooperate with and care for others.
4. Reciprocal cooperation – the individual may have a role in the group where he exchanges cooperation through contractual organization (I help you if you help me). This is aimed towards long-term and short-term group goals.
5. Caring – once an individual has security (protection from harm and discomfort) and adequate resources, he may engage in the care and nurturing of offspring, kin, or other group members.

## Individual power

Animals often hold territories that contain adequate resources and they have more control (individual power) if their territory is clearly defined, that is, the territory has clear boundaries or limits. Owners of property, territories and resources, including humans who own ideas, a job, or a creation, feel a strong sense of investment in these possessions. Usually they don't like to give them up because they have worked so hard to earn and keep them (Krebs and Davies, 1981). Children who have clear focus and boundaries set by themselves, and by adults, and a sense of ownership, are more likely to feel secure and have high self-esteem than children who lack such limits (Coopersmith, 1967; Epston, 1988).

## Status and influence

Group members with higher rank or status and influence have more access to limited resources than individuals with low status. This is well documented in primates (apes and their relatives) and is the 'pecking order' of barnyard chickens. They can have higher status and influence in a group by being related to high-status individuals (de Waal, 1982), and have higher status and influence by belonging to a high-status group. Children need chances to excel in their particular area (niche) and have responsibilities so they feel they have status and influence in the classroom and school.

Adler (1932) argued that people strive to move from a position of inferiority to one of superiority. They use 'private logic' to avoid feelings of inferiority because people become anxious if they believe they are inferior. For example, an unskilled worker on a large estate might use private logic to convince himself that he is not inferior to the landed gentry owner – 'I am an honest worker – he (the owner) has never done an honest day's work in his life. He just married into money'. Students with low self-esteem, Adler's 'inferiority complex', often use this type of 'private logic' and 'put-downs' on their classmates in a misguided attempt to raise their own status.

People generally react strongly to put-downs, especially put-downs about their capabilities in 'love and work' in relation to peers, families, skills or values they hold dear. This reaction is often out of proportion to the potential social harm that is done by the put-down. Put-downs are powerful. Severe teasing can be particularly damaging and can trigger highly emotive and dangerous reactions, such as revenge, in children and adults. We can tell children to ignore teasing but they usually can't ignore severe teasing for very long, and neither can adults. By telling children to ignore teasing, we are telling them to ignore one of their basic biological needs, the need for status.

Why are put-downs so powerful and why do people take certain put-downs so seriously? Why can serious put-downs over a long enough period make people ill? We may have an innate need to avoid low status because, in our prehistoric past, low status meant we were barred access to limited resources, like food or mates, and it could have meant death if we were forced to live away from our tribal group, be it a family, peer, or food-gathering group. That need is still with us, though shaped by modern limited resources and modern signs of status such as success in school, or sports, or belonging to a group that overtly rejects all conventional forms of status.

The obvious message here is that children cannot cope easily with put-downs. Put-downs generate strong visceral reactions and they can create vicious, emotion-driven cycles that exacerbate a child's problems and drive them to avoid feelings of inferiority through behaviour that may harm themselves and others. Staff and students should be taught that teasing and bullying can have long-term emotional effects, and children should be taught how to manage put-downs. Classrooms need a rule about 'put-downs', and schools need a policy about teasing and bullying (Slee, 1992).

Adler (1932) argued that people can overcome the emotional problems caused by feelings of inferiority if they develop strengths (individual power) to compensate for a perceived weakness, and if they develop social interest (caring). They can overcome problems by working cooperatively with and caring for others.

## Belonging

The drive to 'belong' is powerful in group animals, and humans, and their children, are group animals. Students, of course, strive to join a peer group that differentiates them from adults. Dreikurs, Grunwald and Pepper (1982), Balson (1987) and others argued that belonging is the basic motivation in humans. While belonging is a basic motivation, it doesn't appear to be the sole basic motivation. Otherwise, high school students would happily join low-status subgroups. Most high school students try to join a subgroup with some status and some would rather be alone, or gain notoriety through aggressive and disruptive behaviour than join a low-status subgroup. Status, belonging and other motivators interact with each other, and a key to understanding belonging is to understand the goals of the group, even a group of two. Is it to prevail over other teams in sport, or to disrupt and slow the progress of other groups in the classroom?

## Reciprocal cooperation

The Robber's Cave experiment, conducted at a boy's camp in the United States in 1954 by M Sherif, provided a striking example of how changes in circumstances can tap competition between groups of 11- and 12-year-old boys, or tap cooperation between groups (Sherif, 1956). The boys attending the camp were divided into two groups and isolated from each other. Each group chose a name, one the 'Eagles', the other the 'Rattlers'. Each group created special symbols and secret words for their group, and each developed a collective antagonism towards the other group, the groups became enemy tribes. The two groups were brought together in competitive contact, including baseball, football, tugs-of-war, a treasure hunt and other games. As the tournaments continued, tension mounted between the groups; name-calling and scuffles broke out. As the conflict escalated, solidarity, morale and cooperation improved among members of each group as antagonism increased against members of the other group.

After Sherif and his associates showed that they could create conflict between the 'Eagles' and the 'Rattlers', they attempted to end the conflict and establish harmony between the two groups. They first brought them together for 'goodwill' activities, such as dinners and 'National Brotherhood Week'. These approaches failed completely and sometimes ended in fights between boys in the two groups. The psychologists then organized a series of apparent emergencies where the boys either had to cooperate or lose something that both groups wanted. For example, the truck that normally took them to town for lunch wouldn't start. To get the truck to work, boys from both groups had to push and pull it. Also, someone reported that the water pipe-line to the camp had broken. The boys were told that, unless they worked together to search for, find the break and fix it, they would all have to leave the camp.

Gradually, through meeting these cooperative needs, inter-group hostility diminished. Friendships began to develop between individual Eagles and Rattlers, and eventually they sought out occasions to mingle. Some boys from opposing teams even asked to ride together on the same bus. Sherif had organized for the boys to achieve shared goals, to form alliances, and this resulted in cooperation. The 'goodwill' activities failed because they had no common goals. Telling the boys they would lose out if the water pipe-line wasn't fixed did work because the boys were also told how they could regain power by cooperating towards common goals.

Johnson *et al* (1984) and Glasser (1986) argued that cooperative learning in the classroom – organizing students to work in cooperative groups – enhanced learning and reduced discipline problems. Johnson *et al* (1984) claimed that students in each group should be dependent on each other, they should interact face to face, be individually accountable, and use inter-group social skills, as our tribal ancestors probably did. Each group member is assigned a specific role (a niche) to ensure interdependence. Academic tasks (goals) are explained clearly so group members work collaboratively. The children's natural drive to cooperate, form valuable relationships, and reconcile disputes, is tapped by carefully structuring the environment. A key to success in forming groups is common, shared goals. We have seen these exercises fail when one or two members of a group don't care about the goals artificially set by the teacher; their goal is to disrupt. The group is unlikely to work without goals that are valued by all members. It is a teacher's job to identify these goals, as did Mr Faulkner (*see* Chapter 2).

## Caring

According to Edgar (1989), families can be more stable when each child has an essential helping role, a responsibility or niche in the family, such as bringing in money or caring for younger siblings. We created the problems of today's teenagers (they didn't occur 100 years ago) by removing these cooperative and caring responsibilities.

In a one-room schoolhouse or a kibbutz, where children of several ages work together and care for each other, there may be more of a 'natural' family or tribal structure than there is in age-segregated classrooms. Older children care for and help younger children and this helps everyone. Lazerson *et al* (1988) showed how cross-age tutoring, older children helping younger children, gave truanting teenagers an increased perception of control power) over their own lives. This reduced truanting behaviour. Cross-age tutoring can structure a cooperative, care-giving group – members care, and they are cared for.

We can teach love and caring to children, but we can also tap their natural need to care for others by placing them in circumstances where they are needed by others. John Bednall wrote in *The Canberra Times* (8 March 1995) that:

If the most important socialising dynamic in a boys' school is the modelling provided by the older males, this means not only the male teachers but also the senior boys. In a kindergarten to grade 12 school of more than 1000 boys such as mine, this seems to me to say that I should structure my school vertically wherever I can. I must demand of my oldest boys that they exercise compassionate and moral leadership of their younger colleagues. They must recognize that in their own process of values definition they cannot be introspective with their age peers, but must recognize their profound responsibility to those who look upwards towards them. Schools are not democracies – we learnt that in the 1970s – but it is possible to make a distinction between the jurisdiction of the professional educators, and the accountability boys bear to them and those things which impact directly upon student culture and within which student decision makers will stand directly accountable, not to the school, but to their peers for the moral integrity, equity and respect for others they show.

A good boys' school will seek to empower boys to control the student culture themselves within the aims and objectives of the institution. I am now prepared to go a considerable distance in this and to take risks in allowing boys to share with me the managing of the school. We argue to the boys that they, and not the staff, are responsible for the maintenance of a healthy student culture. We have defined precise areas of jurisdiction which the students themselves are responsible for protecting and which impact directly upon the morale, rights and safety of the student body. Boys who disrupt class, who discredit the school in public, or who invade the privacy and rights of other boys, are not dealt with now by the staff but by the student community itself.

---

An aside to finish this section. It is remarkable how often children tell us that the most important thing they valued about their teacher was that the teacher took care of them. Furthermore, parents in counselling, especially whose children are in danger of exclusion, will align themselves to, and cooperate with a counsellor or teacher who they believe is caring for and protecting their child from exclusion. Caring leads to cooperation, and this leads to success in changing problem behaviours.

# Conclusions

As we saw in the Robber's Cave experiment, interventions can fail if they concentrate on one element of the power-caring balance at the expense of others. Interventions can succeed if they balance individual power, status and influence, and belonging with reciprocal cooperation and caring aimed at long-term goals. As teachers we often try to overcome problems by tapping individual power, status and influence or caring alone. By presenting opportunities where all these needs are met, we can tap children's natural drive for reciprocal cooperation and caring, and we can balance their power-caring needs. We can do more than empower children with assertiveness or social skills. We can do more than praise their efforts (status and influence), and allow them to belong. We can structure classrooms and schools so that students have the opportunity to cooperate and care for others.

# 4

# Establishing a regime for positive behaviour in the classroom

In this chapter we consider the promotion of positive behaviour from the viewpoint of the class teacher, and explore some of the measures that such a teacher might take to establish a basic structure on which positive behaviour can be built.

## Child development and ways of relating

The peak period for disruptive behaviour in schools is the adolescent phase – a fact supported, for example, by the dramatic increase in school exclusions during these years (Parsons, 1999). This observation is not intended to diminish the importance or the severity of childhood behavioural problems in the early years (see Bennathan and Boxall, 1996), but it is to highlight the fact that the adolescent years are associated with particular problems that cannot be ignored. For most adolescents the years between 12 and 18 are characterized by a series of challenges. These challenges are related to the inevitable biological changes that occur during this time as well as emergent social and emotional needs which are associated with these changes (Cooper, 1999).

The onset of puberty brings with it the need for individuation – that is the process by which the adult-dependent child begins to establish a distance between him or herself and their parent(s)/carer(s). This is the first important stage in the transition between childhood and adulthood. This is coupled with cognitive changes, in the form of an increased facility to engage in abstract thought and reasoning (Beard, 1969). It is an appropriate thing, therefore, for young people at this stage in their development to become critical and, at times, argumentative. This cognitive shift is associated with the quest for independence and the need for distance between themselves and their adult carers. On the other hand it links to their growing tendency to look for emotional fulfilment and social reinforcement from peers rather than adults.

This is a time of finding a new identity. This is not a smooth or simple process for anyone, as it is fraught with uncertainties and strangeness (Dare, 1985). For some adolescents post-pubertal hormonal changes and the emergence of sexual identity may be directly associated with feelings of irritability and depression (Graham, 1991; Rutter and Smith, 1995). For a minority of children whose passage through the infant stages of development has been unsuccessful, adolescence comes as an additional burden which serves only to exacerbate their unmet attachment needs (Bowlby, 1975). These individuals may well be caught in the strange limbo of being adolescents with infant needs, and may be prone to express their needs in developmentally inappropriate ways, such as through tantrum behaviour or sulking. Added to this group are those individuals with specific developmental disorders, such as autism, Asperger's syndrome and attention deficit/hyperactivity disorder (AD/HD). These individuals too will tend to display behaviours that the teacher would normally expect to see in chronologically younger children, and will therefore present particular challenges in the secondary classroom which is often set up with certain assumptions about how children in a particular age group are expected to function and behave. Inappropriate expectations and demands will tend to exacerbate the problems of these vulnerable youngsters and may well help produce a whole set of additional, 'co-morbid' problems in the form of social, emotional and behavioural difficulties (Cooper and Ideus, 1996).

These and other challenges brought about by the complex nature of the adolescent population make teaching a particularly difficult task. It means, for instance, that whilst the Rules-Ignore-Praise (RIP) technique is often an effective classroom management tool with younger students, it is often not so effective with secondary age students (Charles, 1996). Older students may speak derisively of peers who receive praise from the teacher. Because most adolescents rely more on reinforcement from classmates than from their teacher, public adult praise presents complex problems, even for well-motivated students, and must be used with care. Though, as we noted above, there will be adolescent students who are still operating at an infant dependency stage, and these students may well require the more overt personal approval of their teachers, though not in front of their peers whose acceptance they also crave. On the other hand, the Rules-Rewards-Consequences (RRC) approach does seem to be more effective with most age groups. This may be because the RRC approach is presented in a way that emphasizes the idea that the student has earned the reward or consequence through his or her own efforts, and relies less on the idea that he or she has 'pleased teacher'. The RRC technique, therefore, is more likely to appeal to adolescent sensibilities, and the need for a sense of autonomy. (The Rules–Ignore–Praise technique is when the teacher responds to a student's rule infringement by: 1. ignoring the infringement; 2. identifying a student in the class who is complying with the infringed rules; and 3. making a verbal praise statement directed at the compliant child that includes a statement of the rule, and that can be heard by the rest of the class, including the rule infringer. The Rules–Rewards–Consequences approach is when the teacher responds to a rule infringement with a statement of the rule and the application of consequences, for example, the student who has not completed a task is required to do so in his or her own time; or the teacher responds to rule compliance with a statement of the rule and the application of a reward, such as a preferred activity.)

The foregoing discussion emphasizes the need for the teacher to develop an awareness of different student characteristics, and to recognize the need to be both age appropriate and developmentally appropriate in their behaviour towards students. Thus whilst the RRC approach will probably be appropriate for most adolescent students, there will be others who will still require the individual and private acknowledgement that they have 'pleased teacher', and this acknowledgement should be provided discretely and warmly, though a teacher with high referent power can sometimes use public acknowledgement.

## Foregrounding and backgrounding: verbal and non-verbal communication in public situations

If adolescents find public verbal praise hard to take, then public reprimands are going to be even less acceptable. The giving of praise can be seen as an assertion of higher status, and, therefore a patronizing form of control. Reprimands are usually overtly controlling in their intention. When reprimanded (eg told to 'stop doing that') the student has only two choices: to accept and conform to the reprimand, risking derision from peers, or to reject the reprimand, risking negative consequences from the teacher, but winning the approval of peers.

Given the adolescent need to be *perceived* (especially by peers) as independent of adult influence, the second option is often preferred. In this way the public reprimand, which is intended by the teacher to restore order and control, can have the opposite effect of exacerbating the situation and thus escalating the conflict between teacher and student (Cooper and Upton, 1991; Molnar and Lindquist, 1989). Once this happens there is always the danger that other students will become involved; then we have a group or whole-class problem.

Having said this, the teacher can tap into another source of influence. This is students' desire and need for security and order. Students frequently complain not only about teachers who shout and use bullying tactics, but also they dislike the sense of uncertainty and chaos they experience when taught by teachers whom they see as weak or who 'can't control us' (Cooper, 1993). As

Larry, a 15-year-old attending a residential school for boys with emotional and behavioural difficulties, once put it: 'It would be better if everybody would try to cooperate more with staff… I think it [ie the discipline regime in the school] should be more stricter. But if they [ie the staff] get more strict I'm going to be the one breaking all the rules' (Cooper, 1993: 142–43). There is definitely something obtuse about this statement. It is deliberately framed as a paradox. It illustrates the way in which students are often resistant to adult control but complain when it is not there. The point here, however, is to listen to the use of the words 'everybody' and 'I'. Larry was uncomfortable with the lack of cooperation and stability in the school and the extent to which students were disobedient and disrespectful to staff. His belief was that if staff were 'more stricter' this would not happen. He reserved the right as an individual, however, to resist greater strictness. So here he is expressing the twin needs for security and individuation, or, to put it another way, the need for individual freedom and autonomy within a safe and well organized social structure.

In the classroom situation, we suggest, we can go some of the way towards meeting successfully these potentially incompatible twin needs, by thinking in terms of 'foregrounding' and 'backgrounding'. In the foreground is the thing we want to draw attention to, in the background is the thing we want people to be aware of but not focusing on. In classrooms we usually want to foreground the formal curriculum as well as academically productive and socially desirable behaviour. In short, most people want classrooms to be experienced by the individuals in them primarily as places that are socially and educationally rewarding. In the background is the infrastructure of rules and procedures that help the group to operate in ways that make individuals feel safe, secure and valued.

From this perspective the classroom behaviour management policy should, among other things, take care of the negative part of disciplining so teachers are freed to form positive relationships with their students. The teacher should talk to the students about doing well in their work, about planning and goals, about positive things. The teacher may walk by the student and say 'That's an excellent piece of work John,' (encourager) or, particularly with older students, 'Thanks for working so quietly. It helps the others,' (social concern statement). In contrast the consequences for misbehaviour can be handled non-verbally, as Mr Faulkner did, so the teacher and class can continue with the lesson.

One way of thinking about this is in relation to the difference between the use of verbal and non-verbal communication. When we talk about something in a face-to-face group situation we are making our private thoughts public and demanding that others attend to them. If we reprimand a student verbally in public we are, to all intents and purposes, overtly including the whole class in the communication. We are not only reprimanding the student therefore, we are also saying, non-verbally: 'Hey, stop what you are doing everybody and pay attention to the fact that I am telling this student off!'

We will often also use non-verbal communication to support our verbal utterances, such as posture and gesture, but the intended emphasis is usually experienced as being on the verbal utterance. In fact, we should be careful to ensure that there is strong coherence between our verbal and non-verbal behaviour, otherwise we can undermine our intentions. On the other hand certain kinds of non-verbal communication in a public setting can be subtle person-to-person communications with only limited public exposure. For example, in a lesson where the class is required to watch a video a student is off task, reading a book. The teacher might indicate to the student that he should stop reading and attend to the video, by placing his hand on the student's book and then, if necessary, after having secured the student's attention, gesturing with his hand toward the video. Other students do not even need to know that this interaction has taken place. The student will be able to comply with the teacher's request without losing face before the peer group.

# A systemic approach to disruptive behaviour

In this section of the book we begin to consider the practical measures that might be taken to establish effective teaching and learning, to promote positive student engagement in learning and social activities, and to minimize and prevent disruptive behaviour.

It should be stressed from the outset that there are no simple formulae for promoting positive behaviour in classrooms. At every step of the way teachers and schools are likely to maximize their likelihood of success when they take account of the context in which they are working, and when they pay particular attention to what their students are telling them – overtly and covertly – about how they see the situation. Teachers must also take account of the organizational and historical context, and be ready to admit that before some in-class measures can be adopted it may be necessary for relationships to be established and/or aspects of the wider institution to be addressed and altered. This is the essence of a systemic approach (sometimes referred to as the 'ecosystemic' approach). This is not to say, however, that there are not some important general insights that can be drawn upon in this endeavour. We will be exploring such general insights in the rest of the book, and suggesting ways in which such insights can be used within an ecosystemic framework. The crucial point being made here is that these insights do not, in any sense, comprise a 'magic bullet'. Rather, they represent tools that may be useful to teachers when used in the right ways and in the right circumstances. They must always, however, be approached by teachers in a critical and analytical way, and they must be interpreted in the light of the conditions in which the individual teacher and particular schools operate.

## Skill clusters

Frederick Jones (1987) studied thousands of hours of carefully controlled observations of primary and secondary classrooms and concluded that discipline was mainly non-verbal. He said that classroom discipline depends some 90 per cent on the teacher's effective body language. Most lessons go fairly well until the teacher asks the students to work on their own. Then trouble can start. He advised the use of three skill clusters to overcome these problems.

### Body language
- Eye contact – sweep the room continually and engage the eyes of individual students.
- Physical proximity – move near the student, establish brief eye contact, perhaps stand behind the student, but say nothing (verbalizing can weaken the effect).
- Body carriage – hold yourself erect and move assertively.
- Facial expression – very slight shakes of the head, frowns, and, especially, tight lips and flashing eyes used instead of verbalizations can show that limits are being strained.
- Gestures – palm forward (stop or desist), finger to lips (quiet), or flexing fingers (continue) won't interfere with instructional verbalizations.

A standard technique used by some teachers is to pause and stare at the student, or maybe pause and say the student's name (names are particularly powerful), or ask them a question about the lesson.

### Incentive systems
Like Mr Faulkner in Chapter 1, Jones (1987) recommends group incentives. He uses Grandma's Rule (the Premack Principle) – after a significant period of work, children can have a reward, like free time to talk with their friends. Activities are chosen democratically by a vote to emphasize this group effort. For example, the students may choose 20 minutes of free time at the end of the day. Then, when students break rules and disrupt the progress of other group members, the teacher holds up a stopwatch and turns it on. Children watch their minutes of free time shorten. Peers of the disrupting students may urge them back to the task and group goals at hand. Some teachers may wish to include a separate set of consequence for students who repeatedly disrupt, as Mr Faulkner did, like names or initials on the board leading to a hierarchy of consequences that include time-out.

### Providing help efficiently
Jones (1987) learned from his research that most teachers provide help inefficiently. They create dependent children. He believed that teachers should:

- Organize the classroom so the teacher can easily access students; desks in shallow concentric semi-circles are best.
- Use charts, lists, models, and clear examples of instruction.
- If the teacher attends to a student at his or her desk:
    - find something the student has done correctly and tell him or her;
    - give a clear, brief instruction;
    - leave the student after a maximum of 20 seconds.

This may sound harsh but Jones found that teachers who stayed longer than 20 seconds did not help children any more, and they were more likely to create dependent students.

Bolton (1986) discussed other studies of human communication and, like Jones, found that about 90 per cent of communication was non-verbal. Obviously we need to attend to both our verbal and non-verbal language. It is useful, therefore, for teachers to think about being verbal about appropriate behaviour like work, planning, goals, etc, and non-verbal about misbehaviour. The teacher catches the child being good, talks to the child through and about schoolwork, friends, achievements, interests, but avoids verbal reprimands.

# Verbal and non-verbal communication

The teacher can use verbal interventions to:

- Acknowledge when students do it right, 'Excellent work, John'.
- Remind them in discussion what to do, 'Put the large number over the small number'.
- Tap students' need for individual acknowledgement and for cooperation by acknowledging their loyalty and social responsibility (i) to the group, 'Thanks for working so quietly and helping the others,' (ii) to their friends, 'That was a loyal thing you did for George, and (iii) their teacher, 'Thanks for working well today everybody, it must have been really difficult with the builders making so much noise outside.'
- The teacher may take them aside and tap their drive for caring by asking for help – 'I'm having a hard time with this lesson, and I need your support; can you help?'

The teacher can use non-verbal interventions such as:

- eye contact – to indicate awareness of the student;
- gaze (sustained eye contact) – to indicate expectancy (ie that the student will change his or her behaviour);

- physical proximity (eg standing next to a student) – this can be used to indi- cate to the student that he or she has been noticed;
- hand and head gestures (eg raised first finger, flat palm, thumbs-up/ thumbs down, head nod/head shake) – these are more explicit acts of com- munication which may be used in conjunction with the other non-verbal signals to direct a student's behaviour;
- smile/frown – to indicate approval/disapproval.

This suggested dichotomy between the use of non-verbal and verbal commu- nication is not intended as a hard and fast rule, but as a means of raising aware- ness of how the way we communicate influences what we communicate. The teacher who makes issues of order and rule compliance the most prominent feature of lessons, is not only detracting attention from the business of acade- mic learning, he or she is also communicating the view that the desire to con- trol students' behaviour is of paramount importance. And, as we have noted, this is a red flag to the proverbial (adolescent) bull. Having said this, there clear- ly will be times when the teacher has to bring discipline issues to the fore- ground of classroom discourse when he or she raises their hand palm outwards and says:

'Stop what you are doing everybody. Put your pens down, look at me, and listen to me. We need to talk about rules for a few moments.'

The important thing here though is that this should be the exception rather than the rule. The assertion of control through the wielding of power should always be a means to an end, and not an end in itself.

Another important issue here is the need to make a distinction between the public and the private. What we are talking about in this chapter is some of the ways in which teachers and students interact with one another in whole- class situations. Things should be very different in the one to one situation, as we shall see later.

## A few words of caution about non-verbal communication

The first thing teachers must be aware of, in relation to the use of non-verbal communication of the type we are describing, is potential for misunderstand- ing. There are two main bases for the misunderstanding of non-verbal gestures.

### Culture
Social psychologists have shown that there are some gestures that have mean- ing in one culture, but a different meaning in another. In France, for example, when an individual extends the first finger of their right hand, places this on their face, just below the right eye, whilst making the corners of their mouth

droop, this can be interpreted to mean 'You can't fool me!' (Aronson, 1998). In the United States, Australia, or Britain, however, it is unlikely that this gesture would be understood in this way. To use this gesture in a classroom in any of these countries, therefore, would be more likely to create puzzlement than to communicate meaning.

One thing worse than failing to communicate is to have one's communication interpreted as meaning something other than what is intended. There are some gestures which have different meanings in different cultures. Thus whilst holding eye contact with a person who is speaking to you is considered a sign of respect and interest in most English speaking countries, in other areas it can be construed as being disrespectful, especially between individuals of differing social status, such as between students and teachers. Countries where this is the case include Nigeria, Puerto Rico and Thailand (ibid). Similarly, there are wide variations between cultures concerning what is acceptable in terms of physical proximity and physical contact. Furthermore, some gestures may have opposite meanings in different cultures. For example, the 'thumbs up' gesture means 'OK' in English-speaking countries, whilst in Iran and Sardinia it is an obscene gesture, equivalent to the extended middle finger gesture used as an insult in English speaking and European countries (ibid).

Clearly, in the modern multi-cultural context teachers have to be very careful when they use non-verbal communication. Schools need to take responsibility for ensuring that their staff has access to knowledge about such matters, and that where confusions and errors are made they are rectified. Of course, equal care must be taken with the use of verbal communication and there should be a high level of awareness of the dangers of unintended meaning in all forms of communication.

## Children with communication difficulties

There is a group of school students, the majority of whom are distributed in mainstream schools (in Australia, the UK, and the United States) who, regardless of cultural factors, may experience particular difficulties in dealing with non-verbal communication. This group would include students who carry such medical diagnoses as attention deficit/hyperactivity disorder (AD/ HD), autism, and Asperger's syndrome (AS). Children with AD/HD often have a poor understanding of social cues and may not even detect non-verbal signals (Barkley, 1990). Individuals with autism and AS have particular difficulty with decoding symbols and may be both mystified and distressed when confronted with gestures that they do not understand (Happé, 1994). Students with these kinds of difficulties are not incapable of learning to detect and understand such cues, but if they are to master non-verbal communication they will often have to be given explicit instruction in it.

# The importance of establishing transparent rules

Before the teacher can begin the delicate business of separating the background from the foreground of classroom process, there needs to be clear agreement between teacher and students as to what the basic rules of classroom behaviour and interaction actually are.

A first step may be to broadly define appropriate and inappropriate behaviour. Some schools define appropriate behaviour as behaviour that is neutral or helpful to the student or others, and actively contributes to the smooth running of the class and school, and inappropriate behaviour as behaviour that harms the student or others, and interferes with the smooth running of the class and school.

Rules will help students to access appropriate behaviours, behaviours that contribute to the creation of a constructive, pro-social atmosphere and that do not harm the student or others. These rules will form a continual point of reference that will guide classroom activity, it is essential, therefore, that they are transparent, in the sense that they are fully understood by everyone. As Good and Brophy (1973: 168) put it:

'Teachers who take time early in the year to listen to students and explain carefully the rationales underlying rules and assignments are making a wise investment. This ultimately will establish teacher credibility and reduce the students' tendencies to continue to test the teacher throughout the year'. This sound advice could be handed to every teacher at the beginning of each school year and will underscore the principles laid down here for developing a classroom behaviour management policy.

With Good and Brophy in mind, we will now look at the stages in setting up a classroom management policy.

# Establishing a classroom policy for positive behaviour

We recommend the following four stages in the development of a policy for positive behaviour in the classroom.

## Stage 1 – invite assistance

What are the group and individual goals? Establish incentives and rewards. Students may want free time at the end of the lesson or the week, or they may want to learn something, or keep the teacher off their back. Talk to the students about positive incentives and consequences and organize group goals so you can utilize peer influence and tap their need for cooperation.

Rewards work as well for children as they do for adults. Successful teachers use them. One important thing about rewards, however, is that they must be experienced as rewards by the students who are encouraged to earn them. Ten minutes free access to the computer may be 'hog heaven' for one student, or the most infernal torture to another. Other students may simply be left completely unmoved by the whole ICT experience. The important thing here is to consult the students regularly about what they find rewarding, and to develop a diverse rewards 'menu'. It should also be borne in mind that concrete rewards, such as money or sweets, are less effective for most students than more symbolic rewards (such as positive letters to parents or merit certificates). Rewards are a matter of individual preference and should be explored on both group and individual bases. To facilitate this the whole class should discuss issues around the nature of rewards. The discussion should be followed, however, by students being given the opportunity to provide private responses regarding their personal preferences. This can be done through the use of a questionnaire. There will be situations where students will be unable or even unwilling to identify what they find rewarding. In these circumstances teachers can adopt the strategy of 'sleuthing'. This involves watching students and learning from them.

Where possible teachers should use group rewards in preference to individual rewards, especially with older students, for example, time at the end of class to watch a pertinent video or work in groups with friends. Some teachers use an 'Aim of the Week', or the month, where the whole class works together towards a goal, or groups work towards group goals – an excursion, a party, a video, a sporting event that they will participate in. Teachers are likely to enhance their effectiveness by creating reward and referent power and tapping the students' need for individual power, status and influence, belonging, reciprocal cooperation, and caring.

The rules and consequences decided can later help students obtain some of these chosen goals. Also, to strengthen the teacher's reward and referent powers, they should decide early how they will be verbally positive. It is important for teachers to become overtly aware of their repertoire of verbal encouragers and goal reminders, and to be committed to developing and modifying this repertoire. This is important, not least because students may come to tire of what they see as stereotypical or overly predictable teacher comments ('he always says that'/'she says that to everybody'). For praise to be powerful it needs to be personal. To be personal it needs to sound original.

It is useful for teachers to list what they would like from students, and for students to list what they would like from the teacher. This may sound threatening, but most students want teachers to manage disruptive students so the

## Verbal encouragers and goal reminders

*Verbal encouragers*
Find your own ways of saying things that:

- Praise work: 'That's an excellent piece of work, John.'
- Thank them for Socially Helpful behaviour: 'Thanks for helping your mates out.'
- Thank them for Adherence to Agreed-upon Rules: 'Thanks for observing the rules we agreed to.'
- Solicit Help (Care Statement): 'This is a hard game. John, can you and Robert keep us organized?'
- Express a Social Concern Statement: 'That's not fair to the others.'
- Talk about Work: 'You'll have a test on this at the end of the hour so raise your hand if you need some help.'

*Goal reminders*
Find your own ways of saying things that:

- Set limits: 'Finish page one by two o'clock please.'
- Future statements (these should link to rewards that the child or group strive for): 'Finish so we can watch the video.'

rest of the class can work. Students are often surprisingly conservative, and this conservatism helps teachers if they bring it out into the open and use its power.

Teachers can establish with students the reason for rules, why the class needs them. During a class discussion students can discuss rules in their community and even rules from home. Throughout the discussion it can help if the teacher reinforces the notion that rules help each of us reach our goals and that the teacher will be bound by the same rules. The rules are for the good of the group in the long and short term. Rules help people work together, like on a cricket or basketball team. The teacher will reward this teamwork.

Brainstorming the reasons for rules can help, particularly if the teacher writes the students' statements on butchers' paper or the whiteboard.

## Stage II – agree on rules and consequences

With the class the teacher can write a list of rules and consequences. Some writers claim that rules should always be framed positively, a principle drawn from behaviourism not humanism. We believe this is an appropriate approach if teachers so choose, but there is no hard research evidence for this position and trying to frame rules positively can make them incomprehensible and difficult to remember. Olsen (1982, 1989) recommends the use of short, clear rules like 'No annoying' and Heins (1996) agrees that 'No annoying' is a particularly powerful rule. Teachers may wish to use such a rule and frame the other rules positively. Teachers can just as easily teach the child appropriate behaviours from a negatively stated rule as from a positively stated rule. We suggest that when working with young or particularly difficult students, a mixture of positive and negatively stated rules works best for the following reasons:

- Clarity – some negative rules may be more concrete and clear. Heins (1996) found this was particularly true with younger children.
- Ownership – when teachers ask children to decide on rules, they frame some rules negatively. If teachers aim to empower students, give them ownership of the class rules, it may help, where possible, to use the students' own language.
- Reflecting social reality – many rules in society are framed negatively. Some argue that we are teaching children skills that help them enter society. Does the rule say 'Park conscientiously' or does it say 'No parking'? Teachers need clarity and force in their classroom rules, and euphemisms in place of clearly stated rules can be downright dishonest as well as confusing.
- Negativity – Teachers can let the behaviour management policy do the negative side of disciplining for them, and let the rules and consequences do most of the dirty work. Teachers can be pleasant to a student who has to be sent from the classroom 'Sorry Susan, but you've broken the No violence rule. You know what we agreed to.' (the student is then sent from the room). A teacher's verbal behaviours with the student can remain positive. Negative verbal statements can create resentment because the student hears 'put-downs' and may plan revenge.

Again, we are suggesting that teachers try to be verbal and positive when students behave appropriately, and non-verbal and unobtrusive when students behave inappropriately.

## Eight areas for classroom rules

When deciding rules with students, it is helpful to cover the following eight areas. Students can discuss the eight areas and choose appropriate words for the rules, then rehearse them:

- dangerous behaviour (safety);
- physical or verbal violence;
- staying within boundaries;
- put-downs;
- being assertive (Thank you for not whingeing);
- annoying;
- work hard;
- property.

The above are not rules. Students can develop rules to cover these or any area they think is important. It is helpful to keep the list down to seven or fewer rules. As with other skills, younger students can practise rules they devise. For example, the class may have a 'No annoying' rule. The teacher asks the students for examples of behaviours that annoy, and lists these on the board. Then groups of four students think up role plays about the 'No annoying' rule that show:

1. doing it right;
2. doing it wrong;
3. doing it right;
4. doing it wrong.

When students think of examples themselves, they increase their ownership of the rules. Also, it can help to reverse the roles so certain students, particularly those expected to break the rules, play the teacher and show the teacher and other students how to manage rule-breakers.

Secondary teachers can generate a list of rules from each of their classes, then have a group of students combine these rules into one list. Alternatively, the teacher can present a list to each group and have them revise it by adding, removing or modifying rules. Some secondary students tire of repeatedly establishing rules for each class, and sometimes ask the teacher if they can use those already in place. This gives 'legitimate power' to the teacher, a mandate from the students for teachers to use the existing rules and consequences.

## Consequences

Teachers need consequences when rules are broken, but many teachers believe that the key to classroom discipline is more powerful consequences. These teachers usually fail at classroom management because rules and consequences alone are not discipline, they are not classroom management. To give students ownership of a classroom management policy it is crucial to ask them about consequences. Teachers may find that students prefer Glasser's (1986) approach or they might prefer the list of strategies used by Bull and Solity (1987). We suggest that teachers ask students which approach they think will best manage problem behaviours so the rest of the class can work. It is not uncommon to find that students generally prefer non-verbal consequences, like those used by Mr Faulkner. If we are democratic teachers as Dreikurs, Grunwald and Pepper (1982) advised, we listen to the students in our class.

Charles (1996) listed five types of classroom misbehaviour in order of seriousness:

1. aggression;
2. immorality – lying, cheating, etc;
3. defiance of authority;
4. class disruptions;
5. fooling around, off task, etc.

In our rules and consequences, we would deal with 'aggression' differently to 'fooling around'. For aggression the student may go straight to Step 6 on a consequences hierarchy (see pages 56), because it becomes too cumbersome to have a different consequence for each rule or inappropriate behaviour. Most teachers we have observed try to handle all inappropriate behaviours with one set of rules and one hierarchy of consequences.

Consequences work most effectively when organized in a clear hierarchy. Consequences move from least to most severe, for the least to most severe misbehaviours and from least to most intrusive in terms of teacher behaviour (Bull and Solity, 1987; Jones and Jones, 1990). As mentioned above, students should agree on and help choose these consequences and know them in advance. That is, students know clearly what consequences follow certain misbehaviours before those misbehaviours occur; teachers don't decide consequences after a misbehaviour on an ad hoc basis. The early steps of a consequences hierarchy help the student redirect his or her own behaviour. For example, goal reminders, name (or initials) on the board, mediation essays (see Figure 4.1; MacPherson, Candee, and Hohman, 1974) and other techniques can help students rehearse appropriate behaviour.

As discussed above, when teachers are positive, the rules and consequences can do the negative part of managing for them, and free the teacher to teach. The consequences are a bit like the story of 'Brer Rabbit and the Tar Baby'. The

**MEDIATION ESSAY**

Name: _____    Date: _____

1.    What I did that got me into this situation

2.    What happened

3.    How I feel about it

4.    What I plan to do next time (in this sort of situation)

5.    What will happen then

6.    How I will feel then

Signed: _____

Figure 4.1 Mediation essay (after MacPherson, Candee, and Hohman, 1974)

more the student fights, the more entangled he or she will become. Hopefully, the student wants to avoid this entanglement in future.

Some strategies that teachers may wish to build into their consequences hierarchy include:

- Being physically assertive – one way of doing this is for the teacher to stand upright and look bold with their arms and hands open at their sides (to show that they are not intimidated). The most important point here is for teachers to reflect on their physical presentation: for the physically less imposing person, for example, maintaining steady eye contact can be very powerful.
- Five word (maximum) directions (to limit verbalizing during misbehaviour): 'Feet off the desk' (gesture); 'Enough' (glare); 'No talking please' (walk towards the board to put their name or initials up); 'No' (point).
- Proximity – moving close, into the student's space, and, if necessary, stooping to eye level and make eye contact, or stand behind.
- Movement – Using deliberate, bold, never tentative, movements.

Other strategies discussed below are:

- secret signal (Brown, 1986);
- write rules;
- name (or initials) on board;
- mediation essay;
- time out;
- phone parents.

### Hierarchy of consequences

This example is based on a programme designed by A Owner and J Olsen and used in a number of Canberra schools between 1983 and 1987.

For example, a student disrupts the class; he breaks the 'No annoying' rule. A possible consequences hierarchy could be:

1. Rewards and goal reminders (see above). The teacher rewards the student who is working; uses group rewards; helps the students work towards long- and short-term goals, for example 'Finish so we can go out for a game'; asks the students for help, for example 'I need your help this morning'; ignores small disruptions.
2. Gives a disapproving look, pauses, makes eye contact with the student, but continues the lesson.
3. Says the student's name. This is the first time the teacher has disrupted their lesson. The teacher may choose to use an FWD – Five Word (maximum) Direction:

   'Feet off the desk, please.'

   The student and class know this is serious and the next step is a name (or initials) on the board.
4. Name (or initials) on the board. The teacher continues with their lesson. The student knows he has to see the teacher after class and must write the rules

out in his/her seat and write what she/he should have been doing instead of breaking the rule. The student must also complete the work. (See the comments below by Phil Hopkins about the use and misuse of such a technique.)

5. First cross beside his/her name or initials. The teacher continues their lesson. The student knows s/he must move to an isolated seat near the teacher and fill out a Mediation Essay (see Figure 4.1). The teacher may choose to use a social concern statement like 'That's what we agreed to, the class needs to finish this work'.

6. Second cross beside his/her name or initials. The teacher sends the student to a pre-determined location out of the class. The student has supervised detention at lunchtime. (If the student refuses to go, the teacher sends a message to a designated staff member who comes to remove him/her). Parents are telephoned. They must return with the student the next morning. The student works out a contract (behaviour agreement, see Figure 5.2) with the supervising staff and parents. All stakeholders sign the contract.

At the end of the day, the teacher wipes the board clean.

## 'A name on the board'

### By Phillip Hopkins

Mary, a teacher, works through three scenarios that demonstrate different ways of noting behaviour in classrooms.

**Scenario one**

It had been a long term for Mary. Every day she knew that she had to face the English class from… well, somewhere. She felt after three years of teaching that she had a decent amount of tricks she could use to get students to do the right thing in her class. In speaking with her senior teacher about the class Mary was asked; 'Well, what is it you want your students to do?'. Mary, at home had written a short but powerful list. She wanted them to:

- sit in their seats;
- follow simple instructions;
- keep their hands off fellow students.

Mary had shown this list to a colleague who seemed to think that her list represented some fairly fundamental expectations that a teacher might have in a classroom, and so Mary decided it was time to play it straight, simple and to the point.

9.03am, the bell goes and with it Mary rises to do battle. She collects her roll, whiteboard marker, student books, and brief notes. She has her list of expectations and is off to put them in place with her students. Out the door turn left, 345 paces, turn right, up three flights of stairs, turn right again, 45 paces, turn left, through the door, 'good morning everyone, open your books, I have something to say'. All this is said before she even looks at the students. She isn't game to look at Jason or Kylie. She knows their ability to distract her from her purpose, she knows their ability to be able to sense exactly when they can get the whole class off track. The students seem a little stunned, being first thing in the morning, but the strategy of being authoritative and sharp seems to be working. They are after all, quiet!

'This morning I am implementing a new system. Each time you fail to do one of these things', she writes them on the board, 'your names will appear on the top right-hand corner of the board. This will mean that you will stay back five minutes. Every time you do something wrong I will add a stroke and this will mean another five minutes. Understand, good'. No one actually had time to respond. 'Ah, John, out of your seat, that's five minutes, now sit down'

'But I…'

'Ah, failure to follow simple instructions, another five minutes.'

The lesson continues, already Mary has got Jason and Kylie seething in the back corner, waiting for their moment. 'Miss I have dropped my pen on the floor, would it be alright if I got it?' says Kylie. Mary can sense the sarcasm in

*continued overleaf*

her voice. 'Miss, I am very sorry but Jack just touched me and you didn't put his name on the board,' says Jason. Cheers go up around the room.

What does Mary do, and why has this happened?

- The problem for Mary is that she believed that instituting this system without any explanation, warning, discussion or trial, was going to work. It never will. If students feel they have not been consulted and reasoned with, there is little likelihood that it can succeed.
- By instituting the system out of desperation, in the hope that 'a system' based on rigid structure that other colleagues may say is the cure for all discipline difficulties will solve problems, Mary has given herself no room to move. Students can sense this and some, like Jason and Kylie will be ready to test it.

Mary has well and truly committed herself. To her students it presents as a red rag to a bull. Her treatment of John will well and truly be an incentive for other students to achieve the same result. Why, because they know that Mary is being unreasonable and as such students will invariably want to demonstrate over and over again that the way in which she has presented the 'system' is unreasonable. It may be that the bulk of the class can work together to get everyone's name on the board and to see how much time can be accumulated in a 40-minute lesson. If each misdemeanour gets you five minutes and you are able to achieve two misdemeanours every five minutes, you could accumulate 80 minutes of detention.

If the students choose this path of action, it may be their way of trying to get a teacher who does not want to negotiate, to stop and listen to them.

**Scenario two**

It had been a long term for Mary. Every day she knew that she had to face the English class from… well, somewhere. She felt after three years of teaching that she had a decent amount of tricks she could use to get students to do the right thing in her class. In speaking with her senior teacher about the class Mary was asked; 'Well, what is it you want your students to do?'. Mary, at home had written a short but powerful list. She wanted them to:

● sit in their seats;
● follow simple instructions;
● keep their hands off fellow students.

Mary had shown this list to a colleague who seemed to think that her list represented some fairly fundamental expectations that a teacher might have in a classroom, and so Mary decided it was time to play it straight, simple and to the point.

  9.03am, the bell goes and with it Mary rises to do battle. She collects her register, whiteboard marker, student books, and lesson notes. She has her list of expectations and is off. Out the door turn left, 345 paces, turn right, up three flights of stairs, turn right again, 45 paces, turn left…

**STOP**

Mary checks her body language, she feels tense, nervous, anxious. How is she going to appear in control, considered, authoritative and caring if she feels like this. She takes a moment and says good morning to two students who walk past, takes a deep breath and enters the classroom. She immediately smiles at students, makes a special point of making eye contact with Kylie and Jason, places her books on the front desk and then moves around the room, opens the blinds, moves some chairs that aren't being used, asks people to open their books as she walks, while also commenting on some good work that students completed the day before.

  In starting her lesson this way Mary has done some important things:

● she has shown to the students that she is comfortable in the room;
● by walking around the room she in a sense is bringing the students into the focal point of the classroom, which for now is going to be her at the front.

*continued overleaf*

John responds, 'Oh yer, what good work?'

'All of us at some stage do good work John,' she says as she continues on her way to the front of the room.

'Now all eyes up here please. You may have noticed that I have not been happy about our class. I seem to have to spend huge amounts of time asking you to do simple things that I know you are sick of hearing about too. In order to make sure that this class operates in a way where I can teach and you can learn, I have been thinking about the simple things that need to happen.'

Mary moves to the board; 'I want you to be able to sit in your seats, follow simple instructions and keep your hands off fellow students.'

Jack pipes in, 'I can't stop touching people Miss, it's in me blood.'

'Yes well, Jack there are places that can help you with that,' Mary says as a gentle joke, and quickly moves on.

'Does that seem reasonable?' There are nods of approval around the room, even from Kylie as she senses that Mary has got most people listening and on side. Then John's hand goes up. 'Yes John,' 'Well it's just the hands… ', 'John, please,' responds Mary. John seems to get the message while the class, including Mary, have a quiet laugh.

Mary continues, having completed some simple reaffirmation with the class. Mary has introduced this concept in an understated way and is now ready to implement the system.

'Now I know that you are able to keep to these rules but I have to say that it almost seems that many of you don't even know when you are acting against these expectations, and I can understand that. Sometimes behaviour becomes so ingrained that we don't know we are doing things. So, I'd like to try a system where I will write your name on the top right-hand corner of the board each time you break the expectation. Take that as a reminder, if you do it again, I'll write a line next to your name. That means you owe me some of your time for extension work. We'll decide when that time is but it must be within the week.'

Mary has done a couple of proactive things here. She has put the action in a context. 'Sometimes we forget we are doing the things that disrupt learning' and has couched it in language which means that everyone, including herself, owns the problem. She has also given students a chance to correct the behaviour by giving them a warning on the board. She has even given some power to the student on the timing of the extra time and has spoken of it as extension work, which is productive and positive rather than detention, which implies servitude and boredom.

## Scenario three

It had been a long semester for Mary but at the end she could say that it was a very rewarding one. To know that she finally had her English class working as a team who could joke and work and achieve great results left her feeling that she was a success and that her students were at last enjoying learning and, she hoped, life. Mary didn't care if this sounded a little trite to some of her hardened colleagues, it was the end of the semester, she was enjoying the staff dinner, and in the morning she would have two weeks of, 'do what I want, when I want' bliss.

About half way through the term Mary walked into her class and said;

'You know how we have been writing names on the board when things go wrong, well I think it's about time we wrote names up when things are going right. I think it is important that you know straight away when I think you are doing really good work, or helping someone, or sharing ideas. I don't know how many times I have gone home and thought that I should have complimented one of you. So, from now on when that happens your name goes up.'

John, remember John, sparks up, 'Wait on a minute, if we do something wrong we stay in… or I mean, do extension work. If we do something right, what do we get?'

Mary responds, 'I thought you might ask that John, I don't know, I can't give you an early mark, I've already got in trouble once for that. I could give you chocolate, but I'll go broke and beside I'd probably eat it before I got here. I don't know, we'll have to find something won't we. Anyway, is it a good idea or not?' The class nod in agreement.

Mary has created a class that is a team. A nice moment came for Mary when she wrote the name of Tina on the board. Tina had been working away quietly on her own, as she usually did and Mary had noticed some beautiful illustration Tina was doing around a piece of writing she had done. Tina was quiet and hated being the centre of attention. Mary had written her name up, no one noticed, including Tina until they were packing up when Rose nudged Tina, 'Hey look, your name'. Mary noticed the acknowledgement, Tina looked embarrassed, and quickly looked away. As she left the room Tina said quietly to Mary 'What was that for?', 'Your illustration, it's beautiful'. Tina smiled, walked a few paces, stopped and turned; 'Thanks'.

Every teacher looks for ways by which they can successfully keep students on track, doing the right thing, without them needing to raise their voice, repeat an instruction over and over again, or remind a particular student that once again

*continued overleaf*

they seem to be engaging in the sort of behaviour that they know is inappropriate. There are not many occupations where you are asked to speak publicly for three hours or more five days a week, 40 weeks a year. Teaching is one of them.

Our voice boxes are amazing things. If we exercise them they seem to be able to cope with all sorts of stress and strain, but any teacher who has a lovely quiet holiday where they are able to only engage in civil, quiet conversation, knows that those voice boxes quickly go out of training. So many teachers will spend the Friday evening of the first week back at school soothing a sore throat and a scratchy voice. So, any method that saves our voices is one to be taken note of.

Keeping a list of minor misdemeanours on the board can be a powerful thing, but what are the arguments for using it?

- Given that everyone in the classroom knows why the system is being used, it can give participants in the class immediate feedback on whether they are doing the right thing or not.
- It is a way of publicly presenting judgements of behaviour that are being made by the teacher, thereby objectifying them.
- It can become a motivator for positive behaviour.

What are the arguments for not using it?

- It can give the misbehaving student immediate public recognition.
- You might end up filling the board with names and misbehaviours. This might become a potent message that you can't teach.
- It may appear punitive.

When implementing a system like this there are some ground rules that you need to be aware of:

- The purpose of noting a student's name on the board is meant to save you having to disrupt the flow of the lesson while the misbehaving student gets an immediate non-verbal cue that their behaviour is inappropriate. Therefore negotiation is out.
- Overuse it and it might just become a game for students to see who can get the biggest, 'score'.
- Overuse it and your students might start believing that you can't face problems in the class.

Remember, often in our classrooms we become preoccupied with correcting negative behaviour. Whenever you think of a method to correct that behaviour, always turn the method on its head. The opposite of noting negative behaviour on the board would be to note positive behaviour on the board. Also, always ask; 'Why am I doing this?' And, what is the consequence. Presumably, if you are noting negative behaviour, the culprit will lose something – usually time. If you are noting positive behaviour there needs to be a reward!

In our final scenario Mary has achieved a classroom that is working as a team, where effort is recognized and reward is given. Often the greatest reward a teacher can give is a positive comment. For students, and all of us, recognition that you are doing well carries a great deal of benefit. For many adolescents being told that they are difficult and disappointing is a daily and often hourly occurrence. We know in our own adult work life that we are very quick to tell someone they are doing something wrong, but perhaps not so forthcoming in telling them that they are doing a good job.

Chocolates are nice too, but being told what we can do, rather than what we can't do, carries us long after the chocolate has melted.

Most class rules and consequences will not look exactly like those listed above because each teacher and class will formulate their own. Older students will often say they do not want a consequences step where parents are contacted. Teachers can say to them, 'That's fine, as long as we have consequences that work', and give a commitment to try the consequences developed by the students. The teacher explains, 'If these consequences don't work, we will need to include a step where parents are contacted'.

Note: At one school in Canberra, the Principal and Assistant Principal, Colin Garner and Jim Veal, collected and filed the mediation essays filled out by students. If a child convinced their parents that he or she was unfairly accused by teachers, the Senior Management Team could show parents this record of mediation essays in the child's handwriting. This approach successfully brought many parents on side with the school.

## Stage III – gain a commitment

Teachers can send a copy of the rules and consequences home for parents to sign and return. Along with the rules the teacher can send home a copy of their discipline philosophy, so parents understand the context in which the rules were formed. For example:

---

As a teacher I believe all children have a right to learn and that I have a right to teach. My goal is to help them reach their potential and to help them learn to work together and care for each other. There are no excuses for violent behaviour. Children who are violent or who continually disrupt the learning of others will be removed. The children agree with this philosophy and, with me, have developed a set of rules and consequences. I would be grateful if you could discuss these with your child, sign them and return them to me.

---

After parents return the discipline philosophy, rules, and consequences, the class can have a ceremony where the rules and consequences are adopted and each member of the class signs a large sheet with the rules and consequences on it.

### Stage IV – review and reconsider your rules

During the first few weeks of school it is helpful to review the rules each week. It is also helpful to reconsider the class rules four times a year to make certain that the class believes the rules are working, and so the students can make changes where necessary.

It can also help if the teacher asks that pupil who most often breaks rules, to review, justify, or explain the rules and consequences to any visitors, parents, or new students. Justifying and explaining the class rules and consequences can change that student's views, with respect to the acceptance and ownership of these rules.

Students can, of course, become more disruptive towards the end of the year. So at that time, or any time management breaks down, is a good time for the teacher to meet with the class and ask for their help to review the rules and consequences.

## Handling minor disruptions

Minor disruptions can occur for a number of reasons. Students might find a lesson boring, or show off to their peers, or they may not be involved in learning, or may not understand the task and don't want another failure. Most minor disruptions can be stopped through good teaching practices. Vern and Louise Jones (Jones and Jones, 1990) suggested nine methods for initially responding to minor classroom disruptions. These are modified and summarized below:

1. Arrange desks and chairs so the teacher can see and move easily to be near all students. During large-group and small-group work, the class should face the teacher and the teacher should face the class. At all times the teacher should be able to move around the room without disturbing students.
2. Scan the class frequently. Effective teachers learn to attend to more than one thing at a time, they have 'withitness' in the words of Kounin (1970). They attend to the children being taught, for example, to a student at his/her desk, and, at the same time, regularly scan the room with their eyes and ears to monitor all students in the class.
3. The disruptive influence of the teacher's response to misbehaviour should be less than the student's disruption. As suggested above, some teachers create more disruption by disciplining students than misbehaving students cause in the first place. Effective teachers ignore minor disruptions unless they are repeated, then deal with the student privately before using their hierarchy of consequences.
4. An inappropriately angry teacher creates tension and more disruptive behaviour. Kounin (1970) and Brophy and Evertson (1976) found evidence for a 'negative ripple effect' in classrooms associated with harsh criticism from the teacher. Firmness should be associated with teacher warmth, politeness, and explanation of reasons for firmness.
5. A teacher who responds calmly and immediately causes a 'positive ripple effect'. When teachers react calmly and quickly to a student's disruptive behaviour, other students respond by improving their own behaviour.
6. When misbehaviour occurs, the first step for the teacher is to quietly make contact with the student. The teacher can do this with a glance, by moving close to the student, by touching the student on the shoulder (if allowable) or by asking the student an on-task query like – 'Have you finished?'
7. Effective teachers use effective communication skills when resolving conflicts. Reflective statements (Bolton, 1986) can diffuse student anger, for example responding to 'This work is stupid!' with 'You seem fairly angry about this assignment. Let's see if I can help'.

   Use 'I – messages' coupled with an expectation of appropriate behaviour – 'I'm not happy with this. Can you please raise your hand next time'.

---

Teachers should avoid threats and appeals to authority when stopping misbehaviour through direct intervention. By simply stating how they want the student to behave, teachers communicate the expectation that they will be obeyed. However, if they add a threat ('Do it or else!'), they place themselves in a position of conflict with the student, and at the same time, they indirectly suggest that they are not sure he is going to obey.

(Good and Brophy, 1973: 204)

8. Teachers can remind students of the classroom rule or procedure they are not demonstrating. The teacher could point to the list of rules on the classroom wall.
9. When one or two students are being extremely disruptive it is best for the teacher to focus the other students' attention on their task and then talk privately with the disruptive students. The teacher might say to the class, 'Can you please help me by working quietly on your maths while I help Tom and Robert solve their problems?' By handling the situation calmly and positively, the teacher indicates his/her competence, which in turn has a calming effect on the other students.

## Diversions for impending aggression

To a sound curriculum, the teacher's pleasant manner, encouragers, goal reminders, rules, consequences, routines, and good relationships with parents, the teacher can add diversions. If Johnny comes in to school as dark as thunder and the teacher knows he'll blow by 10am, the teacher may pre-empt trouble by trying some of these:

- Activity circuit – the teacher times how long it takes the students to run a particular circuit, for example run down and touch the fence, then run over and touch the classroom door, do two push-ups, then run back to the group. Students try to reduce their times each session.
- The teacher takes the student aside and uses reflective statements – reflects how he/she thinks the student looks. 'You look a bit upset today, Johnny. I'll settle the others down to some work, then come and talk to you.'
- Relaxation – Children lie on the floor and listen to a relaxation tape.
- The teacher introduces a topic of interest to the student – teachers who know their students well can successfully choose subjects that will divert problems.
- The teacher can make a joke, especially about him or herself – humour diffuses tension.
- The teacher can give the student a job.
- The teacher can use a 'secret signal' (Brown, 1986) telling the student to cool down. Only the teacher and student know that, when the teacher pats his or her arm, or holds one finger down at his/her side, it means that the student is headed for trouble and should go to their special corner.

- The teacher gives the volatile student a way out, for example, lets the student go to a special corner or to the hall until he or she cools off. This has been rehearsed so the student knows where to go and what to do.
- The teacher can send the student with a note to another teacher, a note too complicated for the student to understand. 'Because of differing philosophies on pedagogy, this student is contemplating his position here. Please assist.' This is planned beforehand with the other teacher.
- The teacher can encourage the student to help another student who may be having difficulty with their work. Often students in trouble are good at helping others, especially younger students, and they work hard at it.
- The teacher can alter the speed or structure of the lesson to keep up the student's interest. If things have been slow for a time, speed them up; if things have been too unstructured, structure them.
- If the need arises, the teacher can stop the lesson and completely change the activity; for example, move the class outside for a run on the oval.
- The class can have a game, for example, divide into teams to answer questions about sports. First hand up gets a chance to answer and win a point for their team, a wrong answer loses a point for the team.

With a classroom behaviour management plan in place we can now turn to a school-wide plan. The teacher can influence the school-wide behaviour management policy by showing other staff members the effective strategies used in his or her class. Consequently, some may wish to structure a management plan in that sequence – the classroom policy first, then the school-wide policy.

# 5

# Creating a culture for positive behaviour: the importance of values, atmosphere and attitude

## Effective schools for all students

A group of English researchers (Daniels *et al*, 1999) studied a selection of mainstream schools which had been identified, through the UK government's standards inspectorate (OFSTED), as being particularly effective in terms of supporting students with social, emotional and behavioural difficulties. An outcome of their study was a list of five common features associated with good practice. These were:

- Leadership: heads and other members of senior management teams (SMTs) provided effective leadership, particularly in communicating appropriate values, ethos and aspirations for the school as a whole.
- Shared values: a core of staff worked cooperatively and reflectively with one another and pupils to ensure the active participation of all students.
- Behaviour policy and practice: a common, consistent and well monitored behaviour policy for all pupils and staff was in place. A particular feature of this policy was that there was consistency between approaches to dealing with pupils with EBD and those who were not deemed to have EBD.

- Understanding EBD: there was a key member of staff who understood the nature of emotional and behavioural difficulties.
- Teaching skills and the curriculum: The curriculum was appropriately challenging for all students, and approaches to its delivery were marked by opportunities for children to learn from their own actions, through purposeful involvement in learning tasks.

This echoes the findings of other studies that have been carried out of 'effective schools' (eg: Mortimore *et al*, 1988; Purkey and Smith, 1983; Rutter *et al*, 1979) which all point to the importance of clarity and consistency of vision among the staff of a school. The point made by these studies is that all students benefit, in terms of their social and educational experience, from schools which reflect these characteristics. Furthermore, these studies suggest that the particular measures we referred to in the last chapter will be enhanced in their effectiveness if they are reflected and supported in students' experiences in all classrooms and throughout the school. This is not to say that all teachers in all classrooms should behave like mindless robots. What is being said here is that messages about what is acceptable, desirable, unacceptable and undesirable behaviour need to be agreed and consistently reinforced throughout the school.

# Building positive values and a good atmosphere

The bedrock of such a whole-school approach, which is reflected strongly in the five characteristics described above, is the need to establish a clear and unambiguous set of values that are acceptable throughout the school community and its associated subsystems (eg students' families). All schools (and other institutions) are underpinned by a set of values. And although it is often difficult to pin down the precise set of values that a school lives by, it is possible to detect the general tone of a school in terms of its 'ethos' or 'atmosphere'. 'Atmosphere' provides an especially good metaphor here, because it carries with it connotations of habitability. The atmosphere in some schools is positive and enriching, imbuing staff and students with a sense of well-being, optimism and confidence. In other schools the atmosphere is toxic, giving rise to a sense of demoralization, depression and hostility.

A number of researchers and educational practitioners have recently provided us with first-hand accounts of what they see as the underpinnings of a positive school atmosphere. Grundy and Blandford (1999), writing about an English 'Pupil Referral Unit' which has received conspicuously positive evaluations from government inspectors, emphasize the importance of a number of factors. First, they reflect on leadership of the institution. For them good leadership is characterized by the ability to communicate a coherent and positive vision, in a situation where all staff feel able and welcome to contribute to the leadership of the institution. A crucial factor in this 'vision' is the quality of 'hope' (see Fullan, 1998), whereby even the most difficult situations are construed as valuable learning experiences. In these circumstances 'hope' becomes equated with a sense of power. Similarly, when difficulties occur the emphasis is on finding a solution as opposed to dwelling on causes. These qualities combine with an emphasis on supporting staff and acknowledging and celebrating their strengths, as well as confronting their needs in an honest and positive manner. Finally, Grundy and Blandford stress the importance of the effective management of change. For them, the effective school is constantly aware of its status as an institution in process. This means that schools must always be in a state of reflection and self-analysis, which in turn feed into ongoing collaborative planning.

A second article, by Richard Sattin, an educational psychologist, deals with a special school for children with emotional and behavioural difficulties (Sattin, 1999). Again, this is a school which has received a highly favourable report from UK government inspectors. Sattin echoes many of the issues raised by Grundy and Blandford. He adds to their analysis an emphasis on the constructive use of students' time. This relates to the stress that is placed on providing students with clear, unambiguous behavioural boundaries, which are supported by considered explanations and justifications, as well as incentives and rewards that are accessible to all.

Lucas (1999), writing about her experiences as a head teacher of an inner city primary school, describes the way in which what she describes as 'nurturing principles' can be effectively applied to mainstream schools. Again, she echoes many of the points made by the authors to whom we have already referred. Additional points gleaned from her account, however, highlight the importance of (that much maligned and frequently abused item) the school's 'mission statement'. For Lucas:

> ... the mission statement is more than a form of words. It becomes a constant point of reference. All other aims and objectives for the plethora of curriculum and organisational policies which schools are now required to have, flow from it. There is a continual process of testing new initiatives against the statement wherever they come from... No hasty decision is taken and indeed no decision is taken unless it can be clearly seen by all to be compatible with the agreed aims. The mission statement is binding on all; no one is outside it.

The mission statement is required to reflect the inclusive, person-centred, practical and hopeful values that we have already discussed. Good schools value people, including staff, students, parents, and all the people who come into contact with the school, as well as any persons or groups who may impinge on the awareness of members of the school community. This last point is very important because it draws attention to the fact that (for example) *all* schools should prepare their students for active and positive participation in the multicultural society, regardless of whether or not they are a 'multicultural school'. Another important point made by Lucas is that, in an effective, 'nurturing' school, mechanisms must be in place to ensure that new members of staff and new students are fully inducted into the school's value base and ethos. Finally, Lucas emphasizes the need for schools to adopt a developmental emphasis, whereby historical and maturational factors are taken into account, both in relation to students and the school as a whole.

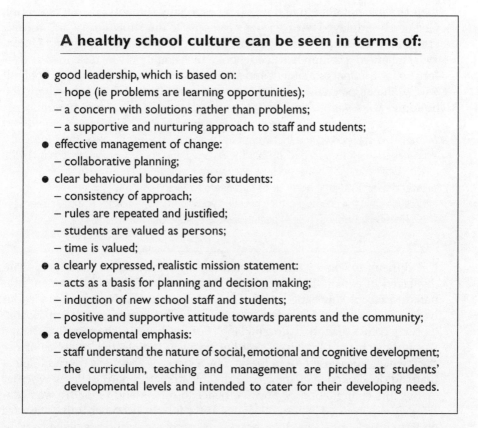

### A healthy school culture can be seen in terms of:

- good leadership, which is based on:
  - hope (ie problems are learning opportunities);
  - a concern with solutions rather than problems;
  - a supportive and nurturing approach to staff and students;
- effective management of change:
  - collaborative planning;
- clear behavioural boundaries for students:
  - consistency of approach;
  - rules are repeated and justified;
  - students are valued as persons;
  - time is valued;
- a clearly expressed, realistic mission statement:
  - acts as a basis for planning and decision making;
  - induction of new school staff and students;
  - positive and supportive attitude towards parents and the community;
- a developmental emphasis:
  - staff understand the nature of social, emotional and cognitive development;
  - the curriculum, teaching and management are pitched at students' developmental levels and intended to cater for their developing needs.

# Getting a whole-school approach started

It may seem odd to be addressing issues of a whole-school approach *after* having given consideration to the individual teacher's own classroom policy. This is not so odd, however, when we recognize that the classroom is the main theatre of educational activity in the school, and that, in the classroom, it is the individual teacher's vision, purposes and practices that are central to what goes on. In short we need to know what it is that we want to be going on in the classroom before we can address questions about what should be happening in the rest of the school to support classroom activity. It is the collective pooling and exploration of individual staff members' views on this subject that lies at the heart of an effective whole-school policy.

In reality, it is not always easy to get staff to focus on policy issues. This can be a particular problem in a school where there is poor staff morale, and where there is a general sense that things (and especially students) are out of control. One newly employed head teacher's response to this situation is worth considering. In this example 'Mrs Lincoln' (Cooper, 1993; Cooper, Smith and Upton, 1994) inherited a comprehensive school which could only be described as dysfunctional. Student attainment and attendance levels were poor; the school roll was falling as parents who could chose to send their children elsewhere; the buildings were scarred with graffiti, and staff morale was at rock bottom:

---

They [the staff] could see that what they were doing was not successful. Nobody comes to work to do a bad job, but they were going home, feeling very dissatisfied with what they had done, because they were not winning.
**Interviewer:** Was that because of bad exam results?
Disruption in the classroom: they believed you didn't really look for results in a comprehensive school... Their expectations were very low.

(Cooper, 1993: 190)

---

It is difficult to convey here the formidable determination that Mrs Lincoln displayed in person. But it was clear that she was not for one moment prepared to accept 'low expectations'. On the other hand, she was also a leader with a real sense of hope (see above), as is illustrated in her remark that 'nobody comes to work to do a bad job'. For this head teacher positive change would be achieved by harnessing her belief in the positive qualities of her staff, which, she sensed, were masked by a sense of dissatisfaction and defeat that had developed over some considerable time. It is hard to know whether or not this combination of positive belief in others and empathy was consciously experienced by her colleagues. What is clear, however, is that she *acted* on it. In other words she did what the research and writing reviewed earlier in this chapter suggests that good leaders do: she turned her positive values and beliefs into practical action.

In this case Mrs Lincoln initiated a series of staff workshops designed to encourage staff to reflect on ways of improving their school. This proved to be a turning point in the school's development. The first workshop was entitled 'What makes a good school?' This led to the generation of a list of qualities which were identified by staff as being attributes of a good school. They included (quoted verbatim from school documentation generated as a record of these meetings):

- strong head with a good sense of direction; obvious and effective leadership;
- a caring community, where there is respect for people and property; quiet environment;
- a desire to do well – a community where achievement in all spheres is encouraged;
- where there is an established disciplinary framework, help and support for new, probationary and supply [substitute] staff;
- where a good public image is cultivated;
- one which is educationally forward thinking and innovative;
- where the school's policy about what it is attempting to do is clear and kept updated;
- able to take any visitor to any part of the school at any time;
- good atmosphere.

Further lists were generated relating specifically to student and staff qualities. These included the need for students to have a sense of pride in themselves and their school, to have positive attitudes toward educational achievement; to have self-respect and respect for others. Staff, on the other hand, were seen as needing to be 'professional', to have high morale, pride in their work and opportunities to practise their specialisms, the ability and willingness to respond to students' individual needs, a consistent approach to behaviour and discipline, good relations among the staff team and between staff and students.

After a period of reflection, during which time these views were collated and distributed, the staff engaged in another workshop. This time the question was: 'Is *this* a good school?' Here the staff were required to explore the extent to which their school lived up to their own ideals of what a good school should be. Predictably, the outcome was that this was indeed a school with enormous shortcomings which were, owing to the original exercise, easily translated into goals for improvement.

Once a school staff has begun to formulate some sense of collective values and the school's mission, it is time to involve the students. Again, the opportunity to reflect on the desirable qualities of an effective school often reveals that students share many of their teachers' values. They too want to attend schools of which they are proud, that reward effort and foster achievement, and where they are treated with respect in an atmosphere that is stimulating, but orderly, safe and secure. Students the world over like their teachers to be consistent, firm and fair in their discipline, as well as being personally considerate and approachable (Cooper, 1993; Druian and Butler, 1987; Tattum, 1982).

Clearly, exercises such as these workshops would benefit most schools, because they create opportunities to discover the values to which staff aspire. Once these values have been identified practical issues present themselves as obstacles are encountered. In the case of Mrs Lincoln's school, direct consequences of these activities were:

- the establishment of a discipline code;
- the creation of a system of rewards for students;
- reform of the pastoral system;
- the introduction of a counselling programme.

The remainder of this chapter is devoted to providing a concrete example of the development of a whole-school policy that is rooted in the positive, humanistic values that we have outlined above, and a sense of the need for a transparent, rational and consistent structure for school discipline. What follows also reflects the findings of research studies which have established the effectiveness of different approaches.

It should be emphasized that what follows is entirely consistent with current UK government policy that is directed at promoting social inclusion. The main issue addressed here is that effective whole-school behaviour policies do not involve simply reacting to behavioural problems, rather they are geared to promoting a pro-social climate which identifies and prevents the development and escalation of problems. As part of this process, the strategies and techniques described also contribute to other evidence based formal measures designed to support inclusion, such as individual education plans (IEPs), statements of special educational needs, and statement reviews.

# Steps to establishing a whole-school behaviour policy

## Stage 1 – gathering evidence

### Constructing a picture of the problem
Systemic problems can take a number of different forms, for example:

- A problem in the classroom, involving interactions among pupils, or between teacher and pupil(s) (eg a pupil who constantly speaks out of turn in spite of repeated rebukes).
- A problem in the school that disturbs the classroom situation (eg a child who misbehaves in class in response to an unreasonable school rule; inconsistencies in staff expectations; because of peer problems, or bullying).

- A problem at school that disturbs the out of school context (eg families; neighbourhoods – a child's anxieties about being bullied at school lead to withdrawn/aggressive behaviour at home and in the community).
- A problem outside the school (such as in the neighbourhood or family) that disturbs the school (eg marital discord leads to collusion in pupil misbehaviour).

In establishing a whole-school approach it is essential that schools start with the element of the picture over which they have greatest control, that is, within-school factors. The first job, therefore, is to define the nature of the within-school issues that need to be addressed.

## Defining elements in the picture

What do the problems look like to those involved? Each perspective should be provided in subjective-emotive terms (ie individuals' feelings), and objective-behavioural terms (observable facts). These perceptions include:

- What are the problems?
- Where are the problems?
- What will things be like when the problems have been addressed?
- What needs to be done?
- What are the strengths in each of the school/community/family sub-systems?

The teacher's *subjective* perceptions can be gathered through the approaches already suggested, such as through staff workshops. The students' *subjective* perceptions can be gathered through various consultation exercises, such as class discussions, student surveys and interviews.

## Testing the perceptions

Those elements of these perceptions that can be measured through behavioural observation should be identified and measured. This can be done through the use of, for example:

- behaviour rating scales (see Chapter 13);
- systematic observation (ie the listing of particular behaviours and the systematic recording of them at specified times and specified places) (see Chapter 13);
- examination of records (attendance; detentions; recorded incidents).

These data are useful for both defining the problems, and, therefore, indicating ways forward, as well as providing a baseline against which the success of intervention can be measured in the future. By repeating these data gathering techniques in a year's time it will be possible to gauge the extent to which the situation has changed, either for better or worse (ie behavioural problems either get better or worse, they rarely remain stable). The involvement of students and staff in these data gathering exercises helps to create a sense of shared ownership and common purpose, and can be the first step on the road to developing a more cooperative atmosphere in the school.

It is important to note that once consultative and investigative exercises such as these are set in motion sensitive and discomforting issues may be brought to the surface. Unspoken rules may be challenged; customary practices may be highlighted as undesirable; traditional power bases may be undermined. For example:

- 'no go areas' may be questioned;
- students' rights of access to certain facilities and areas may be questioned;
- student and staff behaviours (eg lack of punctuality; civility) may be criticized;
- staff may be required to do more supervision duties;
- students may be required to engage in the supervision of other students;
- members of the school management team may be seen as needing to be more visible around the school, and more accessible to staff and students.

Of course there is no point in a school staff embarking on an exercise such as this unless there is a substantial commitment among the staff to responding constructively to fair criticism. To put it more positively, dysfunctional practices often develop out of dysfunctional situations. For example, a teacher may avoid students who are difficult to handle because in the past attempts to challenge or correct undesirable behaviour have failed. As a result, the more the student misbehaves, the more he gets away with it, and so the more he misbehaves. Gradually the teacher's position is undermined, further weakening his or her sense of confidence and efficacy. The best thing to do in these circumstances is to acknowledge the fact that this is what is going on. The avoidance has to stop and the member of staff needs the support of colleagues (as well as students and probably parents) in finding effective ways of establishing positive behaviour.

## Stage II – establishing a discipline plan

The US writers Walker, Colvin and Ramsey (1995) echo Lucas's emphasis on the mission statement as a fundamental step in the creation of an effective school-wide discipline plan. The mission statement should be rooted in the positive aspirations that are associated with what staff and students believe makes a good school, whilst being 'challenging and uplifting' (ibid: p127). For example:

River Primary School is a caring community committed to providing all students with the social, behavioural and academic skills that will help them to lead happy and successful lives both whilst at the school and when they leave. Our goal is to help each child reach his or her highest level of academic success, and to help students learn to work together and care for each other in a rewarding, stimulating and safe environment.

The next step is to show how the discipline plan is going to support the mission statement. Walker, Colvin and Ramsey provide the following example of a 'statement of purpose', that is succinct and widely transferable:

The purpose of the school-wide discipline plan at [this school] is to:

1. establish school-wide structures and procedures for teachers and students to facilitate teaching and learning;
2. encourage student behaviours that enhance the learning environment;
3. minimize student behaviours that inhibit teaching and learning interactions.

(Walker, Colvin and Ramsey, 1995: 127)

On the basis of the investigations carried out in Stage I, staff and students agree on a set of clear behavioural expectations. This can be achieved through staffroom and classroom discussions, questionnaires and focus groups. Efforts must be made during this consultation phase to ensure that statement of purpose is kept in the forefront of staff and student thoughts. Walker, Colvin and Ramsey (ibid) suggest that the number of expectations be limited to four or five, and that they be expressed in positive terms, with examples of positive and negative behaviours. Finally, extensive opportunities will need to be provided to allow students to explore, discuss and understand these expectations, and, where necessary, receive training and practice in them. Additional guidelines may be required for specific settings around the school where particular behavioural problems have been identified (such as dining areas, the playground, school trips).

Further consultation with students should address issues of how compliance with agreed expectations will be rewarded (eg with awards, merit certificates, free time, private praise, posted work, etc). Again, it is essential that the statement of purpose be kept firmly in mind, and the rewards decided upon will have the effect of supporting the statement of purpose and not being a distraction from it. It is often important to emphasize that a reward can be defined as an action or event which makes the recipient feel personally valued.

## Stage III – consultation with parents

At this point it will become appropriate to consult more widely. This is consistent with the statutory responsibility that schools in the England and Wales now have to establish home–school agreements (DfEE, 1999). For this purpose a consultation document can be sent to parents which includes a questionnaire regarding discipline (see Figure 5.1 opposite). The purposes of this consultation exercise are to:

- raise parental awareness of the school's mission statement, statement of purpose, and reward system;
- secure majority parental support for the school's mission statement, statement of purpose, and reward system;
- inculcate a sense that responsibility for discipline issues is shared between the school community and the wider community of parents and carers.

Included in the consultation pack are the school mission statement, the statement of purpose, and reward system, for parents to comment on. In addition the parents can be asked to respond to the following statement:

---

In every community there will be times when some individuals will behave in ways which make others feel frustrated, unhappy or unsafe. Whilst we will make every effort to help students at River Primary to behave as good citizens through positive reinforcement and encouragement, we need to have a clear set of procedures for dealing with students who persistently fail to respond to these positive means, and who make life difficult for others through disruptive, aggressive, violent or otherwise unruly behaviour. The students and staff agree with this view, and are developing a set of rules and consequences for the school. We would be grateful if you could discuss the attached survey with your child, complete it and return it to the school.

---

The form may have to be sent out a second or even third or fourth time before some parents will return it. Some might only respond to a phone call in which a member of staff fills out the form for them. All parents should retain or be sent a copy of their responses, so that they have a record. It is important that the school be aware of possible literacy difficulties or other language issues, and take appropriate steps to deal with these so that all parents are given equal opportunity to participate in this process.

After the form has been filled out by parents it can be helpful to use it when a child is in trouble and refusing to comply with school expectations. For example: 'Mrs Jones, you said that a child who's been fighting on the playground should have one weeks detention. Now Johnny has been fighting on the playground so we know you'll agree that he shouldn't be treated differently to any other child.'

Dear Parents,

We are interested in your views on school discipline so we can formulate a policy on behaviour management. Could you please rate the behaviours listed below on the 1 to 5 scale according to how serious you think they are. Then suggest a consequence and return the form by Friday.

Name: _____    Date: _____

| | not very serious | | | | serious | Suggested consequence |
|---|---|---|---|---|---|---|
| 1. Fighting in class | 1 | 2 | 3 | 4 | 5 | |
| 2. Swearing at a teacher | 1 | 2 | 3 | 4 | 5 | |
| 3. Drinking alcohol at school | 1 | 2 | 3 | 4 | 5 | |
| 4. Cheating in a test | 1 | 2 | 3 | 4 | 5 | |
| 5. Fighting in playground | 1 | 2 | 3 | 4 | 5 | |
| 6. Backchatting the teacher | 1 | 2 | 3 | 4 | 5 | |
| 7. Disrupting a class | 1 | 2 | 3 | 4 | 5 | |
| 8. Being late for class | 1 | 2 | 3 | 4 | 5 | |
| 9. Striking a teacher | 1 | 2 | 3 | 4 | 5 | |
| 10. Skipping school | 1 | 2 | 3 | 4 | 5 | |
| 11. Skipping a class | 1 | 2 | 3 | 4 | 5 | |
| 12. Stealing or damaging others' property | 1 | 2 | 3 | 4 | 5 | |
| 13. Bullying other children | 1 | 2 | 3 | 4 | 5 | |
| 14. Smoking at school | 1 | 2 | 3 | 4 | 5 | |
| 15. Having illegal drugs at school | 1 | 2 | 3 | 4 | 5 | |

Are there any other behaviours that concern you, that have not been listed here? Please write them down here, or phone Ms Z at the school, and say what your suggested consequences are:

Behaviours:

Consequences:

Figure 5.1 Parental views on discipline

The completed form can also be used with children who try to bluff by saying, for example, 'My dad says I can swear at teachers if I want to.' The teacher can reply: 'That's interesting Liam, because the form here shows your parents say that a child who swears at teachers should get one week's detention.'

Some schools have a committee of students collate this information so the students have ownership of the school behaviour management policy. This information can be sifted for the range of legitimate and humane suggestions and combined with data gathered from each classroom and each staff member on their ideas on rules and consequences for the school. A committee of students collate this material, particularly at the secondary level, and use it to generate suggestions for school rules which are then discussed with staff.

### Physical punishment and restraint

Whilst it is likely there will be some consensus about the relative seriousness of most behaviours, the range of consequences proposed is likely to be wide and varied, and sometimes showing scant awareness of the moral, educational, practical or legal parameters in which schools have to operate. For example, although the use of corporal punishment in schools is, by and large, illegal throughout most of the world, there are still parents who employ it and people who would argue for its reintroduction in those countries where it has been outlawed. Clearly, the use of this or any other illegal or morally questionable form of intervention must be challenged. To take one example, current UK government guidance for England and Wales suggests that behaviour management plans for individual students should be cross-referenced with home–school agreements, so as to facilitate both a consistent and humane approach to managing the student's behaviour (DfEE, 1999).

There is of course the potential for confusion on this subject where issues of physical restraint are concerned. Under English law (Education Act, 1996, section 550A) teachers in schools have the power to physically restrain students in order to prevent:

- the committing of an offence;
- personal injury to, or damage to the property of any person, including themselves;
- behaviour prejudicial to the maintenance of good order and discipline in the school.

This power extends to all circumstances inside and outside of schools where the teacher has 'lawful control or charge' of the student. A crucial issue here is the requirement that the teacher must not exceed the application of 'reasonable force' when restraining a student. Reasonable force is defined as: 'The degree of force used must be in proportion to the circumstances of the behaviour or the consequences it is intended to prevent' (DfEE circular 10/98).

The guidance makes the explicit point that 'physical intervention should never be used as a punishment.' The DfEE (Department for Education and Employment) recommends that teachers should receive training in restraint approaches from an accredited training agency.

The DfEE requires that Local Education Authorities (LEAs) and individual schools should publish guidance on the use of physical restraint in their LEA and whole-school behaviour policies. An important point here is that physical restraint should usually be seen as a last resort that is used within the context of a programme of positive behaviour management, positive staff–student relationship and effective teaching. The clear implication of this is that where the need for physical restraint occurs as a result of inadequacies in the overall policies of a school or the failure of groups and individuals to effectively implement an appropriate policy, the legality of restraint practices will be undermined.

## Stage IV – stakeholders' responsibilities

By this stage a practical policy is beginning to take shape. The aims and purposes of the policy are clear and everyone has had an opportunity to be involved in its development. Now it is time to establish responsibilities so that everyone knows exactly what they are expected to do when there is a problem with misbehaviour. The following are examples of one school's stakeholder policy (modified from the policies used at the Methow Valley Intermediate School and George Middle School in Washington, USA). Because of the differences that exist between schools in terms of their organizational arrangements, circumstances, personnel and so on, the precise details of stakeholder responsibilities will need to be expressed in terms of the particular needs of a given school. The following examples could be used by a school as a basis for drafts of their own stakeholder responsibilities which can then be put out for consultation as with other aspects of the policy. A major part of this process should be an open discussion and exploration of the meaning of the term 'stakeholder', with all its implications of identification, status, vested interest and ownership. Stakeholders in a school can be likened to shareholders in a public company: the more successful the company, the more they benefit, though they can only benefit if they are prepared to make an investment (ie take on responsibilities).

One of the authors uses the suggestions on pages 82–89 in in-service training in schools. The staff divide into groups that each list the responsibilities for one or two of the stakeholders. Often the people deciding these are not a member of that particular stakeholders' group, for example, the group deciding the head teacher's or deputy head teacher's responsibilities does not include the head teacher's or deputy's input until the suggestions are later put to the whole staff.

It is interesting to note that these professionally derived principles are in keeping with the principles of the requirements for promotion threshholds

## Students' responsibilities

The importance of students' rights to a voice in issues relating to the regulation of their lives is enshrined in European and UK legislation (The European Convention on Children's Rights, 1996; The Children Act, 1989), an important extension of this is the need for rights to be balanced with responsibilities.
Students have the responsibility to:

1. Participate in learning by listening, sharing ideas, asking questions, working cooperatively, and completing assignments on time and to the best of their abilities.
2. Learn and practise appropriate behaviour for classrooms, buses, common areas, libraries, toilets, and playgrounds.
3. Respect the rights, feelings and property of everyone.
4. Contribute to the positive learning climate of the school by making every effort to understand and practise the school's philosophy and support its goals, and by recognizing and encouraging the contributions of other students and adults to that positive climate.
5. Follow the directions of all staff members and visiting members of staff.
6. Come to class on time and prepared.
7. Settle conflict in non-violent ways, through problem solving and mediation.
8. Actively try to involve parents in the academic, social, and extracurricular life of the school, by encouraging them to attend and keeping them informed of events and opportunities.
9. Keep the school clean.
10. Be civil, courteous, responsible, and act in a safe manner.
11. Participate in the improvement of the school by sharing concerns and ideas with other students, staff, parents, and concerned community members.
12. Be honest and respectful when discussing school issues in the family situation, so as to promote constructive and cooperative ways of dealing with problems when they arise. Do not play the school off against the family or the family off against the school.

and statutory responsibilities imposed on teachers in England and Wales, and Northern Ireland. What is important and distinctive about the following prescriptions is that they were *self-imposed* by a group of professionals. In this way they exemplify something of the professional craft knowledge of practitioners,

## Parents' responsibilities

Parents have the responsibility to:

1. Model a respect for learning and participate actively in their children's educational experience by:
   - attending school events;
   - making every effort to provide a regular time and space for children's reading and out of school study;
   - communicating with the school concerns and relevant information about children (separations, serious illnesses, and other crises which may increase the need for special sensitivity on the part of school staff);
   - requesting and being available for conferences with school staff as needed;
   - ensuring regular and prompt attendance.
2. Make every effort to understand, and support the philosophies, goals and policies of the school.
3. Make every effort to understand and support the discipline plans developed by the Board and staff of the school.
4. To the best of their ability send children to school clean, fed, rested, and ready to participate in school activities.
5. Participate in the improvement of the school by sharing concerns and ideas with students, staff, other parents, and concerned community members.
6. Be honest and respectful when discussing school issues in the family situation, so as to promote constructive and cooperative ways of dealing with problems when they arise. Not blame the school for problems until every effort has been made to engage in reasonable discussion with school staff. Not play the school off against the family or the family off against the school. Communicate concerns to the school without conveying to the child that home is against school.

which emerges from a process of reflection and interaction in the schools where these procedures were to be employed. We offer these, therefore, not as prescriptions to be slavishly adopted, but examples of well thought through ideas that professional readers might wish to engage with in their own schools with a view to producing their own set of ideas (see references to Cooper, 1993, above). We wish to emphasize the importance of the process of generating solutions to school problems from within schools.

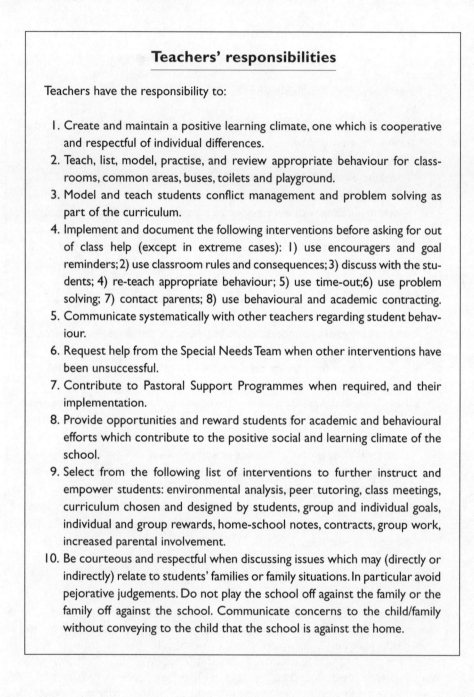

# Teachers' responsibilities

Teachers have the responsibility to:

1. Create and maintain a positive learning climate, one which is cooperative and respectful of individual differences.
2. Teach, list, model, practise, and review appropriate behaviour for classrooms, common areas, buses, toilets and playground.
3. Model and teach students conflict management and problem solving as part of the curriculum.
4. Implement and document the following interventions before asking for out of class help (except in extreme cases): 1) use encouragers and goal reminders; 2) use classroom rules and consequences; 3) discuss with the students; 4) re-teach appropriate behaviour; 5) use time-out; 6) use problem solving; 7) contact parents; 8) use behavioural and academic contracting.
5. Communicate systematically with other teachers regarding student behaviour.
6. Request help from the Special Needs Team when other interventions have been unsuccessful.
7. Contribute to Pastoral Support Programmes when required, and their implementation.
8. Provide opportunities and reward students for academic and behavioural efforts which contribute to the positive social and learning climate of the school.
9. Select from the following list of interventions to further instruct and empower students: environmental analysis, peer tutoring, class meetings, curriculum chosen and designed by students, group and individual goals, individual and group rewards, home-school notes, contracts, group work, increased parental involvement.
10. Be courteous and respectful when discussing issues which may (directly or indirectly) relate to students' families or family situations. In particular avoid pejorative judgements. Do not play the school off against the family or the family off against the school. Communicate concerns to the child/family without conveying to the child that the school is against the home.

## Head teacher's responsibilities

The head teacher has the responsibility to:

1. Ensure that all students, and staff are cared for in a safe positive learning environment.
2. Provide or delegate leadership in staffing and assist in developing and monitoring behavioural plans that involve students, parents and staff.
3. Observe, monitor and assist individual staff with procedures and expectations.
4. Provide timely, consistent feedback to students, staff and parents.
5. Comply with the law, and be fully committed to protecting the rights of all students, parents and staff, without exception.
6. Contribute to Pastoral Support Programmes when required, and their implementation.
7. Select and administer appropriate and consistent consequences which support the school's philosophy and goals.
8. Delegate administrative responsibility as needed.
9. Represent the schools position regarding all behaviour management matters.
10. Be courteous and respectful when discussing issues which may (directly or indirectly) relate to students' families or family situations. In particular avoid pejorative judgements. Do not play the school off against the family or the family off against the school. Communicate concerns to the child/family without conveying to the child that the school is against the home.

## Deputy head teacher's responsibilities

The (or a) deputy head teacher has the responsibility to:

1. Facilitate and lead in the establishment of a consistent school behaviour management policy.
2. Provide for yearly staff review of the school behaviour management policy, prior to the end of the summer term, and make necessary revisions.
3. Distribute copies of the school behaviour management policy to staff, parents and students by the second week of school.

*continued overleaf*

4. Facilitate the planning and implementation of student, staff and parent behaviour management instructional activities.
5. Ensure that Pastoral Support Programmes are provided for students at risk of exclusion, contribute to their development and implementation, and ensure that they are implemented effectively.
6. Approve individual teacher's classroom rules and consequences.
7. Be a member of the school behaviour management committee.
8. Participate actively in the Special Needs Team.
9. Protect the rights of all those involved in behaviour management matters without exception.
10. Communicate effectively with students, staff members and parents.
11. Represent the school's position regarding all behaviour management matters.
12. Follow Department of Education and Employment policy and legislation, and keep staff advised of changes.
13. Provide an opportunity for review of behaviour management policy decisions.
14. Be courteous and respectful when discussing issues which may (directly or indirectly) relate to students' families or family situations. In particular avoid pejorative judgements. Do not play the school off against the family or the family off against the school. Communicate concerns to the child/family without conveying to the child that the school is against the home.

## Pastoral team responsibilities

Members of the pastoral team have the responsibility to:

1. Assist with the design and implementation of educational and behaviour management interventions with other staff, students and parents which are in accord with the school's philosophy and goals.
2. Take a leading role in the development and implementation of pastoral support plans.
3. Consult with parents and teachers regarding the educational progress, peer relationships and behaviour of students with special needs.
4. Assist teachers with the design of special behavioural and academic programming.

5. Provide consistent, ongoing counselling and support for children including individual, group, and crisis counselling.
6. Participate actively in the special needs team.
7. Work with community agencies to develop more available, and effective services for children and families.
8. Facilitate the training, and supervision of conflict mediation, programming, and assist with its integration into the school's intervention procedures.
9. Assist teachers by visiting classrooms and taking classes as a teacher to provide valid consultation about problems with individual students, or groups of students.
10. Be courteous and respectful when discussing issues which may (directly or indirectly) relate to students' families or family situations. In particular avoid pejorative judgements. Do not play the school off against the family or the family off against the school. Communicate concerns to the child/family without conveying to the child that the school is against the home.

## Behaviour specialist's responsibilities

The behaviour specialist has the responsibility to:

1. Provide appropriate, consistent interventions and be a source of specialist knowledge.
2. Clearly communicate staff/student/parent responsibilities.
3. Help monitor at-risk students and/or students who repeatedly misbehave.
4. Contribute to the development and implementation of Pastoral Support Plans.
5. Demonstrate a leadership role in establishing personalized education plans.
6. Comply with current legislation.
7. Participate actively in the special needs team and the school behaviour management committee.
8. Mediate conflicts between students or between students and teachers.
9. Assist teachers by visiting classrooms and taking classes as a teacher to provide valid consultation about problems with individual students, or groups of students.
10. Be courteous and respectful when discussing issues which may (directly or indirectly) relate to students' families or family situations. In particular avoid pejorative judgements. Do not play the school off against the family or the family off against the school. Communicate concerns to the child/family without conveying to the child that the school is against the home.

## Senior management team responses to discipline referrals

The senior management team (SMT) will respond to referrals in a way consistent with the school behaviour management policy and will emphasize teaching students new skills for resolving the problems that led to the student management referral. Responses will include:

1. Develop and implement a personalized education program and Pastoral Support Programme.
2. Counselling student.
3. Notify the parent or guardian. (Should a parent meeting be necessary, teachers will be given one working day's notice by the SMT. Teachers may request representation at the meeting if it appears a complaint is being made that could result in disciplinary action toward the teacher. A teacher can request that a conference be held between the teacher, the student and/or the parents, and the SMT before the student returns to class or when all stakeholders are available. This conference will not disrupt the teacher's class instruction time.)
4. Assign one or more days of lunch time detention.
5. Assign one or more days of after-school detention.
6. Arrange for students to see the behaviour management specialist, or other staff.
7. Refer to the special needs team.
8. Develop and implement a student contract.
9. Arrange staffing for the student.
10. Arrange a conference with parents, students, and teachers.
11. Change the student's timetable.
12. Revoke privileges.
13. Impose fixed term exclusion.
14. Impose permanent exclusion.
15. Refer students for an alternative placement.

These stakeholder responsibilities are only a guide. Each school will develop a set of responsibilities tailored to its own needs. For example, some schools adopt a no-exclusions policy. We would hope that all schools would aspire to such a policy, at least in the long term. At any given time, however,

## Senior management team responsibilities

Members of the SMT will take responsibility for discipline issues referred by staff in the event of (for example):

1. After the teacher has used appropriate interventions for continual classroom problems (ie defiance of authority and chronic rule violation, poor behaviour choices in common areas).
2. Fighting, and/or assault.
3. Serious or chronic threats or harassment of peers (ie bullying).
4. Students possessing weapons, harmful and dangerous objects on school premises.
5. Students skipping class or school.
6. Students leaving school without permission.
7. Vandalism.
8. Smoking.
9. Use, transfer, sale, under the influence, or possession of alcohol, illegal drugs or illegal drug paraphernalia.
10. Assault on a staff member. If investigation shows a student has assaulted a teacher, the teacher does not have to accept the child back into his/her classroom.
11. Using abusive language directed toward another person.

In the case of events 3 and 4 the teacher has the option of removing the student from class immediately; for events 4, 9 and 10 the student should be immediately removed from the classroom and/or school until an investigation is conducted.

there will be schools where exclusion is seen as a necessary last resort and a part of the counselling process used with the child and family, that is, the student receives help from case managers before exclusion to try and prevent this exclusion, during the exclusion process if it comes to that, and after. Essentially these lists of responsibilities should be seen as records of agreements and may be listed in the policy document as: parent/student/staff responsibilities. Each stakeholder agrees to certain things. Staff members, students, and parents refer back to the document if there is a question of someone failing to carry out their part in the school's behaviour management policy. Embedded in these responsibilities should always be measures designed to prevent the mutual blame cycle that can so easily infect teacher–student/school–family relationships.

Before we move on to examine the hierarchy of consequences it must be emphasized that at all times the student's perspective should be sought and appreciated. It is crucial that disciplinary action always be just and fair and seen to be just and fair. It is true that students who are aggressive, violent and disruptive are responsible for infringing the basic rights of others to personal respect and fair treatment, but this must never be taken to mean that the offender has relinquished their right to personal respect and fair treatment.

Disciplinary action against the student should only be pursued if, first of all, the student's 'offences' can be verified as having been committed by the student concerned. Second, disciplinary action should only be implemented if exhaustive efforts to promote positive behaviour through means of positive encouragement and sincere attempts to identify and remove any possible causes of the negative behaviour that are within the scope of the school's influence have failed. The pastoral support programme, employed in UK schools, is just such a personalized approach. It must always be remembered that one of the causes of indiscipline most commonly cited by disruptive students, is the unfair, inconsistent or arbitrary use of discipline in schools (Cooper, 1993; Cooper *et al*, 2000; Lovey and Cooper, 1997; Tattum, 1982). This complaint is usually accompanied by the view that 'teachers never listen' (ibid). Attempts to deal with the student in a 'therapeutic' manner, therefore, should both proceed and carry on simultaneously with the disciplinary methods described below. The message to the student should always be that school staff care about all students as individuals all of the time, and that when problems arise it is solutions that matter rather than the apportioning of blame. In such a caring situation students are far more likely to accept disciplinary measures than in a setting where behaviour is regulated only by a disciplinary system (Cooper *et al*, 2000; Lovey and Cooper, 1997).

## Stage V – agree on rules and consequences

Next, the school needs to agree on rules and consequences. Some areas for school rules that teachers may want to consider with students, parents and staff can include:

- dangerous behaviour;
- physical violence;
- staying within agreed boundaries;
- verbal insults and sarcasm;
- bullying;
- being assertive in an appropriate way;

- behaviour calculated to annoy or inconvenience others;
- property.

Consequences, again, must be in a hierarchy and, like rules, should be agreed to by students, parents and staff. If some parents, students or staff do not wish to be involved in this process, it is understood that they give those who are willing to be involved 'legitimate power' (see Chapter 2). That is, non-participation is taken as assent to the policy. The coordinator(s) of this policy needs to be explicit about this with parents, students and staff from the outset. An example of a consequences hierarchy is presented below.

### Classroom and school consequences

1. Having exhausted in-class measures the class teacher refers the student to a predetermined and supervised location out of the class. The student has detention at lunchtime and opportunities to discuss the situation with relevant staff. Parents are phoned. They are asked to return with him or her the next morning. The student works out a contract (behaviour agreement, see Figure 5.2)

---

Date: _____

I, _____   promise to _____

_____

_____.

If I keep this contract I can _____

My teacher/carer will _____

_____

If I don't keep this contract _____

My teacher/carer will _____

_____

Signed:

Student 1)    _____

Parent 2)     _____

Staff 3)       _____

---

Figure 5.2 Contract

with the supervising staff and parents. All stakeholders sign the contract.
2. If the contract fails it must be renegotiated and commitment reaffirmed. After several consecutive failures, the student is removed from the class and placed near the head/deputy head's office. Parents are phoned. They must return with him or her the next morning (or as soon as possible before or after that). With supporting staff, the parents and the child organize goals and a means of achieving these goals (Olsen, 1997).
3. After five or six such removals, the student is excluded for one week. With supporting staff, the parents and the child organize goals, means of achieving these goals, and a contract signed by the parent, staff and student.

The issue of exclusion must never be taken lightly. It represents the suspension of a student's basic right to education. It should only be used when the student's behaviour is such that his or her continued presence in the school is likely to be seriously disruptive to the education of other students, or pose a threat to the safety of people in the school. On the rare occasions where it is used it must seen as a constructive measure. It should never be seen as a means of 'getting rid' of a student, but rather should be seen as a period of respite and reflection for key stakeholders. The (apparently paradoxical) purpose of exclusion should always be to improve the possibility that the student will be able to return to full-time education, and participate in a positive and effective manner. The exclusion period, therefore, should be a period of serious reflection and activity, both in the school and in the student's home.

The responses from parents, children and staff, regarding philosophy, rules, consequences and responsibilities of each member of the behaviour management team should be incorporated into a coherent document. Older students can help with this task. Of course, a great deal of work will have to go into the construction of a contract, and it is likely that it will be necessary to offer structure and guidance to stakeholders in how to go about arriving at a set of suitable goals (rather than a list of clichés). For example, during the exclusion period, the student and his or her parents/carer(s) can be asked to devote a minimum of three 20 to 30 minute sessions per day to the questions in Figure 5.3 with a counsellor trained in methods such as those advocated by Henggeler (Henggeler and Borduin, 1990) and always with an aim towards returning the student to school.

If exclusion is going to be something more than a message of rejection, and as such likely to fuel further conflict between the student and school, a similar exercise should be going on back in school. Crucially, school staff need to be asking themselves what they can do to support the excludee on his/her return. The questions used by the student and carers in the exclusion activity can be used by staff. In addition they need to review incentive programmes and consider ways in which other students and the staff as a whole might be encouraged to support the excludee. In particular, exclusion itself should be seen as a period of reflection and renewal of commitment marking a new beginning, and not as the

# EXCLUSION ACTIVITIES

Exclusion from school is always a serious and sad thing. We do not take the decision to exclude a student lightly. We only exclude a student when it is clear to us that their behaviour seriously upsets the running of the school. Sometimes students are excluded because their behaviour makes it difficult or impossible for teachers to teach properly and students to learn. Sometimes students are excluded because their behaviour threatens the physical safety of other people in the school. We never exclude a student without trying hard to help them to behave well. If you do not think that we have tried hard enough, and feel you can help in this matter, please tell us.

The reason why we have taken the decision to temporarily exclude [name of student] is to give [him/her] and us the chance to think about what needs to be done to make sure that s/he can put all the problems behind him/her. During the time that [student's name] is excluded we will be thinking hard about what we can do to try and make sure that [student's name] can come back to school and get back to being the good student that we know s/he can be.

It will help [student's name] and us a lot if you will, over the week of [student's name] exclusion spend at least 20 to 30 minutes, three times every day discussing the following questions with [student's name].

We really do want [student's name] back here in school.

1. What reason has the school given for excluding [student's name]?
   (Refer to letter from the school in which the school's reasons are given.)
2. Did [student's name] do the things that the school has said s/he did?

IF THE ANSWER TO THIS QUESTION IS NO, AN APPOINTMENT SHOULD BE MADE TO MEET WITH STAFF AT THE SCHOOL TO DISCUSS THE ISSUES.
IF THE ANSWER TO THIS QUESTION IS YES, GO ON TO NEXT QUESTION.
3. What things have happened in school which have led up to this exclusion:
   – this term;
   – last term;
   – before last term.
4. What things have happened out of school (in the family, in the neighbourhood) which have led up to this exclusion:
   – this term;
   – last term;
   – before last term.
5. Does [student's name] want to return to school?

*continued overleaf*

Figure 5.3 Exclusion activities

mark of a school career in decline. The student, the family and the school all have responsibilities in making sure that this new beginning is successful.

## Stage VI – gain a commitment

It is desirable to have a school ceremony where the new discipline policy is formally inducted and the staff, students, and parents commit to accepting and abiding by the rules, consequences, philosophy and responsibilities laid down.

## Stage VII – review and reconsider school rules and consequences

The philosophy, rules, consequences and role responsibilities ought to be reviewed periodically, ideally once a year. It is inevitable that changes will be necessary over time. It is important that students, staff and parents believe the document is working, and that they feel able to propose changes where necessary. Modifying and reconsidering the school rules and consequences can help students, staff and parents accept and embrace (take ownership) of the policy. The additional value of such a review is to bring the policy back into focus and thereby reaffirm its purpose.

# Staff support

Teaching is hard. School staff are expected to take on more and more socializing of students, and stress levels amongst teachers have never been higher. All staff in the school need the support of the SMT. In addition, at least three further structures need to be built into the school:

1. Behaviour interventions group – this group meets regularly to review and discuss ideas and techniques for classroom management. Evidence of good practice within the school should be identified and disseminated, and links encouraged between staff to support development in this area. The school should encourage and cover for staff members who go to in-service courses, and these staff members can report back the ideas they have learned. Staff should also be given opportunities to visit the classrooms of colleagues in their school and other schools where techniques that work are in place.
2. Special needs department – members of the special needs department or team need to meet weekly and discuss those children who cause management problems in class or elsewhere in the school. The team should provide expert help and techniques for teachers and departments who manage these children. The team aims for shared discipline, where all stakeholders, within and outside the school, have a say in solving problems.
3. Home School Link – each school needs a teacher, counsellor or other colleague who is skilled at working to build cooperation between the home and the school. The main job of this officer is to act as a case manager. The home school link person's job is to ensure that a central record is kept of all aspects of a given disciplinary case, and to ensure that all stakeholders are working in concert. This person will interview parents, bring parents onside with the school, assign tasks to stakeholders, and dates for completion, and help the child, family and school form cooperative goals (Olsen, 1997).

# The playground

Every school should have a playground policy that is understood by the whole school and organized in a similar way to the classroom and school management policies. Some schools, for example, have a playground licence printed for each child as in Figure 5.4, which has the basic rules of playground behaviour that the school has determined printed on the back. If a student violates any of the rules, by, for example, disrupting the play of others, there can be a hierarchy of consequences for each violation, for example:

1. Warning; teacher redirects the student towards appropriate play.
2. Walk around with the teacher for five minutes; student explains what he/she should have been doing instead.

---

## PLAYGROUND LICENCE

*Holmedale Primary School*

Playground licence for: _____ to: _____ (date)

Name: _____                        Photograph

Class: _____

Head Teacher's signature: _____ Date: _____

*Rules of playground behaviour*

The playground is a place where we go to relax, have fun and enjoy each other's company. To make sure that this happens we have agreed that all students should *always*:

help make the playground a safe and tidy place;

respect everyone by being polite;

not interfere with other people's games or property;

tell playground supervisors and other staff if there is a problem;

follow instructions given by playground supervisors and other staff;

Children who keep these rules will enjoy their time in the playground.

Children who break these rules may not be allowed in the playground.

---

Figure 5.4 Playground licence

3. Time-out for remainder of recess on a marked part of the playground.
4. Off the playground for one week, loss of playground licence. During lunch and recess students are taught skills for playing cooperatively, and demonstrate these skills to the teacher supervising these lessons.

## Playground licences

Playground licences work best when the playground is experienced by students as a nice place to be. This means that thought and effort has to be put into making the playground environment attractive to students. This will be easier to achieve in some schools than others. But even in the most disadvantaged schools there will often be opportunities to make the situation better. Furthermore, the act of consulting students about this can in itself be a very good way of helping to establish an incorporative and cooperative ethos in the school. Organized sport is an effective way to do this, especially if much of this is organized, coached and refereed by the students.

We should also remember that with the best will in the world the idea of going outside on a February day in England can be a very difficult concept to sell to anyone. Making sure that there is adequate and congenial shelter and that students have the right kind of clothing will help here. There is also the issue, however, of the need for flexibility in creating alternatives to the playground. This means that there may be times of the year when a 'playtime/ breaktime activity licence' is the appropriate form. The playground/break-time activity licence relates only to these named activities, and should not be revoked for misbehaviour that occurs in any other setting.

The value of the licence lies in the fact that it acts as a concrete reminder of rules and the consequences of compliance and non-compliance. It should also be remembered, however, that it is a symbolic object. Licences can be displayed on a section of wall in the classroom, as a reminder to students of their playground responsibilities. Revoked licences are removed from their place on the wall.

Another important policy area is that of playground violence. For an example see Figure 5.5 overleaf. Though we agree with a 'zero-tolerance' policy on violence and bullying, such a policy should not be established in a school without a framework to support students and their families. In our experience, such a policy is effective only if the school has a comprehensive and intensive counselling programme in place, like that proposed by Henggeler and Borduin (1990), including home visits aimed to help the student and family accommodate the policy and return to school. Without this the policy below tends to become punitive and fails with the students it aims to helps. The school staff, not the students, may come to look like the 'bullies'.

## SCHOOL VIOLENCE POLICY

**Physical violence and dangerous, threatening behaviour are not tolerated at Blunkhead School**

There are a series of consequences which follow the occurrence of physical violence or threatening behaviour. Physical violence includes acts against people (kicking, punching, biting, throwing stones, etc) and property (breaking windows, throwing furniture, etc).

Dangerous and threatening behaviour against people and property involves the use of a weapon (pencil, ruler, stick, cricket bat, scissors, etc).

The series of consequences is as follows:

Step 1. Warning: the student's name and the behaviour are written into the 'Red Book' (Student Management Book).

Step 2. The student is removed from his/her class, the playground, and the rest of the students in the school for the rest of the day. The student will sit outside the head teacher's office.

Parents are contacted and informed of the student's behaviour and may be asked to come to the school and discuss their behaviour with the head teacher.

Step 3. Parents are contacted and asked to come and take the student home for the rest of the day.

Step 4. The student is suspended for three days.

Step 5. The student is suspended for five days.

Step 6. Negotiate, with the Department, and with parents, the student's behaviour and when they can return to school.

*What to do if you are being teased or bullied*
Being teased is not an excuse for using violent or threatening behaviour.

In order to complain about teasing you must give evidence to show that you have worked through the following steps:

● ignore the teasing or bullying at first to show you are not impressed by it;

- keep away from the person;
- make a joke about it if you can;
- politely ask them not to do it;

THEN

- tell a member of staff.

Figure 5.5 School violence policy

This policy gives a clear definition of violence, and a clear set of consequences for violence. In one school where this was used, all the students knew about the 'Red Book' and whose name was in it. The system was part of the students' culture, so it was effective. One of the best ways to test the effectiveness of such a policy is to ask students on the playground to see if they know exactly what will happen if someone is violent.

The policy also deals with both sides of the violence cycle. That is, children tease Noel and, because Noel reacts so well by swinging a cricket bat at their heads, he becomes a target. The other students taunt and tease Johnny every day. It's fun! In this policy, students are taught what to do if they are teased. Everyone in the school practises the five steps, so everyone understands and owns the policy. Now, there should be no excuses for violence, and there should be less whingeing to teachers on the playground – 'Ms Attwood, Ms Attwood, Noel's calling me names.' 'You know what to do Ruth.' The violent child can't so easily say, 'I hit him because he was teasing me', because he should have gone through the five steps first. If the children and parents own the policy, Noel's parents find it harder to say, 'We've always taught Noel to stick up for himself so it's the school's fault for not stopping this teasing.'

So, we have a good start – a behaviour management policy for the classroom, one for the school, and we have also taken the playground into consideration. But usually a management policy needs refinement. Sometimes we need a dramatically different management policy with different students in different years. Some classes are much more difficult than others, so teachers need to try something else. That's where SALAD comes in.

# 6

# The importance of SALAD

Having a school-wide behaviour management policy in place is an essential component of effective behaviour management. It is not, however, the cure-all for problem behaviour in a school. In most schools there will be times when some students will misbehave, sometimes badly. This echoes the point we made earlier about the need for good discipline to begin in the classroom with the thinking and actions of the individual teacher. It is important to remember that good discipline isn't only about regulating students' behaviour, it is also a lot to do with the self-discipline of the teacher. The nature of human beings is that we are sensitive creatures whose behaviour can sometimes be erratic and even contradictory. In order to establish good discipline, however, teachers need to work very hard at ironing out some of those inconsistencies. This is not to say that good teachers are like robots. On the contrary, effective teaching and learning often involves exploiting the unpredictable outcomes that emerge from two or more people engaging in a genuine transaction of thought and action (Cooper and McIntyre, 1996). But just as it is (probably) impossible to engage in a really thoughtful and effective discussion about the use of metaphor in Shakespeare's sonnets while sitting in the middle of a football field, during a game, with a crowd of 200,000 yelling at the tops of their voices, so it is impossible to engage in that same discussion (properly) in a chaotic classroom. Effective discipline is unobtrusive, it takes care of those aspects of classroom life which could detract from the real business of classrooms: teaching and learning. However, teachers are human, and the following section lists some of the ways in which teachers the world over commonly slip up and inadvertently undermine their own lessons.

# Thirteen classic errors (or how to increase misbehaviour in your classroom)

1. Always agree with pleas of 'Don't tell my parents. Mum will go mad', or other efforts by students to pit the home against the school and the school against the home, so to avoid or subvert the classroom rules. (Though one should always be alert to potential child protection issues in these circumstances.)
2. Reverse 'Grandma's Rule', 'Please don't make me go to detention. I promise I won't hit anyone again.' (Then he hits someone and he is let off because he promises never to do it again.) Grandma's Rule means the child does what the teacher wants, first, then the child does what he or she wants, afterwards – always in that order. When this order is reversed, the student learns to escape the consequences that the teacher has laid down for misbehaviour.
3. Use sarcasm. This is better than just about anything to foster resentment, conflict, and the student's desire to be uncooperative. It also gives the student ammunition to use with their parents against the teacher. Sarcasm invites retaliation. Students will often work out ways to 'pay back' the teacher (Rosser and Harré, 1976). Sarcasm is a form of bullying.
4. Belittle, denigrate, or fight with students' parents. Conflict like this is usually guaranteed to alienate the student, who is going to unite with the family against the school even if relationships between family members are abusive. The child's family members will incite each other to action against the teacher and the school. This action could include classroom disruption from the student.
5. Instead of letting the goals, encouragers, rules, consequences and hierarchy do the work when students misbehave, the teacher pleads, argues, or talks too much. Sometimes students try to distract teachers into talking and pleading with them and then these students don't listen to the teacher who is talking and pleading with them. They become 'teacher deaf'. Furthermore, a teacher who uses too many verbal techniques to counter problem behaviours will disrupt their own lessons, creating dissatisfaction, and possibly resentment among students who are trying to cooperate. Teachers who do this are likely to wear themselves out very quickly. Furthermore, we believe that classes that are 'subdued' each day by a teacher who relies heavily on verbal discipline can be particularly disruptive for other teachers who come in to teach the class. Teachers who let the goals, encouragers, rules, consequences and hierarchy carry the discipline for them, however, are saving precious time and energy, and making things easier for others who take their class.

    This is not to say that teachers shouldn't be verbal when things are going well – praise students, 'catch them being good', listen to student's viewpoints, and be prepared to admit when the teacher has made a mistake. The point is that it is essential that there is a time and place for discussions with individual students about their behaviour. That time and place is not usually in the middle of a lesson. The students need to know that they will be listened to, but they must also know when and where.

6. Teach boring, uninteresting lessons. Bored students misbehave. Teachers who do this tend to have more behaviour problems than teachers who make lessons interesting and stimulating.

7. Treat students as the enemy. When an 'us-against-them' attitude forms in the class, students start to attack or undermine the teacher. Students cause less trouble to a teacher they identify with and feel loyal to (referent power).

8. Try to be the students' friend as an equal instead of as an adult. A common mistake some teachers make in their early years of teaching (especially with older students) is to blur the boundary between themselves as adults with a professional responsibility and the students in their classes. Teachers are professionally and legally responsible for what goes on in the classroom. It is desirable for the teacher to groom students so that he or she can delegate certain aspects of responsibility to them, but the teacher is ultimately the one with the responsibility. Students lose respect for teachers who do not shoulder this responsibility.

9. React before thinking – become defensive and take the situation personally. Some students like to keep teachers off-balance, stir them to react in anger or frustration (see Chapter 9). It is easier for students to control a teacher this way. These student ploys fail when the teacher doesn't react. Instead, the teacher continues with the lesson and lets goals, encouragers, rules, and consequences hierarchy take the brunt of this misbehaviour.

10. Use 'time-out' on students in a class that they dislike or find boring. 'Time-out' really means removing the student from a rewarding environment. If Liam hates Maths and the teacher puts him in the corridor every day when he disrupts the class, she isn't using time-out. She is rewarding him for misbehaviour. In fact she could make him into a hero with the other students who stop in the corridor and talk to him.

11. Back themselves into a corner by stipulating consequences they cannot carry out/back the student into a corner so she or he sees no way out. When the teacher promises a student a consequence that isn't carried out, the student learns to 'gamble', to play 'roulette'. The student will keep testing to find out when the teacher will carry through and when they won't. This game can become quite exhilarating for some students. Likewise, when the students are backed into a corner, so there is no way out ('Do this or else!'), they may react with a 'fight or flight' response. They may rebel, defy, and fight to maintain their dignity in front of their peers, or simply abscond.

12. Use double standards – teachers or certain students can do things that other students are not allowed to do. Students, especially high school students, hate double standards. For example, the teacher can swear or arrive late but students can't, or some students can joke with the teacher or call out in class while others are punished for the same behaviour. Students often retaliate against such unfairness.

13. Tolerate colleagues' behaviour that repeatedly causes legitimate offence to students and parents. Change can be painful. A teacher with an offensive manner may not understand (or care) how this causes classroom management problems. Sometimes teachers who behave in these ways are protected from hurt students and irate parents by colleagues or an SMT that acts as a buffer. This ensures that the teacher will not change, but will probably get worse. SMTs should protect teachers from intrusive or irate parents. But teachers who disrupt the smooth running of a school because of their unprofessional or offensive manner are just as bad as (if not worse than) students who do these things. Colleagues who behave in these ways need help to face their difficulties and overcome them. Having a school-wide behaviour policy can help in this, because such a policy sets standards for teacher behaviour as well as student behaviour. Teachers who are not adhering to the agreed-upon whole-school policy are letting down their colleagues and their students.

# SALAD – what is it?

This section, and this chapter, are about analysis. When our classroom or school policy has failed with a particular student, or group, we suggest that teachers analyse with SALAD so that teachers can try something different, increase their power in the classroom, and avoid such errors. SALAD provides a framework that covers five important areas: Systems, Access, Limits, Acceptance and Direction that help teachers structure the school, classroom and interrelationships between the school, the student, and the home. When there is difficulty with a student or a class, SALAD can help you identify and remedy the problem. We suggest that teachers choose techniques from all five elements to construct interventions for those students who need them. The five ingredients of SALAD are:

## Systems

A system can be defined as 'a set of connected parts forming a complex whole'. This is the concept that underpins the whole approach (see Chapter 7). The parts are connected by lines of communication. Only when there is clear and effective multi-way communication between the parts can we be sure of a cooperative relationship. If parents and school staff agree on common goals, consult openly with children, don't have their fights through the child, and communicate successfully with each other, discipline problems are easier to manage.

We use a systems approach to analyse problems when we ask questions like:

- what is the quality of communication like between the stakeholders (conflictual or cooperative)?
- is the quality of communication conducive to the development of common goals and clearly defined roles among stakeholders?
- how can the quality of communication be improved?

## Access

This is defined as the 'right and means of reaching'. The main function of a discipline policy is to provide students with access to the means of behaving in positive ways. Access involves not only knowing what to do, it also requires the inner motivation to do what is required. This inner motivation comes from a sense of ownership. Ownership derives from an investment of the precious commodities of time and effort, and the sense of value that these impart. This is why students (and other stakeholders) must be involved in the development of school policies (see Chapters 4 and 5). When students share in the ownership of problems, class rules, consequences, the curriculum, plans for changing their behaviour, and clear, long- and short-term goals, they are more likely to want to succeed, and, therefore, more likely to succeed, because they have become, through these processes, committed to fulfilling the goal they have helped create. Discipline problems will be easier to manage because the students are contributing self-regulation to the management process.

Similarly, staff colleagues and parents need access to those aspects of the discipline policy that affect them. The same issues of investment, ownership, and commitment apply. They will support the policy in which they have invested, and in so doing will support the student(s) and the school.

The concept of access can help us analyse discipline problems by suggesting questions such as:

- Do(es) the student(s) know what is expected in terms of behavioural goals and how these might be achieved?
- Has the child been taught appropriate behavioural skills?
  - Do students understand behavioural expectations, for example, can they tell you what will happen to a student who strikes another student on the playground, or calls out inappropriately in class without raising their hand?

- Does each student understand the class routines? have they been rehearsed?
- Does the teacher rehearse appropriate sequences of behaviour with an EBD student?
- Do(es) the student(s) have ownership of the problem?
- Have students actively invested time and energy towards an understanding of the problem and plans for its resolution?
- Are there opportunities and is there active encouragement for students to exploit their individual strengths and interests in developing an understanding of the problem and its plans for its resolution?
- To what extent do other stakeholders (staff and parents) have access to behavioural goals and how these might be achieved?

## Limits

If the student has clear behavioural limits (ie boundaries), based on rules, consequences and routines, discipline problems are easier to manage (Jones and Jones, 1990). Again, this applies to all stakeholders.

Questions we can ask about limits include:

- Do(es) the student(s) know and understand the rules?
- Do(es) the student(s) know and understand the consequences?
- Do(es) the student(s) know and understand the appropriate routines?
- Do other stakeholders know about and understand agreed rules, consequences and routines?

## Acceptance

Being treated with disrespect by school staff is a common complaint among students who are described as 'difficult' or 'disaffected', and frequently cited as a provocation to disruptive behaviour (Cooper, 1993; Tattum, 1982). On the other hand, when students experience genuine positive regard from school staff , and the other students, they are likely to reciprocate; as a result discipline problems tend to be easier to manage (Charles, 1996; Cooper *et al*, 2000; Olsen, 1989b). The condition of acceptance, defined as 'to receive or welcome', extends to other stakeholders and will affect their willingness to cooperate.

Questions we can ask about acceptance include:

- To what extent and in what ways do students show that they are aware of being respected and accepted by others?
- To what extent do staff actively communicate a sense of respect and acceptance to students?

- What measures are in place to encourage acceptance and respect among students?
- Are other stakeholders shown acceptance in equal measure?

## Direction

This can be defined as 'the course along which someone moves'. If students are stimulated and engaged in the educational process, if they see themselves progressing in their school work and behaviour towards clear and achievable goals, discipline problems are easier to manage (Charles, 1996). Again, other stakeholders have to be considered in relation to this condition, because they have a significant role to play in facilitating the students' goal-directed progress.

Questions that arise from direction include:

- Is the curriculum stimulating to students?
- Are students substantially engaged with the curriculum?
- Are students making progress in reaching goals?
- Is progress acknowledged and made visible to them?
- Is progress rewarded?
- Are other stakeholders aware of students' progress and their roles in supporting and fostering it?

# SALAD usage

As Charles (1996) points out, teachers seldom use the whole of a single model of classroom behaviour management, such as the Carl Rogers' relationship-listening approach, Dreikurs' confronting-contracting approach, or the Skinnerian rule-rewards-punishment approach (Cooper, Smith and Upton, 1994). They tend to use parts of models. For example, teachers often use only the consequences of a model, the most punitive part, like Glasser's steps for removing a student from the classroom. They ignore other crucial parts of these models. However, when problems continue with a student, they sometimes claim, 'We've tried everything!' They haven't, of course, they have only used parts of certain models. SALAD can help them analyse problems and ensure that the essentials of classroom management are covered. Teachers are able to plan their classroom discipline using techniques of their choice that cover all five SALAD categories. These techniques are presented in other chapters of this book.

Remember the drunken man who lost his keys at the beginning of this book? He was getting nowhere because he only searched in the area where it was easy to search – even though he was not in the area where the problem seemed most likely to be located. Successful schools have staff who are able to change their plans and not be limited by restricting beliefs that prevent them from trying something new. With a misbehaving student the teacher might assume there is a problem in only one area. Consequently, the teacher bases plans for classroom discipline on assumptions like 'We need tougher rules and consequences in this school' (limits). On the other hand the same teacher might say, 'this student needs to feel accepted by his classmates, he needs more friends' (acceptance). Setting limits and making a student feel accepted are important elements but they are usually not enough on their own to structure a behaviour management plan. Another teacher may simply blame the student's home or, perhaps, the lack of support in the school, for the problem behaviour, and thus see themselves as being in a 'no-win situation' – the best they can do is to quietly 'put up' with the problems. Another teacher may blame themselves completely, and put even more effort than usual into making their lessons more stimulating and engaging, only to find their efforts spurned by the students. These tendencies to favour single causes/solutions can generate some of the 'Classic Errors' we discussed earlier in the chapter, and produce interventions that fail to generalize or maintain (see Chapter 1).

Using SALAD (Figure 6.1) to structure and remediate problems with classroom management can help teachers avoid these problems and achieve generalization and maintenance of helpful student and teacher behaviours. Crucially, this ecosystemic approach shares the burden of management between all the stakeholders, by making it in everyone's interest to cooperate and communicate. Our objective in using SALAD is to draw on techniques that give students a sense of well being, mastery and competence, and so raise self-esteem (Seligman, 1995) and therefore to help these students realize their aspirations in and out of school.

# The importance of being bold and caring

A useful way of thinking about the kinds of teacher qualities that can be engendered by the SALAD approach is to consider the suggestion that teachers can place themselves on a continuum from bold to timid, and in their treatment of students, on a continuum from caring to selfish (Figure 6.2).

Bold/caring teachers tend to be resourceful, imaginative, ready to try new things. They are interesting and nurturing to students. Timid teachers can be unassertive, ineffective, unimaginative, meek and unresourceful. Selfish teachers fail to meet the students' needs, they can be rigid, autocratic and refuse to change. Bold/selfish teachers can be harsh and mean-spirited.

**Systems**
1. Good COMMUNICATION enables an ALLIANCE to exist between stakeholders.
2. DEFINED ROLES are in place for stakeholders.
3. COMMON GOALS are in place for stakeholders.
4. STRENGTHS IN SUBSYSTEMS are exploited to redress weaknesses in the system as a whole.

**Access**

*Ownership*
1. Student OWNS the policy and problems.
2. Teacher uses the student's STRENGTHS and INTERESTS.
3. Student has clear GOALS.
4. Other stakeholders have OWNERSHIP too.

*Knowing*
1. Students UNDERSTAND expectations.
2. Students have been TAUGHT necessary skills.
3. Teachers have REHEARSED skills with students.

**Limits**
1. RULES are clear.
2. CONSEQUENCES are clear.
3. ROUTINES are used.
4. Other stakeholders UNDERSTAND rules, consequences and routines.

**Acceptance**
1. Teacher ACCEPTS the student.
2. Student ACCEPTS the teacher.
3. Students ACCEPT each other.
4. Other stakeholders are aware of their roles in COMMUNICATING and PROVIDING acceptance to students and each other.

**Direction**
1. Students reach GOALS (rewarded; visual).
2. Students see GROWTH (rewarded; visual).
3. Classwork STIMULATES and PROGRESSES.
4. Other stakeholders are AWARE of growth and progress.

Figure 6.1 SALAD

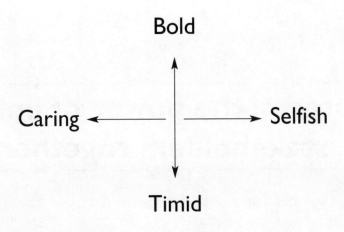

Figure 6.2  Bold/caring teachers

Caring/timid teachers, because they lack boldness and resourcefulness, can lack certainty and any sense of adventure – they are 'wet'.

Bold/caring school staff are divergent as well as convergent thinkers. They are flexible enough to use a variety of strategies from all the SALAD categories. Of course, it works the other way as well: the SALAD approach enables staff to become bold and caring, by providing them with the necessary structures and mechanisms. Effective teaching is not a matter of inherent personality factors, it is the product of an appropriate blend of thought, action and social interaction.

In the next chapter we look at systems in more detail, describing some practical techniques that derive from these concepts.

# 7

# Systems: the power of linking stakeholders together

Because systems is a complex topic, we deal with it in some detail here, and in more detail in Chapter 10. In this chapter we look in a little more depth at the ways in which the quality of communication between these stakeholders can be enhanced. As noted earlier, there is little hard evidence that systemic approaches on their own are effective with managing students' social, emotional and behavioural problems, and cognitive and behavioural approaches alone fail to generalize and maintain. Research evidence indicates that it is when these approaches are combined with considerations of curriculum, school leadership and other educational and institutional factors, that problems with EBD students can be most successfully managed (Henggeler, 1999; Kazdin, 1998; Olsen, 1989a, 1997a).

## A systems approach

One dictionary definition of systems is 'a set of connected parts forming a complex whole'.

The systems approach has its origins in the work of von Bertalanffy who formulated the original 'General System Theory' (von Bertalanffy, 1950; 1968) concerned with the interactions within biological and other natural systems. The application of systems theory to human systems came later with the work of Bateson (1972, 1979) and Bronfenbrenner (1979). The most practical applications of this work, in terms of its success in generating solutions to human social and emotional problems, are to be found in the field of family therapy (de Shazer, 1982, 1985; Minuchin, 1974; Selvini-Palazzoli *et al*, 1973). Much of the work of family therapists tends to involve families in which children are presented by parents as being the source of problems. A major insight from systemic family therapy is that the student's apparent problems are sometimes unconsciously generated by other members of the family system in order to meet certain needs. Intervention in these cases, therefore, is more properly directed at family subsystems (such as the relationship between the parents) than at the student in person. This often extends to the realm of school-based problems, which can sometimes be seen in terms of a problem in the family which affects the school (Lindquist *et al*, 1987). Some therapists have begun to work directly at the interface between the school and the family system (Dowling and Osborne, 1995; Guerin, Katz and Hsai, 1984; Okun, 1984; Worden, 1981). Educational psychologists in some cases have also adopted systemic approaches to school-based problems (Campion, 1985; Provis, 1994), whilst others have advocated the use of systemic principles by classroom teachers in their management of problem behaviour (Cooper and Upton, 1991; Molnar and Lindquist, 1989; Olsen, 1989a, 1997a, 1997b).

Let us look at the way, from a systems perspective, that people can cooperate, unwittingly, to make things worse:

## Terry stops talking to Sherry

Terry Blare has always prided himself on being a good husband and father. He likes to think that he takes an equal responsibility with his wife in the upbringing of their son, Liam. Terry is a teacher who is going through a particularly difficult time because his school is being inspected by the government's educational standards agency. He is very anxious, to the point that his usual calm demeanour at home is replaced by a tendency to impatience, especially with Liam. Also, he is working so late into the evening that far less opportunity than usual is created for conversation between the couple. Secretly Terry is worried that his department will receive a poor report, and that he will be to blame.

Sherry is aware that her husband is under stress, so that when it comes to the date of a parents' evening at Liam's school she decides not to tell Terry – knowing that he is very busy and very stressed at the present time. When Terry returns home to find that the parents' night has taken place he is angry at having been excluded. This, to him, adds insult to the injury of the looming inspection. So when, later, Sherry asks Terry if he has had a good day, Terry ignores her and proceeds to the study, where he slams the door and remains for the rest of the evening. His intention is to demonstrate to Sherry that she has made a serious mistake.

*continued overleaf*

Now Sherry is offended, especially when she has been so considerate as to take the burden of Liam's parents' night all to herself. Over the next week, neither speaks to the other, though both feel aggrieved. Neither will speak until the other has apologized. Eventually, Sherry decides that this is all too juvenile, so, on Saturday morning she initiates a conversation as if nothing has happened. She asks Terry (in her most friendly voice) if he'd like to go shopping with her. He is angry because she appears to be ignoring not only their dispute but what he sees as its cause. Terry explodes in a rage and (for the first time in their marriage) is verbally abusive. Sherry is shocked and upset. Fearing her husband's anger, she packs a suitcase and leaves, taking Liam with her. Now Terry is even more upset and angry.

Because of the paramount importance of the system, it is sometimes the case that an imbalance occurs between an individual's personal needs and the needs of the system, to the extent that one individual in the system becomes severely damaged because he or she is being required to sacrifice more than his or her fair share. For example:

## Terry and Sherry find a way out

Terry and Sherry's son, Liam, is, sadly, a friendless and unappealing student who has always been prone to sulking, but has tended to be an average, though uninspired student. At the age of 14, however, Liam begins to opt out of school by truanting, failing to complete homework assignments, engaging in disruptive behaviour in class, and showing signs of aggression. The deterioration in his behaviour coincides with a particularly difficult period in the relationship between Terry and Sherry, to the extent that they are considering a period of separation.

When the school informs Terry and Sherry of their concern about Liam's behaviour, they are shocked and upset, and, as a result, distracted from their marital difficulties. Without them realising it, Liam's school problems provide them with a situation in which they can cooperate. And so long as Liam's school problems continue, they can avoid confronting the marital difficulties that threaten their family life and cause them such unhappiness.

Consequently, Terry and Sherry form a coalition with Liam against the school, refusing to acknowledge that Liam is at fault in any respect, and encouraging Liam's efforts to blame school staff and other students for the difficulties that arise. Terry and Sherry's responses to Liam's school difficulties, therefore, are unconsciously designed to maintain Liam's problems rather than solve them, because the survival of the family system appears to be dependent on keeping the difficulties going. By blaming the school Terry and Sherry are encouraging Liam's negative behaviour.

In the face of what is unjust criticism the school takes up a defensive position, in which they minimize the importance of their own responsibilities and place blame on the parents and/or Liam. From now on the school is seeking evidence to prove that Liam is a disruptive student, and that his parents are impossible to work with, rather than seeking a resolution to the problems.

The relationship between the school and family subsystem is now in a pattern of escalating hostility, which, if unchanged, will lead to Liam's exclusion.

Liam is being sacrificed to maintain the equilibrium within two subsystems: the home and the school.

Similarly, there are times when teachers may seek, unconsciously, to maintain rather than solve classroom behaviour problems. For example:

## A teacher proves her point

Mrs Kay believes she has too many pupils in her class, and that this poses a threat to classroom discipline. She is having particular problems with Liam Blare. She informed the senior management of this at the beginning of the year, but felt that she was fobbed off. By halfway through the first term she is coping, but only just. Liam's disruptive and uncooperative behaviour is becoming infectious, and there is a small group of students who follow his lead when he acts out. As a result she feels forced to avoid certain activities in the classroom (role play, and self-directed learning tasks) that other students would benefit from, but would lead to chaos if she attempted them with the group of the current size and with the presence of these difficult students. Her frustration

*continued overleaf*

leads her to conclude that by demonstrating that there are behaviour problems in the classroom she can support her case for a reduction in class size.
She now sets out to demonstrate to the senior management that certain students, and Liam in particular, are out of control.

In these circumstances she unconsciously welcomes a degree of disruption,
and may even encourage it. Having decided that class size is the major issue, and
that Liam in particular is a problem, Mrs Kay rejects the advice of the behaviour
support teacher, when she suggests that Liam should be placed on a behavioural programme. 'That will never work, because Liam doesn't want to cooperate,'
says Mrs Kay. 'And not only that, his parents are just as bad as he is. There is just
no place for a boy like that in my class, or in this school, as far as I am concerned.'

A group of people, a system, is different to the sum of its parts, like a loaf of
bread is different to its ingredients (Satir, 1972). Blame can enter a system like
a virus – teachers blame parents, senior managers blame teachers, and parents
blame schools in front of their children, who in turn, blame the school. The
blame in the system results in misbehaviour in students (Minuchin, 1974).

A child who convinces his parents that the teacher treats him unfairly at
school 'splits the executive', he destroys the links binding the school staff and
parents together in an 'executive' (Figure 7.1). Consequently, the student has
no limits on his power. Out of control, he starts to misbehave (Epston, 1988;

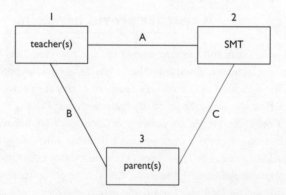

Figure 7.1 Linking the executive. In successful casework, teachers, parents, the senior
management team (SMT) and counsellor set collaborative goals and form effective patterns of
communication. In a systems approach we concern ourselves particularly with A, B and C, the
links between stakeholders 1, 2 and 3 and break unhelpful sequences between these elements

Minuchin, 1974). However, Haley (1987) points out that an organization is not malfunctioning because of cross-generational coalitions, in this case, a student and his parents against the school. The organization is malfunctioning because such coalitions are repeated again and again as part of a system. A mother repeatedly must save her child from the unfairness of the school, and maybe her husband, and the school must repeatedly convince parents that they, not the school, are the cause of the problem.

This can be avoided if the adults in the student's system break these unhelpful sequences and work as a team; if there is clear feedback between the 'stakeholders' – the teachers, parents, and the student. This process can start with Home Notes (Figures 7.2 and 7.3) that cannot be sabotaged by a student who is determined to play one stakeholder off against the other. For example, if the Home Note fails to arrive home or back to school, parents and teachers immediately telephone each other.

It is important to remain a flexible member of the system and realize that everyone (including us) in a school or family tends to see a problem from their own point of view, a view that is usually (on the surface) more favourable to ourselves. It is important for teachers to use the ideas of other stakeholders to fashion an intervention for a class or school problem.

## DAILY REPORT HOME

Name: _____

Date: _____

**Yes   No**

___ ___   Followed our class rules.

___ ___   Did as the teacher asked.

___ ___   Tried hard at school work.

___ ___   Got along well with other kids.

Parent's signature: _____

Teacher's signature: _____

Figure 7.2

**TAKE HOME NOTE**

Week ending: _____

Peter: ◯

Mrs Jones: ✕

| | No | | | | Yes |
|---|---|---|---|---|---|
| 1. Finished my work. | 1 | 2 | ✕ | ④ | 5 |
| 2. Listened well. | 1 | ② | ✕ | 4 | 5 |
| 3. Did not show off. | 1 | 2 | ③ | ✕ | 5 |
| 4. Was kind to others. | 1 | 2 | ✕ | ④ | 5 |

My score: 13

Teachers score: 13

Difference: 0

Peter's signature: _____

Teacher's signature: _____

Parent's signature: _____

Figure 7.3

Some questions we might ask ourselves about systems include:

- Who is the Case Manager in the school?
- What are the strengths in the individuals, in the school systems, and in the home systems?
- Who is on duty in the Time-out room when a student is sent there?
- Do the student, teacher and parents work cooperatively towards goals?
- Do solution-focused special needs teams operate?
- Does the school use homework books, home notes, weekly telephone calls or other techniques to link teachers and parents?
- Do all stakeholders, including parents, have input into school rules and consequences, that is, are teachers flexible enough to use other stakeholders' ideas and beliefs?

- In parent–teacher meetings do teachers show parents the strengths of their child and that they like him?
- Are parents and each staff member clear about their role in the school discipline policy?
- Are problems analysed systemically using conflict maps or the systems-at risk sheet (see Figure 7.6)?

Some examples of techniques that link teachers, parents, principals, and students together so they work on cooperative goals include:

- At the end of the school day the teacher can sit the students down and choose certain students to review what they have accomplished. When students arrive home and parents ask the classic question 'What did you do at school today?' the student will have just reviewed what he or she did. Who knows? The student might shock his or her parents by actually giving them a clear idea of what he or she did at school instead of saying, 'Oh, nothing'.

  Not only does this give students a sense of ownership, and direction (see Chapter 6), but can give parents a favourable view of the school and the teacher.
- Homework books, home–school diaries where parents and teachers record positive and negative behaviours, home notes (Figures 7.2 and 7.3) and joint contracts (Figure 7.4) can link parents and teachers in cooperative two-way communication so students cannot play adults off against each other. Note that if the teacher or parent does not fulfil their part of the contract, the student does not have to fulfil theirs.
- We have seen how some students behave well during the week leading up to parent–teacher night, then behave abominably afterwards. This is because of the anticipated link between home and school before the teacher meets his or her parents. The teacher can reinstate this link by organizing a weekly telephone call with parents so the student knows, for example, that the teacher will speak to his or her mother every Thursday afternoon at 4pm. This differs from a behaviourist intervention that would have the teacher telephone the parents contingent upon (as a consequence of) good behaviour to reward the student, or following inappropriate behaviour to punish the student. Instead, this is a permanent systemic link between adult stakeholders.
- Several teachers can be linked with a record card that the student carries with them. The case manager can review the student's progress with him/her, and with the parents' – was he/she on time to class, did he/she bring necessary materials, and so on (Figure 7.5).
- Parents, teachers and students should have input into school rules and discipline policies, that is, the school staff should be flexible enough to accept

## PARENT–TEACHER–STUDENT AGREEMENT

Student's name: _____

Teacher's name: _____

Parent's name: _____

Date: _____

Area to be improved: _____

_____

The teacher will: _____

_____

The student will: _____

_____

The parent will: _____

_____

Long-range goal: _____

_____

_____

Figure 7.4

and utilize parents' beliefs where this is possible. Systems thinking demands that we be open to new and sometimes unusual ideas (see Molnar and Linquist, 1989).

- Each member of staff should be clear about his or her role in the school discipline policy. This should be carefully coordinated. There are some examples of these responsibilities in Chapter 5 showing the record of agreement between stakeholders in a school discipline policy. If there is a discipline problem, stakeholders can expect others to fulfil their agreed-upon-roles as stipulated in the agreement.
- In parent conferences, it is important that staff convey to parents that they like their student. The student's strengths can be a focus for discussion. Accepting parents and their children is a crucial element in linking the

## TRAVEL CARD

Student: ________________ Grade: ________ Date: ___________

***Desired behaviours***

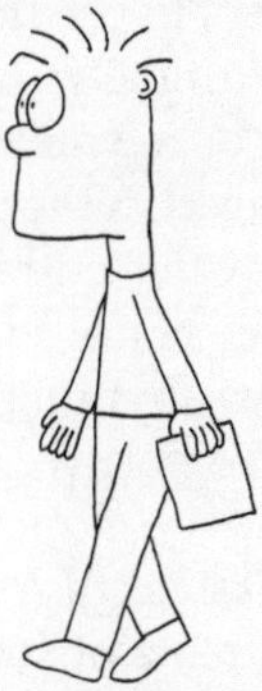

| Period | On time to class | Brought necessary materials | Handed in homework | Obeyed class rules | Participated in class | Teacher's signature |
|---|---|---|---|---|---|---|
| 1 | | | | | | |
| 2 | | | | | | |
| 3 | | | | | | |
| 4 | | | | | | |
| 5 | | | | | | |
| 6 | | | | | | |
| 7 | | | | | | |

Figure 7.5 Travel card (after Jones and Jones, 1990)

home and the school. Parents often refuse to cooperate with a school because the school has been negative about their child, or they feel they are 'talked down to' or mistreated by staff members. Without parental cooperation, long-term, successful management of troubled students is very difficult.

- Problems can be analysed systemically using, for example, a systems at-risk sheet (Figure 7.6). Instead of attributing the student's misbehaviour to one narrow area, such as reading or the home, staff can examine how various people and elements in the student's school life interact and how bickering adults can fuel a student's violent or disruptive behaviour.

- A key to understanding systems is flexibility. If staff are flexible they can easily list at the beginning of each term: what they will do differently this term, and what ideas they will take on-board from parents and other staff members to use this term.

- If an extremely disruptive or violent student arrives in school from elsewhere, or re-enters school after suspension, it is valuable to have previously engaged in the preparatory activities described in Chapter 5. This can be aided by the 'entrance contract' (Olsen, 1989, 1997a). In the contract parents agree to come to the school and take the student if he/she tantrums, destroys anything, or hurts anyone. Parents should also be encouraged to reinforce positive behaviour, through rewards or valued activities, which the school contracts to inform parents about.

- Saint Francis of Assisi Primary School in Canberra has a 'parent network'. Two parents of students in each class are nominated as the school contact for other parents of students in the class. When parents have concerns about the class, or the school, they ring the 'parent coordinator' as their first point of contact.

- Some teachers object to maintaining a working relationship with parents if the school suspects that one or both of these parents are abusing children in the family. We argue that all suspicions of abuse should be passed on to the authorities. However, we cannot see the benefit to students if teachers and the executive in a school refuse to cooperate with parents on other matters. As professionals, we separate out these issues – suspicion of abuse is dealt with as the law directs, but we can cooperate with parents in troubled families around issues of schoolwork, behaviour management, etc. We believe this can help such students, families, and the school. One of the authors (Olsen) was able to move a 12-year-old girl from an allegedly abusive relationship with a stepfather when authorities could not, after five years, gather enough evidence to charge him. The parents cooperated with this move because the school had maintained a positive relationship with them.

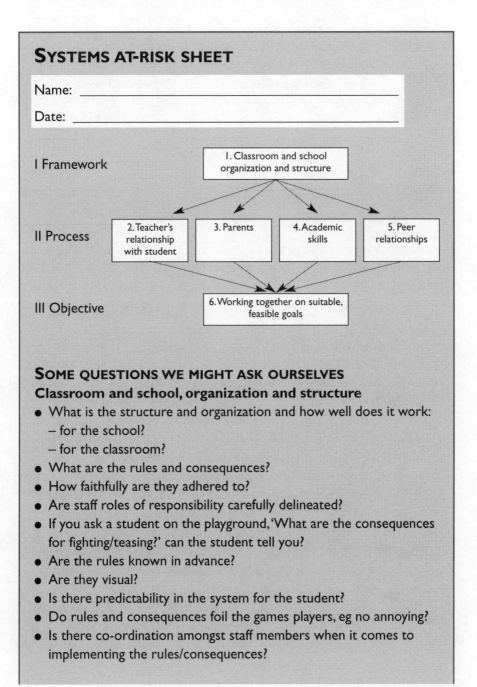

# SYSTEMS AT-RISK SHEET

Name: _____

Date: _____

I Framework

> 1. Classroom and school organization and structure

II Process

> 2. Teacher's relationship with student
>
> 3. Parents
>
> 4. Academic skills
>
> 5. Peer relationships

III Objective

> 6. Working together on suitable, feasible goals

## SOME QUESTIONS WE MIGHT ASK OURSELVES
### Classroom and school, organization and structure

- What is the structure and organization and how well does it work:
  – for the school?
  – for the classroom?
- What are the rules and consequences?
- How faithfully are they adhered to?
- Are staff roles of responsibility carefully delineated?
- If you ask a student on the playground, 'What are the consequences for fighting/teasing?' can the student tell you?
- Are the rules known in advance?
- Are they visual?
- Is there predictability in the system for the student?
- Do rules and consequences foil the games players, eg no annoying?
- Is there co-ordination amongst staff members when it comes to implementing the rules/consequences?

*continued overleaf*

*School staff (teachers, managers, pastoral team, special needs department)*

- Do these people support teachers in developing their skills on how to manage difficult students?
- Do they actively support the teacher and set limits for the student?
- Are they friendly and professional with parents and the student?
- Do they involve teachers and parents in the decision-making process?
- Do they avoid sarcasm at all costs?
- Do they have a high profile (are they visible) in the school?

**Teachers' relationship with the student**

- Do they know how to negotiate and avoid an 'us against them' relationship?
- Do they use humour?
- Do they have high standards?
- Do they take care with praise? (descriptive vs evaluative)
- Do they set consequences in a gentle, totally committed way?
- Do they resort to sarcasm?
- Do they trust students?
- Are they consistent?
- Do they cut down on verbalizing when students are misbehaving?
- Do they speak to students as they would like to be spoken to themselves?
- Do they show neutrality when they manage misbehaving students?
- Do they use positive remarks?
- Do they show that they like the student?
- Do they manage classroom problems themselves and only call in other executive members for extremely difficult students?

**Parents**

- Are the family's views in line with the school's?
- Are the parents operating as a team?
- Are the school and home working towards the same goals for the student?

*1-2-3 lines of communication between adults*
- What are the regular lines of communication between teacher/members of SMT/pastoral staff/specialist staff/parents?
- Are these people working in concert?
- Are home notes used between home and school; are they seen by the members of SMT/pastoral staff/appropriate specialist staff, who discuss them with the student and/or parents?
- Are regular meetings held between these adults?
- Do these people clearly understand and accept each other's views on student management?

## Academic skills
- Is the student succeeding?
- Is there direction for the student?
- Is the student completing set tasks?
- Is there an alternative curriculum, for example off line?
- Are arrangements of groups and classes optimal?

## Peer relations
- Is there equal access for students? (Access here embraces the notion of all additional educational provisions.)
- Is the student's niche recognized?
- Do teachers/students understand how damaging and dangerous sarcasm and taunting/teasing are to the student?
- Is the typical way to respond to teasing 'just go away and ignore them', ie do teachers trivialize the problem?
- Are cooperative games and collaborative learning encouraged?
- Do class meetings have a place in the school curricula?

## Working together on a suitable goal
- What are the student's skills and interests?
- Does the student see direction/purpose in his work and interests? In other words, where is he or she headed?
- Is this clear to the school? Student? Parents?
- What are the goals/objectives that the student, school, and parents are working towards at the moment, eg is it simply to move into the next grade at year's end or even to remain in his/her present school?

Figure 7.6

# 8

# Enabling students to behave well: access, limits, acceptance and direction

In this chapter we examine the practical ways that staff and schools, after they have used SALAD to analyse problems in the classroom or school, can use the concepts of Access, Limits, Acceptance and Direction to promote positive student behaviour. Definitions and a discussion of these terms are in Chapter 6.

## Access – 'right and means of reaching'

Access is the fundamental condition, from everyone's viewpoint. Only when students have a means of access to the nature, purposes and processes of the discipline policy will they own it and become committed to it. At the same time only when other stakeholders have access will they be able to appreciate the demands and responsibilities that are being placed on students, and their own roles and responsibilities in supporting students in their attempts to meet these demands and fulfil their responsibilities.

In order to allow students the fullest possible access to the behavioural outcomes that the teacher (and the school) require, students have to be engaged very closely in the discussion and generation of the policy underlying the intervention, as well as the practical means of implementing the policy.

Access is derived from two interlocking components – ownership and knowing. We first discuss ownership.

## Access part 1 – ownership – 'to hold or possess'

The class can collectively own class goals, rules, consequences, routines, some of the curriculum, etc. The behaviour management plan uses the ideas, interests, and values of the students. Obviously the students will be more motivated to participate in such a policy. Contracts or mediation essays give the students ownership of problems.

Some questions we might think about in regards to ownership include:

- Did the class help decide on goals?
- Have we used the students' interests and strengths to develop the curriculum?
- Did the class help decide on rules and consequences?
- In the rules and consequences did we use the students' language instead of our own words?
- Have we given the student who misbehaves input into the classroom management policy?
- Have we asked that student about the problem? What has s/he suggested we do?
- What are the student's strengths, interests and goals?

The following are some techniques that can enable access by enhancing a feeling of ownership among students:

**Student likes and preferences** Before students have been identified as 'disruptive', it is important to have found out something about them as individuals. What kinds of things do they like? What kinds of things do they enjoy? What are the ways in which they like to spend their free time? This information is best gathered from a combination of observation and inquiry. Asking students (or anyone else for that matter) what their likes and interests are can be a false and sterile activity. People tend to reveal their actual likes and interests incidentally, through the preferences they make, the situations in which we seem to manage best, or in conversation. Having said this, it is not a bad idea to use the questionnaire approach, since it is better than nothing, though it is wise to see this as a fairly superficial first effort. As time goes on all students should be encouraged to reveal their likes and preferences.

Of course, disaffected and vulnerable students may not readily share aspects of themselves with school staff. In these circumstances information needs to be gathered from 'sleuthing' (Molnar and Lindquist, 1989), that is from observing the student, asking his/her parents, peers, friends or whoever might know what his/her interests are.

It should also be noted that school students sometimes complain that their teachers show little interest in them as individuals. This applies to so-called 'disaffected' students, certainly (Cooper, 1993), but also to students who may appear successful in educational terms (Schostak, 1982).

Once some insight has been gained into the student's interests, giving opportunities to work on projects related to their major interests can reveal a student's potential for engagement and commitment. If s/he loves guitar, cricket, horses, computers, motorbikes, or whatever, use this special interest to help structure long-term goals and parts of the curriculum. If the response to this point is that it implies that privileges should be given to disruptive students, our response is that we are not recommending 'privileges' to anyone: all students should be treated in this way.

**Review of class rules** Get student(s), including those deemed the most difficult, to review, explain or justify class rules to new students or visitors to the classroom. The act of explaining and justifying the class rules will enable the

| 1 | 2 | 3 | 4 | 5 | 6 | 7 | 8 | 9 | 10 | 1 | 2 | 3 | 4 | 5 | 6 | 7 | 8 | 9 | 10 |
|---|---|---|---|---|---|---|---|---|---|---|---|---|---|---|---|---|---|---|---|
| 11 | 12 | 13 | 14 | 15 | 16 | 17 | 18 | 19 | 20 | 11 | 12 | 13 | 14 | 15 | 16 | 17 | 18 | 19 | 20 |
| 21 | 22 | 23 | 24 | 25 | 26 | 27 | 28 | 29 | 30 | 21 | 22 | 23 | 24 | 25 | 26 | 27 | 28 | 29 | 30 |
| 31 | 32 | 33 | 34 | 35 | 36 | 37 | 38 | 39 | 40 | 31 | 32 | 33 | 34 | 35 | 36 | 37 | 38 | 39 | 40 |
| 41 | 42 | 43 | 44 | 45 | 46 | 47 | 48 | 49 | 50 | 41 | 42 | 43 | 44 | 45 | 46 | 47 | 48 | 49 | 50 |
| Count your hand raising | | | | | | | | | | Count your talk outs | | | | | | | | | |

Figure 8.1 Count your talking-out versus your hands-up (after Jones and Jones, 1990)

student(s) to reflect on the rules, and create the possibility that they may become internalized. And of course, the act of asking them to do this implies trust and imparts a sense of the student as a valued member of the school community.

**Self-monitoring** It can also be every helpful to have the student monitor their own behaviour. For example, counting a student's hand raising compared to calling out, or how often the student is on task, and tally this for later discussion with the teacher (see Figures 8.1 and 8.2).

**Achievement folder** An achievement folder can be used. Students put into the folder work they are proud of. This can be used in parent–teacher interviews.

**Planning parent meetings** The class can be given a part in planning a meeting with their parents. Each student can organize their work to show parents, and run part of the meeting. Students own this effort, they are responsible for

## STUDENT SELF-MONITORING

| Time | What the class is supposed to be doing | What [student's name] is doing (+ or –) | |
|------|-----------------------------------------|------------------------------------------|---|
| 09.55 | | | |
| 10.00 | | | |
| 10.05 | | | |
| 10.10 | | | |
| 10.15 | | | |
| 10.20 | | | |
| 10.25 | | | |
| 10.30 | | | |
| 10.35 | | | |
| | Teacher's signature | | |

Figure 8.2 Student self-monitoring (after Jones and Jones, 1990)

it, in cooperation with the teacher. This enhances the link between home and school, completing the central systemic triangle.

**Contests** The teacher can tell the class there will be a contest but that they won't tell them what it is about. Teacher draws a vertical line on the board and on either side places ticks or crosses based on good versus bad behaviour, right-hand side of the class versus left-hand side of the class working hard, or whatever the teacher chooses. In letting the students try to figure out what the ticks and crosses are for they are forced to reflect on the issues chosen by the teacher. Of course, victory in the contest has to be celebrated in a way that reinforces positive behaviour.

**Contracts and mediation essays** Contracts and mediation essays, if used properly, give the students ownership of the problem. More long-term ownership can be developed by requiring students to keep longer and longer agreements, for example, working productively for 15 minutes, 30 minutes, one hour, then two hours, then all morning, then all day (Olsen, 1989a, 1997a). A verbal repertoire is an important precursor for such contracts. For example, teachers and students can use the same verbal formulations, such as:

- Is the behaviour that is going on helping the group? (or is the behaviour self-ish and a hindrance?)
- The group, including the teacher, agreed that no one would do that sort of thing here.
- What are we working towards?
- What is in the way?
- How can we (the teacher and students) reach our goal and stick to the rules we agreed on?

## Access part II – knowing – 'showing knowledge'

Some questions we might think about in regards to knowing include:

- 'Can each student name the class rules?'
- 'Does each student understand what is expected in terms of class and individual goals and how these might be achieved?'
- 'What does the student want, and how can we help them get it?'
- 'Can each student name the consequences for rule infractions?'
- 'Can each student name the consequences and formal rewards for positive achievement in academic and social areas?'
- 'Has information been gathered on each student's skills, learning styles and preferences?'

● 'Does the student understand class and school routines? Have these been discussed and rehearsed?

Below are some techniques that can enable access by enhancing a feeling of knowing among students.

**Teasing 'practice'** For the student who fights angrily with students after being teased rehearse with the student how it feels when they are teased. Give them a simple cognitive strategy to use instead of hitting (eg a form of words that rehearses the consequences of committing physical violence in school).

**'Steps to winning'** Some students can be helped with problem-solving strategies. Steps to winning (Figure 8.3) gives a format for solving problems that can be taught to the whole class.

---

## Four steps to winning

1. Snap the rubber band on your wrist, relax and breathe evenly, don't tighten up.
2. Say your goals, and 'I will win'.
3. Count to 10.
4. Seek help.

Now enjoy the view from the top floor.

---

Teachers can use these steps to help students plan strategies, goals and appropriate behaviours. They may want to modify some steps, for example, they may not want to snap a rubber band worn on their wrist. Instead, they can discreetly tap themselves on the leg or arm. The only requirement is that they physically cue themselves to break the hurtful sequence of thoughts.

Language is important in teaching these steps. The teacher can create with the class a special language around the steps to winning and (for example) create a different genre to the language used at home. So, when the teacher is discussing goals and a plan for improvement with a student, she could say – 'You seem to be going downstairs, Patsi. Think about the next step for going upstairs.' Or the teacher can be 'confused' – 'That seems like stepping down behaviour, Liam. I thought you were a stepping-up sort of person.' It is important that the classroom adopts a special language as its own. Students soon adopt and own the special language around this sort of problem-solving technique.

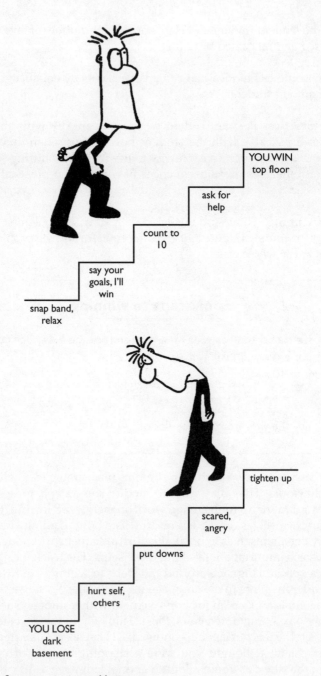

Figure 8.3 Steps to winning and losing

Below are five                    teaching a class steps to winning:

1. Discuss each step           an example.
2. Explain how steps t       g relates to your classroom goals, rules and consequences.
3. Role-play several situations in which a student misbehaves and the teacher uses the steps to winning method with the class rules and consequences to assist the student in taking responsibility for his or her own behaviour. Have the students practise the role of the student and the role of the teacher. Role-play several situations.
4. Provide the class with an example of a violation of a classroom rule and have each student write a problem-solving plan to prevent this violation recurring.
5. Quiz students on the class goals, rules, consequences and steps to winning.

There are many opportunities for the bold/caring teacher to ensure that students know the skills necessary for helping themselves and receiving help at school. In the next section we look at another important SALAD element – limits.

# Limits – 'boundaries'

Appropriate boundaries can be set using rules, consequences and routines. Students feel secure and in control when clear boundaries show them what areas they control. Troubled children feel more secure when they are contained by strong, caring parents and teachers who set limits (Horney, 1972; Epston, 1988). Some questions we might consider are:

- 'Has the class formulated class rules?'
- 'Are they posted?'
- 'Has the class formulated consequences?'
- 'Are these posted?'
- 'Are class routines clear and regular?'
- 'Is the teacher using primarily non-verbal communication when disciplining students?'

In an earlier chapter we discussed rules and consequences but we didn't discuss the third aspect of limits – routines. We define rules as expectations of students that are linked to consequences set by the school, students and teacher. In contrast, routines help us to follow our rules, but they don't necessarily link to consequences. Routines can meet the student's need for fun, belonging and power (control), and help with some of the errors discussed in Chapter 6. For example, the teacher sends a student from Maths class, a class he dislikes, and she calls it 'time-out'. She is actually rewarding him. If her routine for Maths was governed by Grandma's Rule (work first, then play), her class could work for 45 minutes each day, then watch a favourite television programme for 10 minutes. If the student who is sent outside wants to see the film, or be with his friends, the time in the hallway acts as 'time-out', that is, removal from a rewarding situation.

Evertson and Emmer (1982) quoted in Jones and Jones (1990) found that effective teachers in primary schools taught routines in five areas:

- students' use of space and facilities;
- students' behaviour in areas outside the classroom, such as the toilet, dining room, and playgrounds;
- routines to follow during whole-class activities, such as whether to raise their hand to speak, where to hand in work, or how to get help during seat work;
- routines during small-group work;
- additional procedures, such as how to behave at the beginning and end of the school day, or when a visitor arrives.

By establishing routines around certain areas, teachers can enhance their effectiveness in the classroom. Also, it is fun for students, as a treat, when the teacher occasionally breaks a routine and surprises them.

Obviously, we need to find out what the problem is before we try to fix it. So it is important to analyse first. A checklist of some of these primary school routines can help with this analysis and this is summarized in the box opposite.

Jones and Jones (1990) list a number areas for which routines need to be established in secondary classes. We present a composite of these approaches in the box overleaf.

These procedures can be combined with Smith and Laslett's (1993) four rules of classroom management (see overleaf), which say something about how these areas should be managed.

# Areas for primary school routines
(modified from Jones and Jones, 1990)

## I. ROOM AREAS
- student desks, tables, storage areas;
- learning stations;
- shared materials;
- teacher's desk, storage;
- sink, pencil sharpener.

## II. SCHOOL AREAS
- toilet, school office, library;
- lining up;
- playground;
- lunch area.

## III. WHOLE-CLASS ACTIVITIES / SEAT WORK
- student participation;
- signals for student attention from the teacher;
- talk among students;
- handing assignments in on time;
- giving out books, supplies;
- handing in work;
- giving back marked work;
- catching up missed work;
- out-of-seat policies;
- what to do after work is finished.

## IV. SMALL-GROUP ACTIVITIES
- student movement into and out of the group;
- bringing materials to the group;
- expected behaviour of students in the group;
- expected behaviour of students out of the group.

## V. OTHER PROCEDURES
- beginning of the school day;
- end of the school day;
- student behaviour during delays, interruptions;
- fire drills;
- housekeeping and student monitors.

# Secondary school routines
(modified from Jones and Jones, 1990)

## I. BEGINNING CLASS
- calling register, absentees;
- late students;
- behaviour during class announcements;
- getting ready for class;
- distributing materials.

## II. DURING LESSONS
- teacher–student contacts;
- student movement in the room;
- signals for student attention;
- headings for papers;
- student talk during seat work;
- activities to do when work is finished.

## III. ENDING LESSONS
- putting away materials, equipment;
- organizing materials for the next class;
- dismissing class.

## IV. OTHER PROCEDURES
- student rules about the teacher's desk;
- fire drills;
- lunch procedures;
- toilet;
- school bags.

## Four rules of classroom management
(Smith and Laslett, 1993)

RULE 1: 'GET THEM IN'
- smooth, prompt, focused start;
- recap on last lesson;
- preview this lesson (skills to be used, and content to be covered).

RULE 2: 'GET ON WITH IT'
- maintain appropriate and varied pace;
- select stimulating, varied content and tasks;
- ensure appropriate differentiation of tasks and content;
- use pair and group work and encourage cooperative learning;
- provide extension activities.

RULE 3: 'GET ON WITH THEM'
- have clear rules for how students seek help;
- always acknowledge requests for help;
- provide help discretely;
- get to know something about all students;
- be interested and available.

RULE 4: 'GET THEM OUT'
- refresh, restate and reinforce theme of lesson;
- create time for exit phase;
- have clear, tidy routine.

Jones and Jones (1990) also list 'accountability procedures'. Effective classroom managers teach specific procedures related to student accountability for academic work (see overleaf).

Jones and Jones (1990) believe these routines must be taught to children. One way of teaching routines is to follow these four steps:

1. Discuss the need for the routine.
2. Solicit students' ideas.
3. Have the students practise the procedure until it is performed correctly.
4. Reinforce (reward) the correct behaviour.

# Accountability procedures related to work

## I. WORK REQUIREMENTS
- headings for written work;
- use of pen or pencil;
- writing on back of paper;
- neatness, legibility;
- late work;
- missed work;
- hand in dates;
- catching-up with work that has been missed.

## II. COMMUNICATING WORK TASKS
- publicly displaying work tasks;
- making requirements/marking criteria for work clear;
- provisions for absentees;
- long-term work tasks (eg project work).

## III. MONITORING STUDENT WORK
- in-class oral participation;
- completion of in-class work;
- completion of homework;
- completion of stages of long-term work tasks.

## IV. CHECKING/MARKING WORK IN CLASS
- students exchanging completed work with each other;
- marking work;
- handing in papers.

## V. MARKING PROCEDURES
- determining marks recorded on reports for parents;
- recording marks;
- marking stages of long-term work tasks;
- bonus marks.

## VI. ACADEMIC FEEDBACK
- rewards and incentives;
- publicly displaying student work;
- communication with parents;
- students' record of their marks.

Some other techniques for setting limits include the following:

- Predictability is crucial for students to feel secure. This can be achieved by giving students advanced knowledge of class rules and consequences before they find themselves in the situation where the rules apply. This gives students a clear sense of control.
- Requiring the student to write the misbehaviour in a book in pencil, then, if the student stops misbehaving and works hard, he or she erases it.
- When the teacher provides a clear set of rules and consequences, some framed positively and some negatively, this frees the teacher to teach and be positive with students. For example, a rule like 'No annoying' automatically covers many behaviours so the teacher does not have to use negative language each time a student misbehaves. Instead, the teacher simply tells the student that he/she has broken the 'No annoying' rule. For example, the rules for the first class meeting of a group of Year six students might be:

---

### Class meeting rules

- Appropriate posture and eye contact.
- Speak one at a time without interrupting.
- Avoid sarcasm or mockery – respect differences of opinion.
- 'I don't know' responses won't be accepted.
- Respect confidences.
- No annoying others.

---

These rules set limits for the first meeting so the students wouldn't ave responsibility in the meeting, wouldn't violate the rights of other student and would respect confidential information shared by others. Obviousl these rules would change as responsibility for these meetings was hande to the students.

- Using visual (non-verbal) cues for students who may be confused by som verbal instructions or who are predominantly visual learners. Because many troubled students appear to have communication difficulties and take in information through visual or tactile means more easily than through auditory means, teachers can use visual cues, for example 'On the third tick after your initials on the board you leave.' With such students we need to remediate their weaknesses by starting with their strengths. Work routines should be visual, lists and pictures on the board or on charts can show students how to proceed with their work.

- Delineating roles, strengths, and skills of each student. It is useful to allow specialization in relation to preferred learning styles, special interests and personality differences. Each student knows he or she is special because his or her niche is defined in a positive way. This provides boundaries (limits) that empower the student.
- To receive help from the teacher each student writes his name on the board then returns to his seat to work. Then the teacher calls the students name, gives him/her help, and he erases his/her name.

As stated earlier, class goals, rules, consequences and routines should aim, for the sake of all students in the class, to manage the most difficult students. With a consequences hierarchy in place, the teacher should use goal reminders, rules, consequences and routines to do much of the disciplining while he or she talks to the student about his/her work, reminds about goals, encourages, etc, but does not repeat rules back to the student too often. The class should have practised these rules and consequences and should know them by heart. Students learn best if they, rather than the teacher, do most of the work.

We will explore in the next chapter the way in which some students use 'gambits' to try to get teachers to 'come to them' repeatedly on their terms. Teachers can avoid this by using rules and consequences to intervene pre-emptively before things get out of hand. It is important for teachers not to allow themselves to be lured into a trap where they do all the disciplining, all the work, while the student does little but disrupt the class and keep the teacher performing. The misbehaving student comes to the teacher, not the other way around.

Here is a summary of some of the key issues surrounding the use of limits:

- It is very useful to 'catch them being good' rather than focusing on the negative (Walker, Colvin and Ramsey, 1995; Smith and, Laslett, 1993).
- Encouragers and goal reminders keep students and teachers focused on common goals.
- The teacher should try to get in early, before things have developed into real trouble.
- The student should be required to come to the teacher.
- The teacher should visibly enjoy teaching.
- It is better to act preventively than react defensively after inappropriate behaviour occurs.
- Actions speak louder than words.
- It is important to have a formulation of the problem based on evidence before action is taken to 'resolve' it.
- Being non-verbal where possible, in discipline matters, means that teachers are less disruptive in their own lessons.
- Involving parents strengthens the system.

As we noted earlier, it is important that rules and consequences should be planned to meet specific class and individual needs, goals and rewards. For example:

---

Ms ATTWOOD'S CLASS GOALS
1. win the school Maths contest;
2. have a party in Week 8;
3. complete all 12 tasks in this unit of work;
4. make life pleasant for Ms Attwood;
5. make life pleasant for Ms Attwood's class.

Ms ATTWOOD'S REWARDS
1. free time;
2. choice of a video;
3. listen to music while working;
4. more time on the computer, or other activity of choice;
5. note to parents.

Ms ATTWOOD'S CLASS RULES
1. work and play safely;
2. no physical or verbal violence;
3. stay within bounds;
4. be assertive;
5. no annoying, sarcasm or insults.

Ms ATTWOOD'S CONSEQUENCES
1. sit down at the time-out desk;
2. loss of free time;
3. visit the Head Teacher;
4. note to parents.

---

For the bold/caring teacher there is room for great creativity around limits. Each class will have different, democratically determined limits based on the individual teacher, and the students. The same holds true for acceptance, the most important ingredient of SALAD.

# Acceptance – 'to receive or welcome'

Issues of rejection by others often lie at the centre of many emotional, behavioural and discipline problems. Students who are seen as disruptive and disaffected often blame their teachers, and see their own disruptive acts in terms of revenge, retaliation, or retribution against the offences of others who they often see as 'unfair', disrespectful, partial in their treatment of students and unkind (Cooper, 1993; Cooper *et al*, 2000; Olsen, 1989a, 1997; Rosser and Harré, 1976; Tattum, 1982). At the centre of their disruption is a sense of hurt and a desire to experience the sense of ease and security that derives from being accepted by others. In true systemic fashion, however, disruptive students often find themselves trapped in a spiral of escalating conflict. There is a tendency for them to approach the problem of rejection in a reciprocal manner: to offer tit-for-tat. So the more they disrupt the more they are rejected; the more they are rejected, the more they disrupt.

Of course this works the other way too. Teachers can also find themselves trapped into the same negative spiral for pretty much the same reasons. Teachers, just like their students, have a need for respect and acceptance. When they find themselves being rejected, they too may tend to adopt a defensive stance, locate the problem within the student, and retaliate. A teacher who is feeling hard-done-by in this respect may well make the imposition of his or her will on the recalcitrant student(s) a major project which takes precedence over teaching, just as the recalcitrant student makes the subversion of the teacher's intentions his or her major project, which, in turn, takes precedence over learning. Both parties are seeking refuge in a defensive strategy that the other finds provocative – like parties engaged in a race of nuclear arms proliferation, they are on a course of mutually assured destruction.

Some questions we might ask include:

- 'Does the teacher have class rules about teasing, put-downs and bullying?'
- 'Are there clear consequences for students who break these rules?'
- 'Do these rules apply to the teacher as well as to students?'
- 'Does the teacher regularly get feedback about how students see him/her?'
- 'Does the teacher have enough status with students that teacher praise is valued by them?'
- 'Does the teacher teach social skills?'
- 'Does the teacher use self-esteem raising activities?'
- 'Does the teacher use cross-age tutoring?'
- 'Does the teacher use class meetings?'

A major principle underpinning the systemic approach we propose in this book is that change leads to change. In terms of changing problem behaviour, it means that teachers can change disruptive behaviour into cooperative behaviour by initiating cooperative behaviour themselves. Given the status and power structures in most schools it is usually down to the school staff to take responsibility for initiating cooperative behaviour. More importantly, if school staff do not model this approach for students, many students will never gain this insight.

It is useful for teachers to become aware of the kinds of teacher behaviours that are likely to promote positive student engagement, and those that threaten it.

## Accepting and rejecting students: the students' perspective

There have been many studies over the years which have looked at the school experience from the student perspective. The findings of these studies contribute to the compelling case proposed by many writers that the voice of the child/student should play a prominent role in policy development for children and young people (Charlton and David, 1996; Cooper, 1993a, 1996; Davie, Upton and Varma, 1996; Garner, 1996).

In considering the student perspective, several researchers have looked at what students perceived to be disruptive say about their teachers (Cooper, 1993; Cooper *et al*, 2000; Rosser and Harré, 1976; Schostak, 1982; Tattum, 1982). The overwhelming message from these studies is that students resent treatment that they experience as demeaning, impersonal, unfriendly and inconsiderate. By and large these studies show that students claim to work best for and get on with teachers who teach stimulating and well-prepared lessons, who are friendly, but not too friendly, and who maintain well-disciplined and purposeful classrooms.

These points are illustrated by what happened when one of the present authors asked a group of Year eight students what made a good teacher and what made a bad teacher. Their responses were:

- Teachers should make friends with students, make a joke and be willing to laugh. Humour is important; try not to pick on or hate anyone; treat everyone fairly, everyone equal, otherwise some students will feel left out.
- New teachers should not change things.
- We don't like teachers who aren't hard enough; who threaten something but don't carry it out.
- We don't like it when they treat boys differently to girls, especially in PE. (This was to do with the fact that girls had shower stalls while boys didn't.)
- The worst thing a teacher can do is embarrass us in front of our friends. If they do that, we will get back at them (the teacher) eventually. For example, we won't work for them.

- If you do something bad at the beginning of the year, some teachers keep picking on you. We won't work well for those teachers.
- If a teacher makes a promise, they should keep it.
- Kids in the (gifted class) are treated differently. They're squares, crawlers. We lower kids get in trouble for things that they get away with. They're teachers' pets. Teachers make excuses for them.
- The Learning Centre kids (ie students with social, emotional, behavioural and learning difficulties) are treated differently, for example they don't get into trouble if they don't wear a uniform.
- The principal, Mr D., is fair. If teachers don't go along with Mr D.'s approach, they should get out. Teacher's shouldn't make their own rules.
- Teachers should act like they trust you.
- Teachers swear, but if we do we get in trouble.
- Teachers' attitudes need to change; they need to be more cheerful.
- There should be no picking on anyone; no put-downs. Treat everyone fairly.
- If a kid is wagging school, the teachers should sort it out; (find out) why the kid did it, as well as punish them. It may be, for example, because of conflict with a teacher.

This is only one class of students but larger studies reveal similar themes. Students respect teachers who are just and treat everyone fairly. This is not the same as saying that students require teachers to treat them all exactly the same. What they do require is that there is a justifiable reason for differences in the ways in which students are treated (see Sattin, 1999). Teachers should be firm and never use sarcasm or embarrass students in front of their friends.

These student views may strike some readers (as they do the authors) as highly conservative. Like all conservatism, however, this student conservatism is rooted in a desire for security in the face of the experience of feeling vulnerable and exposed. It may well be that it is the most vulnerable of students who have the most conservative expectations of their teachers. This makes sense if we consider security as basic human need from which stems the confidence to actively engage in the world as an autonomous and creative being (eg Pringle, 1975).

Lewis and Lovegrove (1984) studied the attitudes of high school students towards punishment and teachers. Teachers that students evaluated as 'best' were calm and scrupulously fair. They didn't abrogate responsibility to other adults, that is, they managed classroom problems by themselves, instead of sending students to other staff members. An important factor with 'best' teachers was that they never punished the whole class for the wrongdoing of one student. They punished the misbehaving student only. (Note that this is different to the group incentives mentioned above where everyone is rewarded.) These teachers made rules very clear and based their rules on the fact that other students are unable to work when certain students misbehave.

'Best' teachers, according to this research, also put the subject across in a way that students could understand, and in a way that was interesting. They treated students as people. They also exhibited good leadership skills, and were firm for the good of others.

## Ensuring a climate of acceptance

There is a variety of ways in which teachers can ensure that they have covered the acceptance criteria in their classroom management plan.

### Rejection
Students should never be made to feel put-down or rejected, especially in front of their peers. If this happens (as inevitably it will from time to time, either through intent or error) the teacher needs to take the initiative in putting things right by talking to the student concerned, and apologizing if necessary. The teacher and student need to jointly own the problem and solve it without blame. The crucial thing to emphasize is that whilst it may be understandable why a problem such as this has occurred, it can never be justified.

### Respect
Teachers need to have high status or respect so their praise and approval are valued. There is no simple route to attaining this kind of status with students. The primary sources of such respect reside in the school and the classroom, and tend to be built up over a long period of time, during which the teacher shows themselves to be trustworthy and reliable (see Mick McManus's account of 'natural virtues' in Chapter 2).

There is no point in asking teachers to praise students if that praise makes students look foolish in front of their peers. Sometimes it does. In fact, most older students want praise and reprimands from teachers in private, not in public.

Again, this status relates to the reward and referent powers discussed earlier, and teachers need status before they can meet student's need for status. Summarized below from Tauber (1995) are some ways that teachers can increase their referent power:

- Use more self-disclosure.
- Associate with students in non-teaching situations, for example in sports or with special interests.
- Spend time in face-to-face interactions with all students.
- Be accepting, yet not patronizing; recognize students' interests.
- Discipline in a calm, businesslike manner. Avoid the personalization of discipline problems by not taking misbehaviour personally, and by

condemning negative behaviour rather than the perpetrator. Discipline should be administered with dignity so both teacher and student save face.

- Teachers should make themselves aware of any tendencies to react differently to different students. Fairness is essential.
- Use active listening.
- Be a good role model.

Teachers can raise their own status with students by managing most classroom problems on their own with as little help as possible from other staff. Though it should be borne in mind that, at different points in a teacher's career as a whole, or even within a particular school, there may be a need for active public support of a new teacher by more-established members of staff.

## Acceptance

Teachers and other school staff will contribute to their own acceptance by students by extending acceptance to their colleagues. This relates to the kinds of conversations that staff have with students about other staff. Staff who encourage students to 'dish the dirt' on their colleagues are playing a dangerous game that often creates more losers than winners, because it encourages students to play staff off against each other. It is also likely to diminish the respect the students have for the gossip-mongering teacher. Having said this, genuine and well-founded complaints against members of staff should be dealt with in professional ways. Either way, students need to be able to trust and respect staff.

## Feedback

Feedback is crucial. Teachers need to know, from their peers and from students, how they are perceived. Sometimes, a teacher's 'manner' contributes to classroom management problems. Teachers who are brusque or bad-tempered, who do not appear to be concerned with students' welfare, or worse, are experienced as insulting by students or their parents, will create difficulties for themselves and others. In dealing with a colleague who presents in this way it is important for staff to give them the benefit of the doubt, and start from the assumption that their apparent behaviour severely misrepresents their intentions, which are probably positive and professional. If this transpires not to be the case then colleagues must ask themselves: 'what are we doing (wittingly and unwittingly) to encourage and maintain this negative behaviour in our colleague?'; and 'how can we stop maintaining the problem and encourage more desirable behaviours?'

To enhance referent power staff can use the forms below to get feedback about their manner and their teaching. This can contribute to peer evaluation if staff fill out the daily checklist for Teachers (Figure 8.4), then, in pairs, share

# DAILY CHECKLIST FOR TEACHERS

| Today have I: | YES | NO |
|---|---|---|
| Negotiated? | | |
| Used humour? | | |
| Taken care with praise? | | |
| Maintained high standards? | | |
| Maintained my dignity? | | |
| Spoken to the students as I would like to be spoken to? | | |
| Not crowded the students physically or verbally? | | |
| Shown that I really like the students? | | |
| Set consequences in a gentle, totally committed (to the student and standards) but neutral manner (ie, not affected by the behaviour)? | | |
| Acted as if I trusted the students? | | |
| Used the 'us' against 'them' attitude? | | |
| Used sarcasm? | | |
| Used positive remarks? | | |
| Set aside time for private talks? | | |
| Cut down on verbalization when students were misbehaving? | | |
| Used an accusing tone of voice? | | |
| Shouted at the students in anger? | | |
| Used encouragers? | | |
| Used goal reminders? | | |

Figure 8.4  Daily checklist for teachers

| Dear Student, | | | |
|---|---|---|---|
| Please put an x on the line according to how you see your teacher. | | | |
| Thank you. | | | |
| 1.  good listener | | | bad listener |
| 2.  liked by students | | | disliked by students |
| 3.  often uses put-downs | | | never uses put-downs |
| 4.  very fair | | | very unfair |
| 5.  often angry | | | never angry |
| 6.  boring | | | interesting/fun |
| 7.  lazy | | | works hard |
| 8.  stops misbehaviour | | | allows misbehaviour |
| 9.  cares about students | | | doesn't care about students |
| 10.  always picks on students | | | never picks on students |
| 11.  often encourages | | | never encourages |
| 12.  reminds us of goals | | | never reminds us of goals |

Figure 8.5  How my students see me

them with colleagues who have seen them interact with students. Colleagues then, in private, give each other feedback on each category. Colleagues should indicate at least one area, and probably more, where their partner can show improvement.

The 'how my students see me' protocol (Figure 8.5) provides feedback about how students perceive their teacher and their teaching. It is helpful to use this twice a year. The procedures for using this form are: the forms must be filled in anonymously; nobody sees the results except the teacher or someone chosen by the teacher to share the results; and teachers must not single out a student who they believe may have given negative feedback.

These can be painful exercises. But change doesn't come without a little pain. The important thing is that this change can benefit teachers and students, and prevent future problems.

## Negotiation

Students need to be taught how to successfully negotiate with someone more powerful than themselves; this reduces the 'us against them' attitude between students and teachers. This can be addressed through role-play exercises.

## Feelings

Situations from television or movies can be discussed with students to help them understand other people's feelings. For many people imagery of film is more powerful than talk, and narrative is used in all cultures to socialize children. School staff can tap the enthusiasm that students have for television programmes and films, and the interest they have in certain characters; these can be used to teach values and empathy with others.

## Group work

There are many methods for teaching group work. For example, each student writes on a piece of paper five things he or she is good at. Then the teacher hands out random numbers 1 to 5 to each student in the class so each student is in one of Groups 1 to 5. After moving to their groups they nominate a leader, a scribe, and a timekeeper, and design a money-making business venture. They will use each member's strengths to build a strong team. The teacher gives the highest mark, or a prize, to the group with the most innovative plan that utilizes the widest range of individual differences and strengths.

## Social skills training

Social skills training packages, such as those described by Walker, Colvin and Ramsey (1995), and Howell, Fox and Morehead (1993), teach acceptance techniques. These skills can often be taught through games. For example, students can be taught the importance of appropriate eye contact by first asking them to do the skill wrong, then do it right, then do it wrong, then right again. Adolescents can be convinced of the need for certain social skills by using their own values and their subculture to underscore the pay-off for them. For example:

---

'Liam, you know when Mr Woodhead told you off the other day, and you were standing there looking at your shoes?'

'No I wasn't.'

'Actually, you were.'

'So what?'

'Well, Mr Woodhead knew you were dead scared of him.'

'Rubbish! I'm not scared of him!'

'Well Liam, it certainly looked that way to other people, because, if you weren't scared of him, you'd look him in the eye. Like this [demonstrate]. Let's try it.' (Then practise doing it right, wrong, right, wrong.)

---

Social skills, and problem-solving skills, taught to EBD students tend not to generalize or maintain unless: the student practises the skill in the real situations where problems occur (Olsen, 1989a); the student sees and receives some pay-off , for example, the Social Circles Game (Olsen, 1989a, 1997); and parents, teachers, or other care-givers are involved in the training.

### Cross-age tutoring
Cross-age tutoring is an important way to tap a student's natural drive to care for others. Even if an older student is a regular rule-breaker, he or she will often teach younger students not to break rules.

### Conferencing box
If the student sees a problem coming, and they do not think they can solve it, s/he can write his/her name on a piece of paper and slip it into the Conferencing Box. If the note is placed in the box that morning, the teacher will come to help the student solve the problem before lunch. If it is placed in the box in the afternoon, the teacher will help the student before home time.

### Help desk
The student can move him/herself to the help desk (or chill-out chair, or mellow-out corner) whenever he or she feels agitated or hassled by other students. The desk may have some privacy, like a carrel, and each member of the class can rehearse how to use the 'help desk' so they feel comfortable about using it.

### Class meetings
Class meetings have been used for decades (see Dreikurs, Grunwald and Pepper, 1982) as part of classroom management. They are an excellent way to give students democratic acceptance and tap their need for belonging and cooperation. One cautionary note: it has become fashionable to discuss an individual's behaviour in such a class meeting and this can exacerbate problems, even if the student in question agrees to have his or her behaviour discussed. Older students in particular can feel publicly ridiculed if their behaviour is discussed at such a meeting as 'the problem'. The student may already feel 'it's me against them' and live by his or her code of retribution. A meeting such as this can invite retaliation. Though it can be helpful for victims to confront perpetrators in such a meeting, take care with meetings where the whole class appears to gang up on one student. See also the comments on class meetings by Ann Owner on pages 149–51.

Acceptance, the teacher accepting the students, the students accepting the teacher, and students accepting each other is, we think, the most important SALAD area. Readers will understand this most fully if they consider their own experience of schooling, when they felt hurt, or when they felt accepted by peers and teachers. Or to bring things up to date, they might consider the role that acceptance (or lack it) plays in their professional functioning.

# Class meetings: part of a systems approach to the management of students with EBDs

## By Ann Owner

Many teachers run successful classroom meetings, but for others, classroom meetings remain a frightening challenge, a challenge they seldom attempt because when they do, the meetings turn into a disappointing experience. We can look at this problem as two questions:

1. Why are classroom meetings, for some teachers and students, a disappointing experience?
2. Why are classroom meetings, for some teachers and students, a rewarding experience?

In addressing the first question I believe it is because teachers are unable to do a number of things:

Firstly, most teachers are concerned about doing a good job. Fear of being judged a 'bad' teacher can be very threatening. Sad children seem to advertise to the world that they are not happy about a number of things, including their classroom environment. Even though it is not their fault, some teachers feel a sense of guilt or failure about students' displaced anger and, when this happens, the teacher turns his or her anger against the children in their care, blames the students for not making them feel successful as a teacher. In a paradoxical way, teachers may really be saying – 'You're a bad kid because you make me feel like a bad teacher!' Whatever the reason, it seems that few teachers feel comfortable about caring for a student's emotional difficulties, particularly if anger is directed against the teacher or members of the class. They believe they are experts at handling academic problems, not problems of emotional pain. Understandably, teachers often feel at a loss.

Secondly, teachers could in class meetings, but sometimes don't:

- recognize feelings – to do this teachers and students can learn 'active listening';
- validate feelings – children need to know that their feelings are real and justified;
- accept feelings – in a non-judgemental way;
- allow for the release of feelings – children often need to release strong feelings, like pain, anger and fear;

continued overleaf

● give children the opportunity to make their own decisions, give them a chance to find alternatives. Teachers don't necessarily need to give advice; advice carries a built-in obligation.

Thirdly, teachers often fail to recognize their own skills as communicators, their skills in the art of negotiation, their abilities to resolve conflict in a win/win fashion. These skills may need to be strengthened, but, with a bit of reading, the situation is not lost. Refining these skills will benefit teachers and more importantly, their students. Teachers can use class meetings to reinforce, even give awards to students who exhibit appropriate:

● social skills;
● skills for dealing with feelings;
● skill alternatives to aggression;
● skills for dealing with stress;
● skills for dealing with conflict.

All these can be dealt with in a realistic context. Situations abound in schools which teachers can seize upon and utilize to teach these skills. This use of dilemma or conflict from the playground and classroom needs to occur naturally so as to increase the likelihood of the student learning to manage such dilemmas or conflicts, and therefore generalize the experience back into natural settings.

Fourthly, the distinction between merely abiding by the agreed-upon rules set for a class meeting, and actually 'setting limits' has to be clarified. Keeping order does not necessarily mean we have ensured the rights of all students who are involved. A meeting can be totally ruined if one self-righteous or pushy individual is allowed to dominate and trample over the rights of others. We need to recognize that: rights need to be paired with responsibilities; and teachers have the ultimate responsibility for the welfare of the group.

Without resorting to harsh and punitive measures, the teacher should maintain the pre-determined standards and limits (rules, consequences, and routines) in a firm but caring way. These standards and limits give the group a sense of security, give the teacher a measure of authority, and put control back where it belongs, ie not with one pushy individual, but with the whole group via the standards and limits set by the group.

In addressing the second question, 'Why are classroom meetings successful experiences for teachers and students?', we have answered this in part with the suggestions above. Successful class meetings vary from one group to another because of the dynamic nature of the affective needs of the group (students/teachers/school). However, they do share a number of common features. The inclusion of these features, and the suggestions discussed above, can ensure a degree of success, particularly when teachers deal with feelings as well as facts in the content of their class meeting.

Successful facilitators of class meetings attempt to come to terms with situations that cause their students some discomfort, distress, or dilemma. In turn, this provides an opportunity for students and teachers to 'grow' in a climate of trust. Class meetings can provide an awareness of alternative communication techniques. In turn this provides the opportunities for them to 'grow' in a climate of trust based on the basic elements of human need. Class meetings should provide an awareness of alternative strategies in the resolutions of their own personal conflict or problem situation. Class meetings should provide children with the means of access to these strategies and an opportunity to practise these strategies. It is therefore important that class meetings have:

- an agenda;
- rules that set working frameworks for the meeting, preferably established with student input;
- a chairperson or convenor;
- a recorder of events and proceedings;
- circular seating arrangements for all participants;
- the same place and time for regularly timetabled meetings;
- a timeframe known at the beginning of the meeting, for example, 'We will have 30 minutes this morning for our meeting';
- an observable beginning (set the scene), middle (content) and end (closure) to each meeting.

Before students can open up and share their thoughts and problems with their teacher and peers, an atmosphere of trust and safety must be in place. All students need to know that someone is interested enough to listen to them, and capable enough to manage those difficult situations that sometimes present themselves in classroom meetings (see Mosley, 1993).

In the real world of school problems both the home and the school influence classroom behaviour. The point of the approach outlined in this book is that it shows how teachers can overcome classroom problems that may have their origin in the home. It also shows how teachers and other staff can (unwittingly) exacerbate these problems.

In the next section we consider the role of direction in SALAD.

# Direction – 'the course along which someone moves'

## Growing and going somewhere

The direction criterion is all about pace and purpose. This is what Smith and Laslett (1993) are talking about when they exhort teachers to 'get on with it'. Getting on with it requires that the teacher has a clear idea of where they are going; where they want their students to go, and what they will have achieved when they get there. It also requires pace, in the form of a well-judged sense of momentum, by which students have a sense of progress that transmits feelings of urgency without anxiety. The antithesis of 'pace', in this context, is 'going through the motions'. And although a scatological reference here would not be thematically inappropriate, the key (intended) emphasis is on the need to avoid mind-numbing routine in the classroom.

Some questions we might consider include:

- Does the teacher have clear, visual goals, lists and targets so that progress towards task completion can be seen?
- Are the goals easy to measure, display and graph, for example, the number of sight words, maths skills, physical skills or good behaviours he achieved?
- Are clear instructional materials used so students can see themselves progressing?
- Does the teacher use time lines?
- Has the teacher tried points cards?
- Does the teacher form new goals and rewards before existing ones have lost their power?

Charles (1996) pointed out that children need to experience success and recognition of their success. This can be accomplished by: using clear goals as targets; using a curriculum that progresses; encouragement and urging from teachers; using good instructional material; developing *esprit de corps* (morale or group spirit). He suggested that teachers chart group (class) gains using graphs, class diaries or class murals, and that they display these gains in the classroom.

Teachers and parents can help children know accomplishment by setting clear goals, and standards that enhance the child's feelings of competence, success, curiosity and completion of tasks. Teachers need to build direction into their classroom so students can see change. This helps students avoid boredom, maintain a sense of excitement and taps their need for power, fun and status. In the beginning help them achieve short-term goals, then urge them to complete long-term goals.

Many troubled students seem to have communication problems. Talking may not always work with them. Teachers' speeches and warnings seem to go in one ear and out the other. They appear to be 'teacher deaf'. So what do some teachers do? They shout – even though it doesn't work. And the more it doesn't work the louder they shout. The result is to escalate the problem.

Many students with learning and/or behavioural problems prefer to work through visual and kinaesthetic means. Of course, many of our most successful students are quite happy with the more literary/analytical approaches favoured by schools these days. Most teachers realize that the approaches which work for their most successful students don't necessarily work for all students. Good teaching involves working in harmony with the learning strengths of students. If a student has a weakness, like a communication problem, then education should start with their strengths, not their weaknesses. Weakness can be addressed by first using the student's strengths. Once the student experiences success in one domain, they have a basis for taking on challenges in other domains: they have an experience of success that gives them confidence. This relates to the idea that the formulation of goals, on its own, seldom works. Many children need to see movement towards a goal after the goal is formed, and some need to see it daily, or even more frequently. Movement is demonstrated by success.

## Other techniques for enhancing direction in various age ranges

**Narrative and metaphor**  Using narrative and metaphor, the student can be asked tell a story about their life so they see direction in their efforts. This can take any form, including a short story, poem, or a rap (in writing; on a video or audio cassette), depending on the interests and aptitudes of the student. Imagery in stories and film can be very powerful for helping a child identify (and thus own) the challenges they face and define, and the dreams they pursue.

**Skills list** Students can be asked to compile lists, displays and so on, of skills they've acquired. For example, they can chart their reading rate, number of sight words learned, maths accuracy, computer competencies, or their physical skills. Help them set goals to utilize these skills and then give them a sense of competence and completion of these goals.

**Wish lists** Students can be asked to define dreams, hopes and aspirations of what they and their friends will be when they grow up. Discussion around hope is crucial to this process (Seligman, 1990).

**Work predictions** Students can be encouraged to predict how much work they will complete in a day, or a week, and compare these predictions on a chart to the amount they actually complete. The central issue here is that they are competing with themselves rather than with others.

**Time lines** Time lines show how much a student's behaviour has changed (Figure 8.6). For example, over a six month period the teacher may mark on the time line early problems – not completing work, hitting students, swearing at the teacher, etc – and show at what point these problems stopped. The visual representation of this accumulated progress acts as a reminder and an encourager. This also creates a base from which the teacher can begin to focus the student on their future, mature behaviours.

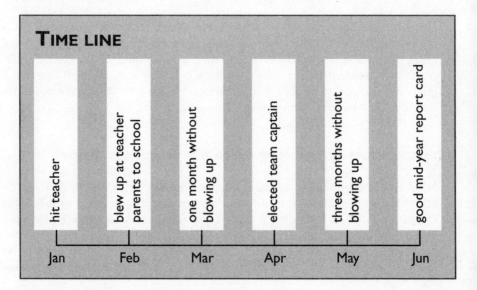

Figure 8.6 Time line

**Help points** Help points involve showing the student visually how often they help others. For example, in a kindergarten or reception class situation, the teacher has each child's name listed on the wall. When a child is seen to help another person, the teacher sticks a coloured pin next to the helper's name. As the number of pins accumulate, students can earn immediate, short-term (daily), medium-term (weekly) and long-term (monthly) rewards. For example, after they earn four pins, they can choose a friend and play a game on the computer. Keeping parents informed of positive progress is an essential part of this strategy.

**Sheep** 'Sheep' is ideal for use with younger students. A cutout of a paper sheep is pinned on the board with each pupil's name on it. Each time the pupil completes all of his or her work for the day he or she can glue a ball of wool onto the sheep until, eventually, the sheep gets its fleece (Figure 8.7).

Figure 8.7 Sheep in need of a fleece

**Points card** Another technique is to make a points card with one square for each day. The pupil can stamp a smiley face on each day that he or she maintains a particular pattern of desired behaviour, for example, not throwing a tantrum (Figure 8.8).

## POINTS CARD

|  | Week 1 | Week 2 | Week 3 | Week 4 |
|---|---|---|---|---|
| Monday |  😊 |  😊 |  😊 |  |
| Tuesday |  😊 |  😎 |  😎 |  |
| Wednesday |  |  😊 |  😊 |  |
| Thursday |  |  |  |  |
| Friday |  |  |  |  |
| Full week |  |  |  |  |

Figure 8.8  Points card

**Targets** Visual goals can be used to teach independent work habits. Each pupil can write a list of tasks in the morning and cross out each piece of work as they complete it to the teacher's satisfaction. Or, each day the pupil can write their work into the stages of a rocket, or a dinosaur or whatever appeals. The pupil colours in each stage as they complete each piece of work (Figure 8.9). The teacher helps the student at first but gradually leaves the student to complete this planning and work on their own.

**Cumulative graphs** Cumulative graphs – If the student has a Daily Home Note (see Chapter 7) with four items to be marked by the teacher 'yes' or 'no',

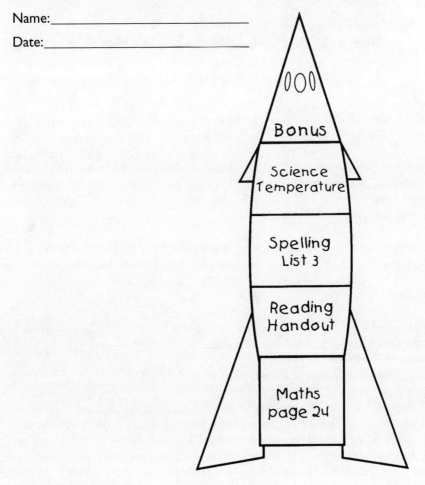

Name:_____

Date:_____

Figure 8.9  Targets

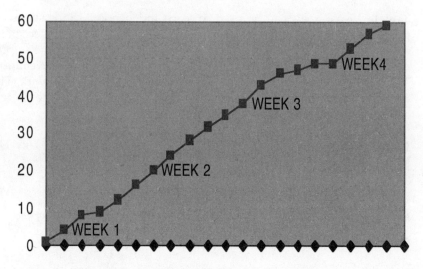

Figure 8.10 Cumulative graph of number of 'yes's' on the Home Note

the student can be given a target average, say three out of four 'yes's' over a month. Then the student (not the teacher) marks every day on graph paper the cumulative number of 'yes's' he gets (Figure 8.10). The student can see that if they have a bad day, for example, receiving one 'yes' and three 'no's', they can raise their average back up to the required three out of four by gaining four 'yes's' each day over the next few days. This method can be highly motivating to students.

**Caterpillar** When working with younger children, the teacher draws a caterpillar head on the board. Add one segment for each time period when the class works hard. When the caterpillar has 10 segments, the class can have a group reward (eg free time).

**Raffle tickets** On the playground young children can receive raffle tickets or play money when the teacher sees them play cooperatively. At the end of the term, children can have a 'raffle day' where they can win prizes or a 'shopping day' when they can spend their play money.

**Displays** Each day the teacher writes the instructions for work clearly on the board, using pictures if necessary, so children can follow the list and complete their work independently. Some teachers like to give the class one tick on the board for starting their work, another for maintaining hard work, and a third for completing their work. After three ticks the class is given a group reward (eg a class game).

**Physical factors** To keep young people working steadily and achieving their goals, it is important always to consider the physical factors in the room and the extent to which they affect students' attention and comfort: Warmth – heat, sun, air-conditioning, fans, etc; Sound – noise, corridor, chairs, etc; Visual – quality of light, colour, etc; and Space – desks, wet areas, how close children sit, movement, etc.

Some students have a greater capacity for coping with distraction than others. With this in mind it is best to judge the overall level of comfort and distraction in relation to the student(s) who show attentional problems, rather than those who usually cope.

# Summary

SALAD is not the answer to all discipline problems. There is only one certain way of avoiding behaviour problems in classrooms, and that is to stay out of classrooms. What SALAD can offer is a framework for analysing and understanding classroom behaviour which, in turn, leads to some straightforward, but powerful, means of preventing behavioural problems and intervening positively with such problems when they arise, as they inevitably will. The strategies we have outlined are suggestions, some of which will appeal to some readers, whilst others do not. We would welcome it if readers took the framework and experimented with strategies from each of the five SALAD categories to generate their own interventions.

# 9

# Gambits: understanding and dealing with the games students play

---

### Liam winds up the teacher

Liam sits at his desk looking at the floor and he won't start his work. He sulks, he won't speak to his teacher who, unfortunately, is you. But, you're a caring, concerned teacher so you continue to urge him – 'Please Liam, tell me what your problem is'.

No response. Ten minutes of this – Liam sulking, refusing to make eye contact while you plead with him. This isn't just a caring inquiry, you beg him to share his problems – 'What's troubling you Liam?'

---

Suddenly he slides his chair back, grating against the floor, bolts out of his seat and runs out of the classroom. Of course, you chase him. After all, you're concerned that he might get out into the road and be run over by a car. No matter that he's much more likely to be hit by a car while you chase him than when you're not. Anyway, he's too fast so you eventually return to your classroom and send a child to the head of year with a note saying what has happened.

Then you look up from your desk and there's Liam outside your classroom. He's pressing his nose against the window and making faces at you. So far you've lost 15 minutes of lesson time.

This is an example of a student 'gambit' (Olsen, 1992, 1993, 1994, 1997b). 'Gambit' is a term used in chess to describe a strategy whereby one player sacrifices a piece in order to tempt the second player into making a move that gives the first player a positional advantage. The term derives from the Italian word *gambetta*, which is used in wrestling to describe clipping an opponent's heels to put them off balance (Hooper and Whyld, 1992). We use it to describe the misbehaviours that school students sometimes use to take power from teachers and keep them off balance.

This gambit falls into a cluster of behaviours called 'annoy/disrupt'. In our example Liam is using the 'wind up', through which he disrupts the class and controls the teacher's attention. He's using a particular variant referred to as 'calling the dog'. This involves the student tricking the teacher into repeatedly coming to the student on the student's own terms. In this case the student is exploiting the teacher's interest in and care for students, and the closer the teacher gets to the student, the further the student takes him or her. This displays a classic example of escalation in which the teacher's behaviour acts as a reinforcer to the student's misbehaviour.

This example also shows the basis of all gambits: 'pursuing – distancing'. The student gets the teacher or parent to 'come to him', metaphorically, and physically, and the teacher pursues him or her and/or does all the work. So, one of the basic tenets in managing gambits is to reverse this pattern by the adult at first resisting the bait to go to the student, and second getting the student to come to the adult.

Students use gambits to keep the teacher struggling for power ('No, I won't do it') and status and influence ('You're an idiot!') so they can more easily control the teacher and keep him/her on the defensive. Sometimes students can exploit the teacher's determination to play fair whilst refusing to do so themselves. To avoid such gambits teachers need to reframe the situation. One way of doing this is to change the conflict from one between the teacher and an individual student, to one between the individual student and the class as a whole. For example: 'The class needs to finish this so they can have their game of football.' This approach is calculated to tap into the student's need for cooperation, caring and belonging.

Not all misbehaviour in the classroom can be seen in terms of a power conflict, but some of the most intractable problems can be seen in this way. Teachers will be in the best position to deal with gambits if they are aware of power issues, know how to create their own power base (see Chapter 2), and can identify gambits when they occur.

It should also be noted that it is not only students who use gambits to keep others off balance. School staff sometimes use gambits with students, as well as with each other. The principles for detecting and dealing with gambits are appropriate in all situations where gambits are used. There are four main gambit clusters each containing many variants:

- annoy/disrupt;
- victim–persecutor–rescuer;
- put-downs – 'you're inferior';
- underfunction.

Gambits are used to keep the person they are aimed at off balance and focused on short-term, instead of long-term goals. Their aim is to disempower. The four gambits fall into two groups based on how they make the recipient feel: those that make their victim feel threatened or hurt; and those that excite sympathy and the need to care for the perpetrator.

Both types, however, can eventually make the victim feel frustrated. If the victim feels threatened or hurt by the student behaviour, and the student is using a gambit, the behaviours are likely to fall into either the annoy/disrupt, the victim–persecutor–rescuer, or the put-downs – 'you're inferior' cluster. If the victim feels deep concern, a need to over-help and over-nurture the perpetrator, the gambit is likely to come from the underfunction cluster.

Some misbehaviour combines all four gambits.

# Gambits

There are a number of ways we can describe these four clusters of behaviours, for example, attention seeking, power seeking, etc. We use these four descriptors because they show the teacher's and parents' involvement in certain problems and because they can be linked to rules like 'No annoying' (annoy/disrupt), 'No put-downs' (put-downs), 'Be assertive', (victim–persecutor–rescuer) and 'Work hard' and 'Grandma's Rule' (underfunction). It is harder to make a rule about 'attention seeking' or 'power seeking'. Each of the four gambits clusters is defined below.

Gambits that make teachers feel threatened or hurt:

- Annoy/disrupt – 'I'll have some fun at your expense.' The student finds the 'grey area between rules' by persistently annoying, disrupting or using intimidation to keep the teacher and/or students off-balance and get them to react.
- Victim–persecutor–rescuer – 'My mum will get you.' The student convinces others that he is a victim because the teacher persecutes him or her. Then parents, or peers, come to the student's rescue and attack the teacher.
- Put-downs – The student laughs at people or uses insults to hurt or make them angry. People's need to be safe from social attack takes over, they become defensive, and the student can control them.

Gambits that tap the teacher's need to care:

- Underfunctions – 'I can't do it.' The less the student does for him- or herself (underfunctions), the more the teacher does for the student (overfunctions), until the student is doing very little, and the teacher is doing a lot.

Behaviours in each of these gambit clusters can take several forms, so it may not be obvious, at first, which type the student is using. Over time, however, it will become easier to recognize each gambit cluster immediately. Here are examples of some common 'syndromes' that might be associated with each gambit.

## Annoy/disrupt

### Limits testing: 'The mosquito syndrome'
Ruth pokes Danny sitting next to her. When the teacher says to her 'Stop that please', she starts tapping her pencil. When the teacher says, 'Stop tapping your pencil please', Ruth begins to giggle. She persistently tests rules and people to see where limits are and how the teacher will enforce them.

### Showing people he cannot be controlled: 'The cutting your nose off to spite your face syndrome'
The teacher tells Liam, 'If you hit anyone again, I will send you straight to the head of year'. He walks straight over and hits Noel and looks back at the teacher, as if to say, 'You can't control me'. By actively defying the teacher, Liam shows that he cannot be controlled.

## Victim–persecutor–rescuer

### Getting adults to fight with each other: 'The set-up syndrome'

The teacher tells Tony to stop messing about in class. He goes home that night and tells his parents, 'The teacher was picking on me today'. Tony's father comes to school the next day and complains to the head teacher about this 'incident' – 'That teacher picks on children in her class, singles them out for ridicule if she doesn't like them'. The teacher denies this and says, 'Tony goes home and makes up stories like this to draw his parents into fights with the school'.

In this example Tony has tapped his parents' strong drive to protect him, their innate drive to care (Olsen, 1993) and, when the teacher says Tony's claims aren't true, the teacher is working against this strong parental drive. The disruptive behaviours grow worse because the student's loyalties are split between home and school (ie 'executive sub-system') (Figure 9.1) (Minuchin, 1974).

Sometimes the student's 'ally', the person who has formed an 'us against them' coalition against the school, isn't one of the parents. It could be a grandparent, an aunt, a welfare officer, or a 21 year-old friend who has been set up by the child as his 'rescuer'. In these circumstances it may be that the student has portrayed him-/herself as a 'Victim' of the school and parents forming a working coalition that has weakened his or her power to divide and manipulate others, a power base that he/she had originally drawn from splitting the home and the school. If the student succeeds in structuring another victim–persecutor–rescuer triangle that gives him/her a sense of power against the 'executive' (home + school), the student may continue to misbehave and draw support from this new 'rescuer'.

## Put-downs

### Getting adults to defend themselves: 'Perry Mason syndrome'

When the teacher puts Ruth's initials on the board for talking in class, Ruth responds – 'You don't care about us kids, you're just trying to be boss'. She

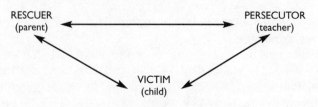

Figure 9.1 The victim–persecutor–rescuer triangle

baits and argues (annoy/disrupt + put-downs) until the teacher is drawn to defend him or herself. The teacher defensively tries to explain to the class – 'I really do care about you kids. It's not true what Ruth says…'

## Underfunction

### Getting the teacher to do everything: 'The horse and cart syndrome'
Jarvis 'can't' do his schoolwork and 'can't' think of goals or rewards. 'I can't do it. I can't think of anything good as a reward if I get it done early', he says.

So the teacher, or teaching assistant, does more and more of Jarvis's work (overfunctions), and Jarvis does less and less (underfunctions). 'Now remember Jarvis, you can't take the large number from the small number so put the small number on the bottom. Now, how about five minutes with Lego if you finish this early?' Eventually, the member of staff is doing most of Jarvis's thinking and planning for him (overfunctioning), and Jarvis is doing very little (underfunctioning). He has no interest in his schoolwork, or the goals and rewards for his work because he has no sense of ownership or investment in them.

We will now turn to some strategies for avoiding and managing gambits.

# Avoiding and managing gambits

The most effective measures are preventive and they are directed at meeting the student's needs. Below are some questions and principles that give specific help with each gambit. It must be emphasized that these techniques are only likely to work for a teacher who cares for, accepts, and is accepted by children, has a good curriculum with clear, strong goals, a behaviour management framework that prevents behaviour problems in the classroom (see Chapters 4–7 above), and has a good working relationship with parents.

It is important to be analytical. A teacher should try to be alert to the possibility that he or she is the target for a gambit. Inevitably, in the hurly-burly of the classroom situation teachers will often act on instinct or impulse rather than on the basis of a cool appraisal of the situation. It is useful to consider afterwards, however, if these non-reflective forms of behaviour are having a positive or negative effect. This may help the teacher over time to adjust their routines and patterns of classroom behaviour, so that they are less open to manipulation by student gambits.

There follows a set of questions and principles that are designed to help the educational professional address their own handling of gambits.

Five questions for teachers to ask themselves:

1. What is my power base (Chapter 2)?
2. Am I letting encouragers, goal reminders, rules and consequences do the disciplining for me?
3. How is the child getting me to come to him/her?
4. Who (caretaker, aunt, TA (teaching assistant), other teacher) can successfully manage the student and what do they do that is successful?
5. Do I have a good relationship with the student and the student's parent(s)/carer(s)?

Thirteen principles for managing and avoiding gambits:

1. Get the student to come to you – Don't repeatedly go after the student who misbehaves. You metaphorically and physically stay where you are. The child comes to you.
2. Never get defensive or 'score points' – Be neutral, unaffected, the 'Teflon teacher': nothing sticks to you. Use humour about yourself.
3. Respond to the gambit with as little disruption as possible – keep the direction of the lesson going, even speed it up and set goals. For example, 'At 12:15 those who are finished can go out for a game. The others can stay behind and finish.' It is important to follow through.
4. Have authority – Be like the Rock of Gibraltar: so solid that nothing moves you and so strong that you have plenty of strength to give to an out-of-control student. Don't show fear. Lower your tone of voice, modulate it; lower the volume of your voice; speak as though you expect students to comply.
5. Future/social concern statements – Act for the good of the group, in the long term, and model this for students. If a child disrupts the class, he is told that this hurts the long-term needs of the group (Chapter 3). For example, 'Sorry, but it's important that we finish this. I can't let you wreck the lesson for the other kids';

   'Your friends won't pass the test unless we finish this so I have to ask you to stop the noise.'

   Sometimes the teacher cannot use an immediate consequence with a student's behaviour, for example, a serious fight on the school playground. But it is always necessary to try to follow-up an incident such as this later. The other students will see 'justice done,' in the long term, if there is follow-up and visible consequences.
6. Time and a face-saving way out – Give the disruptive student time and a way out of the confrontation that won't embarrass him/her. Give the student space and choice: 'You can go outside and come back when you're ready. I'll ask you in a couple of minutes what you've decided' (about staying).

7. Use non-verbal strategies – Never over-verbalize or discuss misbehaviour at length. It is important to know when to do nothing (ie when that point is reached where enough has been said, and more talking will add nothing, even be counterproductive. Have the rules (both negatively and positively stated) and a consequences hierarchy do the work for you. Use the body language we discussed in Chapter 4. For example, 'Feet off the desk, please', and point his or her feet off the desk.

8. Deflect – change the direction of misbehaviour using reflective statements or activities (see Chapter 3). For example, 'Julie you seem tired today.' (But don't continue to nag the child); 'John, can you take a message to Ms. Jones please?'
9. Reflect the gambit – Use reflective statements about the gambit because it is harder for a student to keep a gambit going when you reveal its purpose. For example, 'It seems like you want to show everyone that you are in charge in this classroom.'
10. Paradox – don't disagree with defiant 'I don't care' statements. If he says 'You can put my name on the board, cos I don't care!', take the student at their word and respond with care and concern for the group. For example, the teacher could say: 'I'm glad you don't mind. I have to do it to be fair to the others,' or 'I'm pleased that you don't mind going to the head teacher's office because that's the consequence we all agreed to.' The teacher must always follow through.
11. If… then choices – for example: 'If this doesn't improve, you will have to stay in during break time and work. It's your choice.' or 'if this continues, your place at camp will be reconsidered.' Again, the teacher must follow through.
12. Rewarding classroom – with fun, ownership, direction, goals, and encouragement, make yourself and your classroom activities highly attractive so exclusion (eg through time out) is something students want to avoid.
13. Broken record – repeat the instruction over and over without responding to the child's excuses or argument.

       'No.'
       'But I...'
       'No.'
       'But you said...'
       'No.'
or
       'Feet off the desk please.'
       'But...'
       'Feet of the desk please.'
       'You said...'
       'Feet off the desk please.'

The story on pages 169–73, *Foot on the Table*, by Phillip Hopkins shows the complexity of interactions in a high school class between students and a teacher, how contracts can inadvertently feed the annoy/disrupt gambit, or help remediate it if used properly. The teacher also uses an alliance with another student to help remediate this gambit.

    Below are some ideas to help school staff manage or avoid each of the four gambits. Many of these techniques will be familiar to experienced educators. It is useful for teachers to identify the gambit that bothers them most and learn the ideas for that gambit. Then pick another gambit, read about it, and develop a strategy for that one.

    It must be emphasized that these are broad suggestions only, and we hope that teachers will tailor, from the ideas listed below, and from other ideas in this book, strategies to prevent or correct gambits, strategies that fit the teacher's values, and the needs of the students in his or her class.

## Gambit cluster 1 – annoy/disrupt

### General principles
The teacher should act, instead of reacting to the student's attempts to keep the teacher off balance.

### Preventive strategies
Teachers should use rules, consequences, encouragers, and goal reminders. Have the rule 'No annoying' posted with your rules and hierarchy because it is difficult for students to get around this rule.

### Corrective strategies

1. Proximity – The teacher walks close to the student and stands behind him, at his side, or stoops to make eye contact.

## The case of the foot on the table

### By Phillip Hopkins

John, a student, finds it necessary to put his feet on his table the instant the teacher begins to introduce the lesson of the day.

David, the teacher, walks in to start his maths class. He scans the room, and quickly senses that the students are in a good frame of mind, are already fairly settled, and no one appears aggravated.

Then just as he outlines the goals for the lesson and how the class will achieve those goals, John's feet go on the table. What does this communicate to David and the rest of the class? A whole lot! John is saying:

- By putting my feet on the table I am clearly indicating that I have no intention of doing the work, as my feet are on the workspace available to me.
- I am challenging expected social behaviours and authority because I know that it is a social convention that we don't put feet on tables.

David immediately has a confrontation that he needs to decide how to deal with. His options are, among many others:

1. Immediately blast John, telling him to get his feet off.
2. Give John a warning, reminding him that if he does it three times he will be on a contract.
3. Ignore it.

Remembering that every action will bring a reaction, David needs to think about the consequences of his actions. The first possible action is to 'blast' John. David has decided to use the 'big gun'. The value in this is that it sends a clear message to the rest of the class that this is an inappropriate behaviour, and that may be important. The problem with it is that John's reaction could be unpredictable. In these times of blurred notions of authority John could simply turn to David and say, NO! the stakes have risen, David has been challenged. What is his next move? By now the whole class is watching, hoping for something dramatic. The whole situation is on a downward spiral where David's next option, if he is to save any face, is to ask John to leave the class. Problem solved? No it isn't, it has just been moved.

*continued overleaf*

The second option is the use of a contract system as a way of achieving resolution to conflicts and as a way of getting students to take responsibility for their own behaviours. This seems like a good idea. Let's look at the language used by David in his second option. 'I'm warning you, if I warn you three times about this behaviour, you will be on a contract!' The key words here are 'warning' and 'contract'. The word 'warning' can be seen as a negative word, it tends to suggest that, if you do not take note, something bad will follow. The word 'contract' can have mixed messages but tends to be a positive word suggesting that parties have agreed to a positive outcome to the benefit of all.

David has really just exchanged the 'big gun' for the 'contract'. He is just challenging John to get three warnings and then move to the next step. For John this is a victory, he gets to do the inappropriate behaviour three times (in some ways David has sanctioned this), he gets to hold up the learning programme for other students longer, and probably gets talked about in the playground more, and among some students increases his status.

We can assume that John continues on his course and in turn David removes him from the class, as he did with the first option, and asks him to fill in a contract. John has to answer a number of questions on a contract similar to the following:

---

*Teacher's statement of the problem:*
John continues to put his feet on the table. He has received three warnings.
*Student's statement, what I did:*
I put my feet on the table.
*What rule I broke or infringed:*
Don't put your feet on the table.
*What should I do to fix the problem:*
Don't put my feet on the table.

---

We need to ask what this has achieved, and whether it represents a contract. There has been no discussion between David and John about the problem, it simply states the obvious, and neither David nor John probably believe that this 'contract' will result in any behaviour change, after all, the 'contract' has not even begun to look at the cause of the behaviour.

Unfortunately this is often how a 'contract' is used. It is a failed attempt to be authoritarian when other forms of authority are not operating for teachers who would be more comfortable if they were to have absolute authority. When John breaks this 'contract', David is able to legitimately pass the problem onto the senior teacher, because 'the contract' between student and teacher has failed. David has again got rid of the problem, but for how long?

In the third option David chooses to ignore the behaviour. This is a move full of risk. The danger is that the message to the rest of the class is that David does not care if you have your feet on the tables, and it could then be generalized that David does not care if you break all sorts of social conventions, it could be generalized that David is 'slack'. It could lead to chaos!

David is not about to open himself up to that sort of risk. He recognizes that John's behaviour is happening for a reason and also recognizes that John is doing it at a strategically pivotal time in the lesson, at the very start. David wants to keep the momentum of the lesson going, and as he moves around the room checking that all students are getting on task, he quietly says to John, 'I'd appreciate it if the feet could come down', and moves on. He says it just loud enough to make sure that some students are aware that he has noted the problem and is on to it.

As the lesson progresses, David notices out of the corner of his eye that John still has his feet on the table; he chooses to 'strategically' ignore it. During the ensuing few minutes David notices that Sally, sitting next to John and a very able Maths student, is starting to laugh at John, jabbing a ruler into his side.

'Everything all right Sally?' asks David. 'Oh it's just John and his feet, they're annoying me'; the class snickers. David's experience tells him that Sally may be a player in this game. For some reason she wants John to get in trouble. The reality is that Sally will learn easily whether John's feet are on the table or not (even though there is the chance that they might smell a bit). 'Yes it is a bit of a problem, John and I are going to have a chat later about it, move if you want', says David.

David has just been very strategic. In that one sentence he has put some important messages across to Sally, John, and the rest of the class:

- To Sally – David has given legitimacy to Sally's concern, even though it may not be warranted, and has also told her that she is not going to control the problem, and that she is able to remove herself from the problem, unless that is, she wants to be a player in the problem.
- To John – David has reminded John that he is accountable for the problem and that in his own time David will respond to and solve the problem. John has been reminded of all this without receiving status or losing face. David has also shown to John that he recognizes that Sally may be part of the problem. This could well be the key to a resolution.

*continued overleaf*

- To the class – David is reassuring them that he is dealing with the problem without any grandstanding by any players and with minimal disruption to their learning programme.

The class continues. David is at the part of the lesson where students work in groups on a problem solving project. He incorporates this into his lessons for a whole range of reasons. He knows how important it is in Maths to give students the opportunity to work together to solve problems. Today he waits till everyone is working and then quietly asks John to come and have a chat.

---

'What's going on John?' asks David. David, without saying anything to John about contracts, has started the contract negotiation period.

'Nothin', I'm just bored, I hate Maths,' says John.

'Well let's do something about it. What is it you are bored with, is there stuff you don't understand?'

David has given legitimacy to John's concern, he also senses that the word, 'bored', is used to cover all sorts of things, and he has given a gentle challenge to John by asking if there is something in the curriculum that he does not understand.

'I don't understand stuff because Sally is always talking at me and getting me to do stuff', says John.

'What sort of stuff, like putting your feet on the table?' In this sentence David has removed the behaviour from John. The behaviour is now the result of things that are happening in the classroom. If John accepts this, it is probable that there will be a solution.

'Well, yes, it shuts her up, and in other classes I get sent out so at least she can't get to me then'.

---

David can now move to a resolution. He says to John, 'I think you need a break from Sally, John, and a chance to learn without the hassles you have been putting up with. What do you think?'

The solution to this issue was in this case a simple one that could not have been achieved if David had not allowed the situation to unfold. David did not ignore the problem, in a systematic way he worked to achieving a satisfactory resolution that demonstrated that the successful learning of all his students was at the heart of his practice. It could well be argued that a written contract between David and John was not necessary, that both knew what was going to happen and why.

David explained that he felt that they had reached a resolution and that a contract would be a good way of documenting what they had achieved, and for also having a reference point to work from, should the problem arise again. David organized for John to see him at the end of the lesson. They went down to the canteen together, got their lunch and returned to the classroom to write up the contract, and eat lunch. The writing only took 10 minutes, so John still got 45 minutes of his lunch break to go and play touch footy, which he really enjoyed.

What did the contract look like?

---

*The choices that I made were* – I put my feet on the desk during class time.

*The changes I need to make to my behaviour are* – I shouldn't put my feet on the desk because it is pretty hard for me to learn with them there.

*What I have negotiated with my teacher to help me make the changes* – we've decided that I shouldn't sit near Sally, and that I have to make sure that I ask for help when I need it, even at the end of the lesson, as long as it is not for more that ten minutes, and that I make sure that the stuff we learn relates to something that I am interested in.

*Teacher's comment* – I am confident that the problem is solved. John knows that his behaviour was the result of things that were happening in the classroom. I also know that I have to work to make sure that John understands what we are doing and that he is able to apply what is covered in class to things that interest him.

---

2. Reflective statement – The teacher uses a reflective statement to acknowledge what the student is doing and, then, set standards. For example, 'It looks like you want some attention from me but we need to be getting on with this work'; 'Seems like you want your friends to stop and look at you. Wait until after this is done';
3. Name or initials on the board.
4. If there is a tick after the student's name, the student is required to write out the rules in his seat.
5. Choice – Give the student a choice and be neutral (ie showing neither approval nor disapproval) about which choice he makes. Without the teacher's approval or disapproval the choice remains owned by the student (ie the

student is not doing it to please or annoy the teacher, because the teacher cannot be affected in this way by these behaviours). Choice is most important for the 'cutting the nose off to spite the face' syndrome. For example, 'As we discussed, you can work quietly or miss out on break time. It's your choice.'

6. Send the student from the room. The teacher must follow through, and not argue or plead if the child is upset. For example, 'I can't deal with you when you are upset. You need time to calm down. I'm sure we can sort this out after class.'

7. Speak to the student afterwards to resolve any problems and maintain teacher/student cooperation, and structure a contract showing what the teacher agrees to do, and what the student agrees to do.

## Gambit cluster 2 – victim–persecutor–rescuer

### General principles
The teacher always works for the good of the group, tries to make an alliance with the rescuer (open up good communication with parents), and prevents the formation of two opposing camps, that is, avoids feeding the victim or rescuer with ammunition.

### Preventive strategies
Teachers can use rules, consequences, encouragers and goal reminders.

1. Surveys – Teachers can use surveys and meetings to get all parents' views on rules and consequences for children who misbehave in their school (see Chapter 5). They can use the completed surveys when there's a confrontation with parents, for example, 'This is what the other parents, including you, decided to do about children who hit other children in the playground.'

2. Teachers should avoid put-downs – Teachers should aim to be completely professional, and to never lose their temper. Let's be honest – for some of us, this is very difficult. Sometimes it helps when teachers remember that when they do lose their temper, they give the students ammunition to use against the teacher and the school. It is essential to form class rules that apply fairly to everyone, and to stick to them.

3. Parent/teacher responsibilities – It is important that responsibilities for teachers, parents, etc are clearly delineated in the School Discipline Policy (see Chapter 5). This could be as straightforward as having a sheet that states: 'The head teacher will…', another that states, 'The teacher will…', and another that states 'The parents will…'. List the responsibilities of all people in the system and, include among the parents' responsibilities, the need to 'communicate their concerns to the school without conveying to their child that home is against the school'.

## Corrective strategies

A possible sequence could include:

1. Reflective statement – 'Seems like you are trying to get me into an argument with your parents.'
2. Egalitarianism – Tell the student that he or she can't be treated differently to other students (most children and parents don't want double standards). For example, 'It has to be the same rules for everybody'.
3. Phone call – If a student is misbehaving, swearing for example, phone the parents to first get their support, then say to them, 'I would be grateful for your help. Can you please tell Liam over the phone that you won't have him swearing at teachers.' Then ask Liam to come into the room and hand the phone to him while you wait there for him to speak to his parents.
4. Meet parents alone to establish common ground, (as it is counterproductive to have parents fighting with teachers in front of the child), then bring the child into the meeting, and, if necessary, confront him/her about his/her accusations.
5. Explain to parents that the school can't have separate (lower) standards for their child. It has to be clear, however, that this is different to saying that the school will not cater for individual differences. The crucial point here is that staff and parents must be prepared to work together to give the student 'access' to the patterns of behaviour to which the staff, students and parents have collectively agreed. Take on board, where possible, the suggestions that parents make for helping their child maintain school standards.
6. Speak to the student afterwards to resolve any problems and maintain teacher/student cooperation, and structure a contract showing what the teacher agrees to do, what the parents agree to do, and what the student agrees to do.

## Gambit cluster 3 – put-downs

### General principles

Never get defensive or try to 'score points' back.

### Preventive strategies

Use rules, consequences, encouragers and goal reminders. Have a classroom rule about 'No put-downs of others or the efforts of others'.

### Corrective strategies

A possible sequence could include:

1. Ignore them.

2. Make a joke about yourself.
3. Reflective statement: For example, 'It looks as though you are trying to hurt my feelings.'
4. If they break the 'No put-downs' rule, invoke the consequences.
5. Speak to the student afterwards to resolve any problems and maintain teacher/student cooperation, and structure a contract showing what the teacher agrees to do and what the student agrees to do.

## Gambit cluster 4 – underfunction

### General principles
Get the students to do progressively more and more work and take progressively more responsibility for their work and good behaviour independently, without others reminding them to do the work or doing the work for them. Be positive and encouraging, about their work and good behaviour, so that they make positive associations about both.

### Preventive strategies
Use rules, consequences, encouragers and goal reminders.

1. Coach students; structure goals for students; discourage excuses if they don't complete their goals, and redirect students to continue to pursue their goals.
2. Structure visual goals to teach independent work. Write a student's daily work into stages of the rocket, or whatever appeals to him/her (Chapter 8). The student colours each stage as it is completed. Help students at first with this but eventually let them take over monitoring the completion of goals.
3. Insist – If a student refuses to try, it is important to insist once or twice that they do the task just to give them a sense of completion and success. However, repetition of such insistence will keep the Underfunctioning–Overfunctioning cycle going. Also, be open to the possibility that the apparent refusal to try may be masking a fear of failure or belief that the task is beyond the student's competence. In such cases the student's refusal should be reframed as a call for help. The help should be given in the form of a modification to the task that the student can complete without help.
4. Shaping – Catch even the slightest indication of taking responsibility and shape it by reinforcing it with appropriate praise, acknowledgement and rewards.
5. Praise – Thank them for any effort – For example, 'That's an excellent piece of work. I'm glad you finished everything today.'
6. 'Grandma's Rule' – For example, 'At quarter past two, if you have finished your work you can play a game with a friend.' By setting a clear time limit in this way, the teacher will enable all students to complete the main task and get access to the reward.

### Corrective strategies

1. Reflective statement – 'Seems like the more I do, the less you do. What can we do about that?'
2. Directions and limits 'Finish this by midday or you have to stay in.' Again, the time scale has to be realistic.
3. Contact parents.
4. Speak to the student afterwards to resolve any problems and maintain teacher/student cooperation, and structure a contract showing what the teacher agrees to do, what the student agrees to do, and, if appropriate, what the parents agree to do.

# Conclusions

These strategies and micro-behaviours tend not to work in isolation, they form a small part of a larger behaviour management programme. But this chapter can help teachers recognize, avoid, and manage gambits. With practice, we suggest, many little problems can be managed before they escalate into big problems.

A key to managing student behaviour is to first guide the child's ascendancy towards mastery and competence within a supportive group that includes the adults in his or her life.

# 10

# Working with parents: systems theory

## Introduction

We noted in Chapter 1 multisystemic therapy (MST) shows some of the best outcomes results with troubled youths. Swenson *et al* (1998) note that MST owes much of its theoretical foundation to the work of Bronfenbrenner (1979). Individuals are viewed as nested within interconnected systems, for example, the individual, family, school and community. Problem behaviours are maintained by transactions within one or more of these systems, or between any combination of them. For example, a father might fight the school when the school attempts to stop his child from hitting (defending himself from teasing) because the father is feuding with families in the neighbourhood, and these neighbourhood children are teasing his son in the playground. This provides a difficult barrier to overcome. On the other hand, individuals from various systems in which the child is embedded bring certain strengths to the process of change. An older sibling, as in the case study on school refusal (Chapter 12), or grandparent can help while parents are overcoming certain barriers. Perhaps the schools can use the parents' strong need to protect their child from teasing as a systemic strength.

Henggeler and his colleagues base much of their hands-on work, their interventions, on problem-focused approaches that have some empirical support in the research – strategic family therapy (Haley, 1987), structural family therapy (Minuchin, 1974), behavioural parent training (Munger, 1993) and cognitive behavioural therapies (Kendall and Braswell, 1993). Used alone, many of these approaches are not powerful enough to overcome the more serious cases we find in schools. The problem is that many teachers, and many parents, particularly those with older children, will not readily come into parent-training programmes or follow expert advice. When parents are called in to meet the head teacher about their child's behaviour, they often feel blamed for the child's problems. They feel defensive. Systems theory can help us understand the dynamics in these home/school relationships, and help us align the family with the school so they can jointly assist the child. This chapter aims to help us understand some of the work of Minuchin (1974) and Haley (1987), and why combining these approaches with behavioural and cognitive approaches can help the school achieve long-term change with troubled students. Much of this chapter is about alliances between home and school and about helping parents reach the point where they agree to work cooperatively with the school. Haley (1987) discriminates between a coalition and an alliance. A coalition between people acts jointly against a third person; an alliance between people might share an interest that is not shared by a third person.

Most would agree that a child should not be caught in a war between two or more systems, for example, caregivers in the school versus caregivers in the home. The adults in a child's world need to form alliances with each other so the adults convey to children their agreement about goals and expectations. Most importantly, we need, with difficult classroom problems, to enlist the help of powerful family members or other members of the child's community, to use strengths in various systems because we may not have the power, within the school system alone, to manage certain problems. The problems can often be managed if the adults in the system use each other's points of view, the strengths in individuals, and in systems, to establish common goals.

A major contribution that systems theory has made to our thinking is to shift the focus of problem-solving away from the individual to interactions between systems, that is, between family members, the school and home, members of the school, or the community.

Families and schools are rule-governed systems and Minuchin (1974) focused his attention on the way in which a particular family was organized or structured. Functional families, he said, consisted of a parental alliance in an executive subsystem with children as a separate subgroup in a sibling subsystem. The executive subsystem allowed parents to assume the parenting role, that is, take authority and responsibility for certain aspects of their children's lives. In dysfunctional families the executive subsystem is split when certain children and adults form a coalition against the other parent, or another caregiver. These are known as coalitions across generations. Dysfunctional families can become functional if the interactions between adults and children are restructured so adults remain in an executive subsystem separated by a boundary from the sibling subsystem (Figure 10.1).

Structural family therapists also describe disengaged family members who are separated by 'too rigid boundaries' from other family members, that is,

EXECUTIVE SUBSYSTEM

mother and father


---------------------- boundary


SIBLING SUBSYSTEM

daughter

Figure 10.1 Mother and father in an executive subsystem with the daughter in a sibling subsystem


they are distanced from other family members, and they do not communicate with them or contribute freely. Enmeshed family members, in contrast, are separated by diffuse boundaries that are too easily breached so individuals or family subgroups lack autonomy. For example a father and his 10-year-old daughter may be extremely close and share secrets that they keep from the child's mother. As a coalition, they overrule the mother's decisions and she becomes progressively distanced from family interactions. The enmeshed father–daughter may sometimes operate as a parent–child but at other times as two children, arguing with each other with no clear rules and no sense of who is the parent and who is the child (Figure 10.2).

However, Haley (1987) pointed out that an organization is not malfunctioning because of fixed cross-generational coalitions, for example, a child and his parents against the school. The organization is malfunctioning because such coalitions are repeated, again and again in a repeated sequence. A mother repeatedly must save her child from the unfairness of the school, and maybe from her husband, and the school must repeatedly convince parents that they, not the school are the cause of the problem. Haley, and his wife Cloe Madanes (Madanes, 1981), built on Minuchin's notions. They contend that case managers need to devise a 'strategy' (their approach is termed Strategic Therapy) for solving the family's or school's problems. They clearly set goals, they plan in stages how to achieve these goals, and the problem is defined so it includes at least two or three people, or in cases involving schools, at least two or three


father + daughter
-------------------------- boundary
mother

Figure 10.2 Enmeshed father–daughter and disengaged mother

systems. This means the problem is anchored in the interactions between people, not in one person's head or in one person's faulty perceptions, as cognitive therapists believe, or driven solely by a lack of skills, reinforcers, or punishers, as behaviourists believe. The problem, be it conduct disorder, eating disorder, depression, or whatever, is seen as serving a purpose in the family structure. The family or school may organize itself around repeated unhelpful sequences. In trying to fix the problem, the thrust of an intervention is to shift the family, or school, or home/school interactions, so that the presenting problem no longer serves a function, and unhelpful sequences no longer repeat.

This does not mean that children in functional families, families with clear rules and clear boundaries between the executive and sibling subsystems, are left out of the family's decision-making process. The important point about functional families is that children's developmental stages, and opinions, are carefully considered, but the final responsibility for a major decision lies with the parental executive until children are old enough to take on that responsibility. In addition, clear feedback loops maintain the system in a flexible mode that allows individuation but also allows security and growth for each family member. As children grow older, parents take in information about the changing needs of their children, including the child's increased need for peer contact and independence. Parents, then, can respond with changed rules, and changed family structure, and children can make more decisions on their own. The system, that is, the structure influencing interactions between family members, can change as the children and parents grow.

# The school and the home

There have been many behavioural techniques published for managing children in classrooms, and many are effective, but these techniques can be undermined or rendered ineffective by parents who form coalitions with their children against a school, the head teacher or the child's teacher. The family unites to 'white-ant' the school's efforts in repeated, unhelpful sequences. For example, a child may complain to his father that the teacher doesn't really like him: 'She tries to make me look stupid in front of the other kids.' This complaint to his father may structure the interactions between the child, teacher and parent so as to create conflict between the home and school, and therefore result in a split executive. The structure is in the form of a victim–protector–persecutor triangle (also called the victim–persecutor–rescuer); the sequence often is that the child tells his or her parents that s/he is a 'victim' who is then saved by father or mother, the 'protector', from the teacher, who is the 'persecutor' (Figure 10.3). The parent rushes to the school to confront the teacher and protect their child, fixing the child in a repeated cross-generational coalition

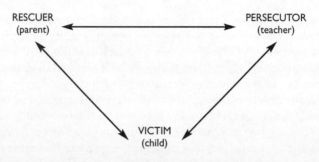

Figure 10.3 The victim–persecutor–rescuer triangle

sequence with his parent against the school. The executive subsystem (parents and teacher) has been split, so the child can be expected to continue misbehaving until the executive subsystem (home and school) reunites. As the gap between home and school widens, communication becomes increasingly negative, and the child may feel a divided loyalty, trapped between the two warring camps. But the child also has a sense of power and a reason to keep this power by keeping the two camps at war. Because the child is tapping, in his or her parents, an essentially biological drive (to protect one's offspring), the emotions and motivation of the parents can run very high. Clear-sighted reason on the teacher's or head teacher's part and the use of rational argument to try to convince parents that their perceptions are wrong, can be counter-productive in these situations. It is exactly the wrong thing to do; it will reinforce the sequence, and the unhelpful pattern will be repeated.

Systems theorists try to combine parents and school personnel into a unified executive who set, in consultation with the child, clear boundaries (rules and consequences) for all members of the system (Figure 10.4).

This does not mean that when parents and the school unite in an executive subsystem, they are united in a coalition against the child. The child helps to formulate a solution to the problem through joint discussion with these adults. But the major responsibility for the decision and outcome of these discussions lies with parents and teachers, assisted by the case manager, until the child matures to the point where he or she can take more responsibility for these decisions. It is the job of the case manager, or team, to formulate these interventions and keep the participants moving towards each set goal. This can sometimes mean watching for opportunities, and recognizing 'problems' or crises, as opportunities to help the family and school restructure. For example, the child is still attacking other children in the playground, behaviour that is strenuously defended by his or her parents. Then, other parents come to the school and threaten to remove their children unless the head teacher deals with this 'problem child', a crisis that many schools would try to water down. But, to a case

EXECUTIVE SUBSYSTEM

parents and teachers

---------------------- boundary

SIBLING SUBSYSTEM

child

Figure 10.4 Parents and teachers in an executive subsystem with the child in a sibling subsystem

manager, this may look like an opportunity to speak to the parents of the alleged offender about a slightly different matter than the concerns broached in past stormy meetings. The problem now is that other parents (who remain unnamed) are complaining about their child, that is, the case manager does not protect parents from the truth. The result, if handled properly, can be that the parents of the alleged offender, who had previously refused to cooperate, may vent their anger against these unnamed parents. The school and home have a common goal, the concern of the school and these parents for the welfare of the target child, a *strength* in the home–school system. Their common goal is to keep the target child in the school and stop the complaints of other parents.

# Referral systems

How we define a problem determines what we do about it. How the school perceives the problem of a troubled child will determine what the staff will do about it. Let us look again at the student who is hitting other students in the playground. In a 'linear' referral system, a student's problem may be referred from the class teacher to the senior teacher, to the assistant head teacher, to the head teacher, to the behaviour support teacher, and perhaps to an outside agency for psychological assessment. Each person or agency will get, from each referring stakeholder, some description of the problem as the case moves up the referral line, each person referring the student on to someone else. Parents may receive a telephone call somewhere along the referral path where school personnel alert them or ask to see them about their child's behaviour (Figure 10.5).

However, this sort of referral process can have at least two unfortunate outcomes, and both result in a split executive, leaving some stakeholders battling with each other. One outcome is that each stakeholder who refers the problem to a second or third stakeholder expects that second or third stakeholder to solve it. The classroom teacher may expect the senior staff or support teacher to solve it; the deputy head may expect parents to solve it. The parents may expect the school to show competence in managing children, particularly in situations where the parents believe other children tease their child who 'justifiably' retaliates with violence. A second outcome is that *blame* will enter this system much as a virus enters a body, or a computer.

## The blame cycle

With blame running rampant through the system, the relationships within the school (head teacher versus behaviour support teacher versus teacher) and between home and school (teacher versus parents) become poisoned, and communication and constructive interaction in the system are destroyed – the executive is split. A strange form of logic operates here – the 'tyranny of either/or'. Parents believe 'the teacher is wrong so the school must be to

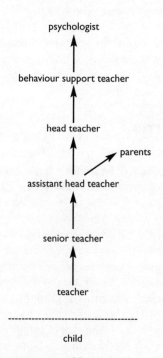

Figure 10.5 Linear referral system – prone to blaming

---

## The blame cycle

*Teacher* – 'the behaviour support teacher just talks to the kid. What good does that do?'

*Head teacher* – 'if the classroom teacher had interesting lessons there'd be no discipline problems; good teachers don't seek outside help for behaviour management problems in their own classrooms.'

*Teacher* – 'if the head teacher would back us up when we send a kid to him, instead of just patting the kid on the head, we wouldn't have these problems.'

*Psychologist* – 'I give these teachers all these ideas but they never bother to use them.'

*Senior teacher* – 'the problem with psychologists is that they have no idea what it's like in the real classroom.'

*Parent* – 'I just wish the school could learn to handle these problems on their own without phoning us. Why don't they just use the cane? It never did me any harm!'

---

blame'. The teacher believes 'the parents are wrong so the home must be to blame'. For some reason, the parents and the teacher need to make certain they identify who is the victim and who is the villain. For them, attributing blame is necessary to their construction of the problem. Blame is a way to gain short-term moral high ground. It might not occur to these stakeholders that both sides could be wrong, or that both sides could be right, or that it doesn't help to blame, or that they are repeating unhelpful sequences of behaviour.

Violent children in a school often trigger infighting between the adults in the system, about who is to blame and what is to be done about the problem. Boundaries and limits blur while the child's misbehaviour increases. More blame enters the system and the cycle escalates, the sequences are repeated, increasingly entrenched by the escalating blame. In our experience, the highly disruptive or aggressive child triggers infighting amongst the adults in his life because he or she directly threatens their values, their feelings of power and their status. He or she makes them feel impotent and foolish. The child disrupts the system, the system becomes destabilized, boundaries are blurred and the child becomes more disruptive; unhelpful sequences repeat.

## Breaking the cycle of blame

How can we break this cycle? We need to unite the stakeholders into a working executive with common goals. The case manager at the school, that is, a teacher, behaviour support teacher, assistant head teacher or other person trusted by the family, can best coordinate suggestions from various advisers and stakeholders. This person should have some training in counselling, working with parents, and a thorough understanding of cognitive, behavioural and systems theories, preferably those with the best track records, like the work of Scott Henggeler and his colleagues (Swenson *et al*, 1998). The case manager need not expect any one person to fix the problem. Seldom in our casework is a difficult problem helped by a referral to any one individual, inside or outside of the school. In most cases, parents and other stakeholders can be enlisted as co-managers of the case who share responsibility for solutions and outcomes. But the responsibility for coordination rests with the case manager or team.

The first priority is to remove blame from those relationships inside the home and school, and between the home and school, and to find common goals for the important stakeholders. All stakeholders, including the child, need to contribute as equals to solve the problem and not expect someone else to fix it. Teachers, behaviour support teachers, head teachers, and parents can influence the problem by offering their different views about how to solve it (Figure 10.6). Because parents dislike being told what to do with their children, it is more productive to enlist them as coworkers and equals than to bring them in, tell them how much of a problem their child is, and then tell them what the school thinks they should do about it. Do not argue with parents about their child. Almost always, this harms the collaborative process.

One important principle in working collaboratively with parents is to use, as much as possible, the family's beliefs, ideas and language. A first step is to listen carefully to the family's explanation of the problem and search for common language (hurt feelings, lowered standards, fairness, etc) and goals (learning, stopping fights, avoiding double standards, etc) between the major stakeholders.

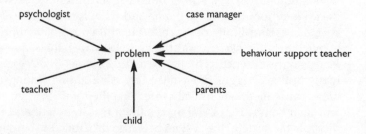

Figure 10.6 Problem management that reduces blame entering a system

Head teachers, teachers and parents are usually reluctant to abandon their own beliefs and values about a child's problem. The teacher wants to believe the student is disruptive because he can't read and he comes from a bad home. The parents want to believe the student is not as disruptive as some other kids in the school, and other victimizing students cause his problem. Consequently, home versus school coalitions form and are maintained.

Head teachers, teachers and parents have invested heavily in these beliefs and they will strenuously protect their investment. To admit they are wrong about the cause of a problem can make parents or teachers feel inadequate, and worse, it can make them feel that their beliefs and values are threatened. However, professionals in the collaborative process, including teachers and head teachers, have to put aside their personal feelings. Parents might not see the same 'logic' that teachers, head teachers or case managers see, but arguing can make parents dig in their heels and vigorously defend their logic. It is important for the case manager to explore carefully the father's, mother's, teacher's and child's explanations of the problem, and the explanations of the other major stakeholders:

---

Dad – 'They should be stricter on him.'

Mother – 'He is a very sensitive boy whose feelings are easily hurt.'

Teacher – 'We need more support from the parents.'

Child – 'Kids pick on me and the teacher doesn't like me.'

Head teacher – 'Teachers need more stimulating lessons.'

You – 'What a mess.'

---

After an initial stage of exploring, at face value, various explanations of the problem and reporting these back to the group, it is important to introduce 'reframing'. One way to find a common goal for everyone concerned is to 'externalize the problem'. Michael White, an Adelaide family therapist, 'externalizes the problem' by putting it outside the conflict and giving the problem an entity and life of its own, so participants can use a number of techniques to jointly overcome it. For example, the problem might be that the 'explosive tempers' in the family cause the family so much trouble. So the family must unite to fight the explosive tempers before they cause further harm to the family.

White (1986) also uses 'relative influence', that is, he asks 'what percentage of the time the temper is in control of the family and what percentage of the time the family is in control of the temper'. 'Relative influence' gives us a measurable way to look at progress and change.

There are other ways to reframe problems as common goals. For example, instead of saying to a child, 'If you do this one more time you will be kicked out of school' you could say, 'Ruth is on step five of the seven steps of the school's discipline hierarchy. We cannot treat her differently to the other students and she will have to leave the school if she attacks children two more times. How can we beat this problem?'

Reframing removes blame and provides a common scale for all participants to examine the conflict, that is, it uses the same facts we already have about the problem, but gives participants a totally different view of it so they are less restrained by previous values and beliefs. The problem, not the people in the system, is the focus of group problem-solving. The Norwegian family therapist, Tom Andersen (1990), believes a family or person tries to maintain the integrity of their beliefs at almost any cost. If explanations and reframes of a problem are too unusual in relation to what the person already believes, they will reject these explanations as too different or threatening to their beliefs. For example, if the parents believe the problem is caused by the teacher, and the school tells the parents that the problem is caused at home, the parents will likely reject the school's explanation (reframe) of the problem. Andersen said that if explanations are not unusual enough, for example, parents believe the problem is caused by the teacher, and they are told that the child's problem is due to a personality conflict with the teacher, then the parents' view of the problem will not change. They still believe the problem is at school.

Participants, according to Andersen, need explanations (reframes) that are appropriately unusual, that is, not too different and not too close, to their original beliefs. Perhaps, if it was explained carefully to the parents and teachers that the *difference in opinions* between home and school confused the child, made him or her feel insecure, and this difference of opinions maintained the problem (a blame-free explanation), the participants would begin to explore strategies for solving this joint problem (Figure 10.7). The problem is defined (reframed) as: 'The difference in opinions between the adults in Johnny's life maintains Johnny's aggressive behaviours.'

Action based on the reframe would involve creating similar rules and consequences at home and at school. The problem is that some schools interpret reframing as convincing the parents to do what the school wants. This seldom works. Instead, the home and the school can be asked to borrow some rules, consequences, and ideas from each other so part of the plan comes from home, and part comes from school, as in the following case study.

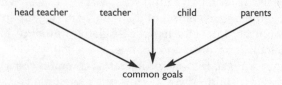

Figure 10.7 Stakeholders need to find common goals

# 11

# Working with parents: a case study

The following case study uses the values and perceptions of the child, parents and teachers as the raw material for finding common goals, breaking unhelpful sequences and constructing a successful outcome to a problem. In the initial stages of the counselling process, we gather as much information as possible, we never argue with parents, even if they argue with us, but we ask ourselves: 'Will I look for obstacles in the opportunities that arise, or for opportunities in the obstacles that arise?'

When we worked with these schools, parents and children (Olsen, 1989a), we didn't know about the work of Henggeler and his associates, but we now understand that the principles of multisystemic therapy (MST) (see overleaf) better explain this sort of work than do the principles we adopted at the time. The reader will be able to see many of these principles at work in the case study below.

## Case study: Greg – as described by the case manager

### General background

Greg was a 10-year-old boy in Year four, in a government school where I was behaviour support teacher. His father, John, was born in Poland and his mother, Mary, was born in Australia. He had a nine-year-old brother, Chris, in Year three. Greg's behaviour during his time at school had been described by his teachers as aggressive, stubborn and non-compliant. Early in the year his misbehaviour escalated and he became particularly violent in the playground. Teachers' reports included the following comments:

I observed (Greg) attempting to punch and choke another child. I separated them and made the other child leave the area. About three minutes later (Greg) picked up a bat and began to flail it widely about at almost everybody... I called for help and attempted to wrest the bat from (Greg). I required assistance to hold (Greg) and remove the bat. During the struggle a Year five boy was hit quite hard on the hand.

The next day another teacher reported a fight where: '(Greg) had (John) around the neck and was saying he was going to kill him. (Greg) had to be physically restrained... When I let (Greg) go he ran into the trees at the top of the playground'. The teachers reported almost daily incidences of Greg fighting, 'losing control over temper', refusing to leave the playground when asked and swearing at teachers.

As the head teacher was preparing to suspend Greg, I was asked to interview Greg and then his family.

## First interview – Greg

I discussed the above incidents with Greg who explained that the violent outbursts came from his 'bad temper' but the outbursts didn't occur at home because, Chris, his younger brother knew not to tease him. At school 'kids tease me and it gets on top of me and I can't control myself and I get in trouble'.

I asked Greg for an example of a time when the problem didn't occur so we could test his assertion that he was out of control. Greg said 'Yesterday I didn't let it beat me, I stood there and teased back and I didn't hit them. I can do it when I want to, I have to think hard'.

Because Greg was interested in sport, we set up a simple game based on 'externalizing the problem' (White, 1986). In this case, the problem was his temper. It was 'us against the temper'. We were in a coalition against the temper, using Greg's sporting strengths; he could score a point on a card when he felt really angry but behaved responsibly instead of hitting or throwing a tantrum. If he did hit someone or threw a tantrum, the temper got a point.

After a week I discussed Greg's progress with his classroom teacher who said there had been some improvement but still one major blow-up. Another major incident occurred the day after I spoke to the teacher. Greg swung a cricket bat at a boy and narrowly missed his head and Greg had to be restrained by a teacher.

### Comment

In this first interview the case manager had attempted to form a relationship with Greg by listening and gaining Greg's trust, exploring his beliefs about the problem and looking for contradictions between his explanation of the problem and what actually happened. It is crucial at this stage for the case manager to be 'confused' or 'curious' about these contradictions and not blame the child or the family. The discussion with Greg, 'externalizing the problem' and the game with the temper did not seem powerful enough on its own to stop his aggressive behaviour. This first intervention was essentially cognitive, not systemic and Minuchin (1992) tells us that talk alone is seldom successful at helping children with such problems; action with the family is necessary. The temper, it seemed, was 'winning' and it was time to contact John and Mary, Greg's parents.

## Second interview – Greg, his teacher and parents

I met with Greg, his teacher and his parents, John and Mary at the school, a week after my first interview with Greg, to discuss the incident with the cricket bat and the two other fights that had occurred. His parents expressed considerable anger at having been 'summonsed' to the school and they asked if other parents of fighting boys had also been called to the school. They shouted angrily at the teacher and me while Greg sat next to them and looked at the floor. We explained that Greg had endangered other children and again both parents expressed anger that the school did not successfully manage those children that 'ganged up on him' and caused these problems.

Mary, Greg's mother, said that she had Greg checked out by a paediatrician and there were no medical problems. She believed that other children knew about his bad temper and used this knowledge to 'set him up'. She explained that Greg had always experienced problems mixing with children and he had a 'complex' – he often thought people hated him. His father, John, had instructed him to walk away when teased but to fight when children tried to fight him. John's Polish extraction, he believed, had led to his own persecution as a child, so he understood how his son felt. Both parents agreed that Greg's incidences of violence were becoming more frequent and that some action had to be taken.

John and Mary accused Greg's teacher of taking the other child's side during the recent fight and said that Greg had come home very upset about this unfairness. I decided to question Greg about this story in front of his teacher and his parents and I expressed some confusion as to why his teacher claimed this incident never occurred. Greg conceded that, in fact, the incident had never occurred and he had told the story to get his parents to help him with the kids who kept teasing him at school, that is, according to systems theory, to form a coalition with his parents against the school. Greg's parents said nothing about this admission, but Mary later told me that they were shocked and couldn't understand why Greg would make up such a story.

We decided as a group that Greg should stay off the cricket pitch and the playground for one week. If Greg felt upset or was aggressive, Mary would come to get him. The teacher would telephone Mary after 2 o'clock each afternoon (a systemic intervention) to report on Greg's behaviour (uniting the executive in an alliance that Greg could see). In addition, we decided to take him off sweets and chocolate for two weeks and make certain he had a sandwich at morning recess in case swings in blood sugar were influencing his behaviour. To further unite the executive, we organized a daily home note (see Chapter 7) between the teacher and the parents. John and Mary asked that both good and bad behaviours be included on the note.

## Comment

It may have been a mistake to include Greg in the first part of this interview because he heard the accusations made by his parents against his teacher and would have seen how badly split the executive was. However, it probably helped to confront Greg, with the teacher and parents present, about his untrue stories.

At least two major problems would require additional reframing. Greg and his parents still believed that other children caused him to lose his temper and Greg probably saw in this interview that the executive was split and that he could successfully keep the adults fighting with each other. When he misbehaved at school, his parents would continue to see this as an expression of Greg's unhappiness. If the executive remained split, his behaviour could worsen. But the strong bond between Greg and his mother was a strength that the case manager could utilize to help remedy the situation.

## Between second and third interviews

The incidents of aggression continued after this interview. In one day, Greg stabbed a pencil into a boy who slipped in front of him in line, he pushed some girls on the playground, he punched another boy in the stomach and he refused to do some written work in class. Greg told me that he felt sad and angry that day, but didn't know why. He agreed that he didn't like people 'getting the better of him' and he was very worried about what people thought.

I phoned Mary who said that Greg's grandparents, John's parents, were both ill with heart trouble and that Greg, who was close to his grandparents, worried about this. Greg had two bad tantrums at home and Mary let him go away and cool off. Mary believed that pressure from school was causing these problems at home, but she also revealed that John often hit Greg and his brother so she usually didn't tell John when the boys were in major trouble. She said she felt very sorry for Greg and she could understand how frightened he was of his father.

In the same week Greg threw a serious tantrum at school and was sent to the open area in front of the head teacher's office where he continued to slam his head against a table and scream for about one hour. This unnerved the staff and I was called to the school to help. I did not restrain Greg, but, instead, spoke to him briefly during a break in one of his bouts of screaming and sat and waited for his tantrum to subside.

As a result of these later episodes, two sets of parents came to the school and told the head teacher they would remove their children if the head teacher didn't force Greg out of the school.

## Comment

The cognitive approach, Greg winning points against his temper, combined with a meeting with Greg's parents and other systemic interventions, the weekly telephone call and the daily home note, seemed to have failed. Haley (1979) pointed out that transition points in a family's life, like adolescents leaving home or the death of grandparents, could result in destabilization and, sometimes, an escalation in the sort of violent behaviour they saw in Greg. In addition, the parents were still blaming the school for Greg's problems, there was a split executive at home and the influence of another system, Greg's ailing grandparents. It seemed that Mary saw the two boys, especially Greg, as victims, John as the persecutor and herself as the rescuer of the two victimized boys. Greg could have been trying to maintain the split between home and school and between his mother and father. Through dividing and conquering, he could maintain his control over adults in the home and the school. Or perhaps Greg's problems still served too important a function in the family structure and this purpose was yet to be revealed.

These systemic explanations could explain why Greg maintained his aggressive behaviour at school. But behavioural theorists can add to this understanding. Subjects who are accustomed to reinforcement for a behaviour, when suddenly this 'payoff' is stopped, can increase this behaviour for a while before it finally disappears (Sulzer-Azaroff and Mayer, 1977). This is called an 'extinction curve'. Greg may have received attention from his parents for his troubles at school, but then he may have sensed this attention disappearing, that his parents were 'siding with the school', so tried harder to regain his position and this rewarding 'payoff'. About this time a violence policy was introduced at the school (see p. 195).

## School violence policy

### Comment
This policy may appear harsh but it was assumed that all children who breached this code through violent behaviour, and their parents, would receive counselling help. The policy dealt with both sides of the violence cycle. That is, other students tease Greg and, because Greg reacts so well by swinging a cricket bat at their heads, he becomes a target. The other students taunt and tease Greg every day. It's fun! In this policy, students were taught what to do if they were teased. Everyone in the school practised the five steps to use if they were teased and everyone understood and owned the policy. So the policy showed clearly: 1) what would happen if students persisted with violence and 2) what they could do as an alternative to violent reactions if they were teased.

Consequently, no excuses were allowed for violence and there should have been less complaining to teachers on the playground –'Ms Attwood, Ms Attwood, Johnny's calling me names'. Moreover, the violent child could not so easily say 'I hit him because he was teasing me', because that child should have followed the five steps. A child's parents would find it harder to support claims such as, 'We've always taught Johnny to stick up for himself so it's the school's fault for not stopping this teasing'.

The procedure was aimed at stopping teasing and retaliation through violence. It allowed teachers to know what to expect and it meant that decisions could be made ahead of time, rather than under pressure and that children and their parents could be counselled about adhering to this policy. Another advantage of this approach was that the hierarchy of consequences acted as a deterrent – not as a punishment. However, if a student moved quickly to Step 3 or Step 4, then it was clear that the behavioural hierarchy by itself was not helping that child and that other action was called for.

# School violence policy

Physical violence and dangerous threatening behaviour are not tolerated at this primary school.

There are a series of consequences which follow the occurrence of physical violence or threatening behaviour, the final stage of which is permanent exclusion from the school.

Physical violence includes acts against people (kicking, punching, biting, throwing stones, etc) and property (breaking windows, throwing furniture, etc).

Dangerous and threatening behaviour against people and property involves the use of a weapon (pencil, ruler, stick, cricket bat, scissors, etc).

The series of consequences is as follows:

Step 1. Warning. Your name and the offence are written into the 'Red Book'.

Step 2. You are removed from your class, the playground and the rest of the children in the school for the rest of the day. You will sit outside the head teacher's office. Your parents are contacted and informed of your behaviour and may be asked to come to the school and discuss your behaviour with the head teacher.

Step 3. Your parents are contacted and asked to come and take you home for the rest of the day.

Step 4. You are suspended. You may not come back to school for three days. You must stay at home.

Step 5. You are suspended. You may not come back to school for five days. You must stay at home.

Step 6. You must leave the school for good. You will have to find another school.

*What to do if you are being teased*

Being teased is not an excuse for using violent or threatening behaviour.

In order to complain about teasing you must give evidence to show that you have worked through the following steps:

- ignore the teasing;
- keep away from the person;
- make a joke about it;
- ask them not to do it;

then

- tell the teacher.

## Third interview – Mary, John and, later, Greg

I met with Greg's parents alone. They said that Greg had stayed off chocolate and sweets as agreed and they had decided to stop him from using his computer until his behaviour improved. Both parents still believed that the problems were caused by the school and that Chris, his younger brother, was also being teased at school, but that Chris could put up with more provocation than Greg. John and Mary were also concerned that teachers might be discussing Greg in the staffroom and that he was gaining a bad name in the school (they were right about this). I told them I would ensure, through the head teacher, that this would not happen. This concern for Greg's reputation was another strength in the system that we could engage to help remedy Greg's problems. Moreover, if we could stop the staffroom gossip, this could strengthen the alliance between the head teacher and the parents.

Greg apparently had been somewhat better at home, but his parents described this as him being 'subdued, scared, quiet'. Mary wanted to ease up on Greg. She felt sorry for him again and thought he was very sad. My thinking was that if she did this Greg would further split the executive. But her own parents had urged her and her husband to continue to expect 'higher standards' from Greg. I then asked Mary and John why they were using a lower set of standards with Greg and had lower, but obviously more modern and progressive standards, than Mary's parents had with her. I also asked John why he tolerated behaviour from Greg that his parents would never have tolerated from him. At first Mary went to her parents' defence and argued that their standards weren't old fashioned at all. She then suggested that both her and her husband could, perhaps, expect the same standards from Greg as their parents had expected from them, although she felt that hitting children, as John and Mary's parents had done, was wrong. I agreed with her ideas about standards and said that, whether hitting was right or wrong, teachers and head teachers could not hit children at school. Other techniques would have to be used. If we wanted to make certain that the boys weren't confused, then we should try to have discipline at home resemble, as closely as possible, the discipline at school. Time-out was used at school, so perhaps, instead of hitting, John and Mary could use time-out at home.

The desire for high standards seemed to be another common strength, a goal in the school–home system. I then explained how the school was raising standards and how, by using the Violence Policy, the staff was going to come down much harder on any acts of violence in the school or playground. Because Greg's behaviour did not meet these standards, trouble could be expected from those other parents whose children did meet the higher standards about violence. Already, I said, two sets of parents had come to the school and told the Head teacher that they would remove their children unless Greg was excluded from school.

Both John and Mary became angry at hearing this news and, after discussing this new problem and blaming these parents, they asked me if I could help. I agreed to do everything possible to keep Greg in the school and, in essence, protect Greg as best I could by talking to the head teacher and maintaining the policy about no discussion of Greg's problems in the staffroom. John and Mary agreed that these new standards about violence and about staffroom gossip, were probably a good thing and that they would urge Greg to aspire to the standards against violence. In the meantime, Mary would visit a local private school, with Greg, to see if she could enrol him there as a safety measure, in case things at this school didn't work out.

At this point Greg was brought in and told by his parents and me, as an alliance, about the new standards at home and at school. We also told Greg about the other students' parents (without naming them) who had complained about him to the school and how his mother would organize enrolment for Greg in another school if he could not meet the new standards on violence. We would help him meet the new standards by expecting more of him, but would not treat him differently to other children.

I described Greg, in front of his parents, as a particularly astute boy who was a bit 'fragile' and not 'big enough' yet to look down on those who teased him. Other students seemed to be stronger in this regard. Unfortunately, he was a 'brilliant divider' who had successfully split mother against father and home against school; he was good at dividing and conquering (an 'appropriately unusual' reframe around intelligence that they hopefully would accept, but would hopefully want to change). This 'smartness' was a strength that could be used to beat the problem of being forced to leave our school (an externalized problem that we could battle together) not only because the school, parents and Greg wanted Greg to stay (common goal) but because the school and family agreed on new standards about violence.

I also suggested that John and Mary confer with the boys about major decisions that affected them, but that they, the parents should make the final decisions in private, as we had done today. They could tell the boys afterwards what they as a couple had decided. John, Mary and Greg agreed to this new process.

To finish the interview I reminded Greg in front of his parents that he wanted a separate set of rules to those used by other students in the school, but, as the school was trying to raise standards, we could not do this. We would not accept lowered standards. I also reminded Greg of his earlier goal to beat the temper (externalized problem) and stop the temper from beating all of us by forcing him out of our school.

## Comment
By including the violence policy the case manager has influenced a third system in addition to the parental and school systems, that of Greg's peers. The case manager attempted in this interview to unite the school, parents and Greg around common strengths and goals so his parents would not continue to undermine each other or the school.

Those parents who wanted Greg excluded from school may have helped to diminish the previous split executive between home and school. This may not have happened so easily if the head teacher and case manager had acted as a buffer between John and Mary and these other parents. That is, telling John and Mary about the complaining parents instead of buffering them from this information could have helped us move forward.

They reframed the problem as Greg being a brilliant divider and conqueror, a partly positive description and 'appropriately unusual' according to Andersen (1990). That Greg was in danger of losing his place in the school undoubtedly gave the case manager and head teacher some leverage. Without this crisis, the parents may have been less likely to work cooperatively with the school.

## After the third interview

Teachers and parents reported no aggressive incidents after the third interview. Greg twice refused to do classwork but changed his mind after his teacher reminded him that this refusal would be reported on his home note.

Greg's parents started to work with a clinical psychologist and they told her that the two most important things that helped Greg change his behaviour in school were that they (the parents) now agreed and worked together on parenting decisions and that the head teacher and I had tried to 'protect' the family from those parents and teachers who wanted Greg out of the school. We were 'on their side'. This perception seemed critical to the changes they made.

When I spoke to Greg near the end of the school year, he praised his own success in cognitive and behavioural terms –'beating the temper' and 'not letting the temper get the better of him'.

## Conclusion

It was clear that just talking to Greg, 'externalizing the problem' and using cognitive strategies did not reduce his aggressive outbursts. It did help, though, to combine strategies, 'externalize the problem' so we could later fight it, use strengths in the systems to break unhelpful sequences and restructure elements so that Greg's problem no longer served a function in the home, perhaps that of distracting his mother and father from strong differences of opinion, or difficulties in their marriage. We created common goals and united John and Mary as parents. Combining these cognitive and systemic strategies with behavioural strategies, like the clear set of rules and consequences about violence, adopted for the common good of all children in the school, resulted in long-term success in this case.

# 12

# School refusal

Most of us in our teaching careers meet 'school refusers', students who prefer to stay at home rather than go to school, but often we don't realize that the problem is anchored in the home, or in the relationship between the home and the school, at least as much as in the school alone. Here we discriminate between 'school refusers', who remain home and/or with their parents, that is, parents know where they are and 'truants', who may be with friends and/or roaming the city or countryside, that is, parents may not know where their children are.

Below, we outline a systemic theory to explain school refusal and we use two case studies to show how systems theory can help us understand and remediate cases of school refusal.

## A theory of school refusal

'School refusers' can show a 'fear' of classmates, teachers, or something in the school. This fear may be genuine, but often school refusal is related to family–school dynamics – things are not as they seem. Hawkes (1982: 129) described family structures that often characterize 'school refusing' children:

1. an over-protective relationship between the school refusing child and one parent (usually, but not always, the mother), which incorporates ambivalent swings between closeness and anger (though typically maintaining an overt closeness);
2. a similar ambivalent relationship between the over-involved parent and his/her own mother or father;
3. a disengaged (passive) position for the other parent (usually the father).

According to Hawkes, the rules and underlying beliefs in these families can include:

1. an overt stress on the importance of family closeness;
2. an underlying belief in the danger of abandonment and separation and consequently;
3. a restraint on showing anger within the family (which might lead to abandonment); and
4. it is the child's task to attempt to solve the family dilemma thrown up by these
   rules/beliefs (closeness versus differentiation) by acting as a companion to his/her
   parents.

Children can refuse to go to school for many reasons, including bullying or
unfair treatment from teachers and these causes need to be explored. But if the
school refusal is related to the family dynamics described above and the
teacher, behaviour support teacher and head teacher take the child's claims of
bullying or unfair treatment by the teachers at face value by intervening only
at the school level, other stronger forces may undermine the school's effort.
The child's school refusal may get worse.

With the above theoretical considerations in mind, we present two case
studies below that are rewritten from Olsen (1989b and 1990).

# Case study: Tony

Tony was in Year four and the youngest of five children in an Italian-speaking
family. A low achiever in school, he nonetheless was well liked and presented
with no school behaviour problems. However, midway through Year four,
Tony started to miss a number of days from school and when the head teacher
checked with his mother, she learned that Tony claimed the work was too difficult and children were making fun of him. The head teacher decided to take
Tony 'under her wing', give him special privileges, organize easier work for
him and, by doing so, make school a more attractive place. For the first part of
the week Tony seemed to enjoy this special treatment, but then he started to
run away from school before midday and would even run away from the head
teacher. She described him to the school behaviour support teacher as 'very
disturbed with a crazy look in his eyes and in need of psychiatric help.'

The behaviour support teacher met with Tony and his mother in the head
teacher's office to try and form a working relationship with both Tony and his
mother and clarify the family's perception of the problem; convey this perception to the school; find some common goals to draw together Tony's parents and
the school; and unite all stakeholders to work towards a common goal.

After chatting pleasantly for half an hour, Tony and his mother had explained
their concerns about teasing and the difficulty of schoolwork for Tony and Tony

had promised not to run away from school again. The behaviour support teacher greeted this promise with some scepticism. Had Tony become so strong so quickly that he could beat his fears of schoolwork and teasing from children? Tony assured the behaviour support teacher that he had beaten these fears, but the behaviour support teacher offered him the use of his office telephone so Tony could speak to his mother from school any time he felt frightened. His mother later reported that Tony said he had liked the idea of using the telephone.

However, Tony refused to come to school on the following morning. As happened after the head teacher's intervention, Tony seemed more frightened of school after the behaviour support teacher's meeting than before the behaviour support teacher had offered to help. Tony's mother agreed, reluctantly, to bring him to school but she was visibly upset at having to escort a crying little boy to the very place he most feared. By midday Tony had bolted from the school in such apparent terror that he left behind his much-loved school bag.

Tony was so upset about the school bag that for most of the day he cried and pleaded with his mother to go to school and retrieve it. It wasn't clear why he was so worried about the bag, as he had nothing of obvious value in it. Besides, the head teacher wanted Tony, not his mother, to come to school for the bag. Tony grew steadily more upset, almost as if part of him had been left behind at school, a part that needed to be safely home. So the behaviour support teacher asked him and his mother to come to the school together and retrieve the bag, a great relief to them both of them.

The behaviour support teacher asked his mother if he could visit their home on the following day. She agreed but explained that Tony's father was unlikely to attend. He worked long hours as a builder, left home early and arrived home late. This led to Tony and his mother spending a lot of time in each other's company because all the other children had either left home or were working.

When the behaviour support teacher arrived at Tony's home, his father was present, as well as Tony's 17-year-old brother. The behaviour support teacher was able to establish that the family believed, still, that the difficult work and teasing at school were the basis of Tony's problem. They said that the school did not cater for Tony's needs. However, the behaviour support teacher knew that the school still considered Tony 'a psychiatric case in need of psychiatric help'. So, perceptions in the home and the school were very different – there was very little common ground and no common goals.

During the home visit Tony's parents said very little to each other and Tony was completely silent. The older brother confirmed that he'd had similar troubles at school and he could understand Tony's anguish. Schools, according to the older brother, were often insensitive to the needs of slow learners. The family appeared to have formed a coalition against the school. Within the family, the mother seemed to be distanced from Tony's father and enmeshed with Tony, similar to Hawkes' (1982) characteristic family pattern. But the family members were so non-verbal that the behaviour support teacher felt that traditional discussion-based counselling would not help join the parents and the school towards a resolution of the school refusal.

The behaviour support teacher agreed with the family about schoolwork and promised to convey these concerns to the school. The school and the home could jointly tackle the problem and start moving forward by using a Home–School Work Report (Figure 12.1) that would be transported between home and school by Tony in his coveted school bag. Each day the teacher was to sign the book and note Tony's progress. Then Tony's parents would, together, discuss the report with Tony and mother and father could each sign it. Clear communication and common goals, would hopefully develop between the home, school and between Tony's parents, with Tony and his bag acting as courier.

Tony's older brother consented to help his parents discuss the report and escort Tony to school every morning. Blagg (1987) noted the importance of a reliable escort for school refusers. Tony was keen on the idea of the home–school work report being transported via his bag and keen to see his brother act as escort. Tony was told he could use the school telephone to ring his mother anytime (he never did) and that the behaviour support teacher would check on his progress daily.

## HOME–SCHOOL WORK REPORT

**Date:** _____

|  | Yes | No |
| --- | --- | --- |
| Finished school work: | ___ | ___ |
| Worked hard: | ___ | ___ |
| Did not run away: | ___ | ___ |
| Did as the teacher asked: | ___ | ___ |

Comments: _____

_____

_____

Teacher's signature: _____

Mother's signature: _____

Father's signature: _____

Figure 12.1 Home–school work report

Tony took very seriously his task of transporting the work report in his bag and brought the note home every day. The school refusing ceased and there was only one 'hiccup' when his father was angered by a remark made on the report by the teacher. The behaviour support teacher intercepted the father at the front office and was able to cool him down so he didn't enter the classroom and vent his anger against the teacher. The situation was reframed for the teacher as 'very delicate', because the home was blaming the school for Tony's school refusal, so we had to bend over backwards to avoid giving the parents ammunition to use against the school. The teacher understood this and was very careful after this incident.

After being escorted for two weeks, Tony began walking to school on his own. The home–school work report continued to the end of the year and Tony missed no school during that time.

As noted by Hawkes (1982), Tony's school refusal could have been solving a family dilemma thrown up by issues of closeness versus differentiation. Tony may have been acting as a companion to his mother after the other children left home or went to work and Tony's father had disengaged and was seldom at home. It is difficult to pinpoint reasons for success, or to understand why Tony was so determined to retrieve his school bag, or know exactly what precipitated and maintained his school refusal. It seemed 'better to join them than to fight them' and the home–school work report helped us structure cooperative goals and achieve this.

## Case study: John

John was an 11-year-old who was repeating Year five. His teacher said he had learning problems throughout school but was popular with his peers, good at sport, and appeared not to be overly concerned about his learning difficulties though he took pains to hide them. John had shown no major problems at home or at school.

One day, quite out of the blue, John started showing a reluctance to attend school. Because his parents thought he was ill, he was allowed to stay home but, after some weeks, the teacher and parents realized he was school refusing and made efforts to force him to attend. At school he refused to enter the classroom and, when pressured, he dug his heels in. He threw one particularly noisy, violent tantrum after his mother and teachers pressured him to stay at school and not return home with his mother. John appeared completely irrational to staff members and no amount of coaxing, threatening or talking from parents or staff members succeeded in keeping him in the classroom. The head teacher described a 'crazy look in his eyes' as if he had 'gone mad' so the case had similarities to the case of Tony above.

John had become dirty, unkempt and smelly and started bed-wetting. His mother said he had lost confidence in sport and stopped all team involvement. Also he suddenly refused to ride in the car with his father to the family business and, instead, rode with his mother in her car. When he arrived home from school he insisted on travelling to the family business with his mother and did not want to stay home.

The school behaviour support teacher could not interview John because he (the behaviour support teacher) had just broken his ankle in a rock-climbing accident. By telephone the behaviour support teacher asked the staff to examine two areas that seemed to be related to John's school refusal; 1) his learning difficulties; and 2) his close relationship with his mother. John had been teased by his classmates and, just before the school refusing started, he was at the beach with some relatives' children who had also teased him about his lack of school achievement; John asked to come home. Several interventions were organized to stop his classmates from teasing him and to renew John's confidence in the classroom. None helped. The teasing stopped but he continued to avoid school and the classroom.

The close relationship between John and his mother was discouraged. She forced him to go to school and would not allow him to remain home with her. He was treated with great care at school and allowed to work in the head teacher's office, instead of in the classroom which appeared to terrify him. In spite of his mother's apparent resolve to break John's over-dependence on her, he still became upset when she left him at school and he refused to enter the classroom.

Because things were so bad for John at school, the behaviour support teacher, though convalescing, agreed to interview John. He hobbled in on crutches, explained his broken ankle to John and used this to lead into a discussion of fears. If this case followed the classic forms outlined by Hawkes (1982) and Haley (1987), John's behaviour could have been triggered by some major fear related to home. The behaviour support teacher asked him to talk about the most terrifying thing that had happened to him in the months before he started school refusing. John said his mother was coming to pick him up one day after school and he was left waiting for over an hour. He later learned that she had had a car accident on the way to pick him up. Soon after that he was riding with her and they narrowly escaped smashing into another car. This frightened both of them. John's mother confirmed these events when the behaviour support teacher spoke to her and she pointed out that John had been billeted on a football trip with a family who had just lost their father. He had accidentally fallen from the roof. John was distressed about that incident and about the car accident. There was a further incident: John had been at a car rally, watching his uncle drive, when a small girl was struck and killed.

During this interview, the behaviour support teacher decided to reverse the previous policy of encouraging John to be more independent of his mother. He organized with the school and with John's mother, to allow John to telephone his mother any time from school. When he felt worried or frightened, she would be as accessible as possible to him every day. This could either 'prescribe the symptom' if the problem was related to the parental/child relationship (Madanes, 1981: 127), or it could give John an avenue to control his anxiety if he feared for his parents' safety. For example, Eysenck and Eysenck (1981) reported that 'Dental patients given a button to press when discomfort becomes unbearable prove far more tolerant of pain than patients not given a button to press (perhaps) because the feeling of being in control prevents arousal from peaking'.

John never asked to telephone his mother. She and the teacher reported that the school refusal problem totally disappeared on the afternoon the behaviour support teacher spoke to him about the car accidents and had organized the telephone intervention. John's mother and teacher were convinced that the dramatic change was a result of the discussion and telephone intervention. John had, just as suddenly, stopped bed-wetting, taken up football with renewed confidence, resumed riding in the car with his father and renewed his friendships at school.

At the time of writing, three years after the behaviour support teacher's discussion with him, John has showed no recurrence of the school refusal or other behaviours.

# Conclusion

Results with 'systemic' interventions on 'systemic problems', like school refusal, are often counter-intuitive. They don't seem to follow the normal rules that we use to guide us in our work with behaviour problems in schools, so the interventions used in these two case studies, at first glance, don't seem to make a lot of sense. But 'systemic interventions' do follow a certain logic and they are highly effective once teachers and other school staff understand their rather strange ways.

# 13

# Evaluating progress

In this brief chapter we give consideration to the issue of evaluation. We not only consider this to be a vital component of any behaviour management plan, but of any educational intervention. The process of education, whether it is concerned with academic knowledge or social behaviour, sets out to foster change. If the desired change has taken place, then the intervention has been successful; if there is no change, or an undesired change has taken place, then the intervention has not succeeded. And as we have noted so many times in the course of this book, there is no value in pursuing interventions that do not work. On the contrary, a failed intervention, if repeated, will often exacerbate the problems it is designed to counter.

In this chapter we look specifically at the ways in which behavioural change can be measured. We will look at the ways in which an individual student's behaviour can be assessed, as well as ways in which the behaviour of groups (classes and whole schools) can be assessed. We will be concerned with ways in which change, as well as people's beliefs about or perceptions of change, can be recorded statistically. In keeping with the systemic theme of the book, we will also be concerned to suggest ways of involving a wide range of stakeholders in the evaluation process. In this way we will suggest that a good evaluation strategy can make a very practical and positive contribution to the change process, since it provides, among other things, a means of sharing the goals of intervention with stakeholders, a means of valuing their views and thus helps to foster a sense of shared ownership in the intervention and its outcomes.

The strategies described in this chapter were developed in consultation with teachers, UK-based Local Education Authority (LEA) advisers and educational psychologists working in Essex and Cumbria LEAs.

The following need to be specified before beginning the process of evaluation:

- What kinds of outcomes are intended to be achieved by the intervention being evaluated?

- Where the aim is behavioural change, the specific change or changes should be specified in clearly observable behavioural terms, such as: a reduction in the frequency of physical violence between students; and an increase in prosocial behaviour. In all cases terms, such as 'prosocial behaviour' and 'violence', need to be clearly defined in behavioural terms.
- Where the aim is to change less tangible factors, such as attitudes, again there is a need for clarity of definition. The question needs to be answered: what is the evidence for attitudinal problems at the moment? Can this evidence be described in observable terms, or is to do with the perceptions of certain people (eg staff)? If so, how are these going to be recorded?

- How will we know when the desired change has taken place? What will be different in terms of measurable, physical evidence (eg specific behaviours, amount of graffiti on school property)?
- What is going to be done to promote this change? What strategies are being implemented to foster change?
- What is going to be done to maintain the change when it has happened? What medium-term and long-term strategies are in place for monitoring and, where necessary, intervening in the situation?

Figure 13.1 provides a summary pro forma for recording basic information about the target, nature and outcomes of an intervention.

# Evaluation tools

## Goodman Strengths and Difficulties Questionnaire

The Goodman Strengths and Difficulties Questionnaires (teacher, student and parent versions) (Goodman, 1997) are reproduced in Appendix 1, see page 229.

This is a norm referenced behaviour rating scale, developed by Professor Robert Goodman of the Maudsley Hospital in London. It has 25 items each of which is rated as 'applies'; 'applies somewhat', or 'does not apply'. The 25 items break down into five subscales (emotional problems; peer difficulties; hyperactivity; conduct problems and pro-social behaviour. In addition the scale has an 'impact supplement' (Goodman, 1999) which requests information about the perceived seriousness of the child's behaviour in terms of the level 'burden' that is placed on the child, school and family by the child's difficulties. The scale is designed for use with children and young persons between the ages of 4 and 16 and has a teacher version, a parent version and a student version (for 11- to 16-year-olds only). It is easy to complete (taking

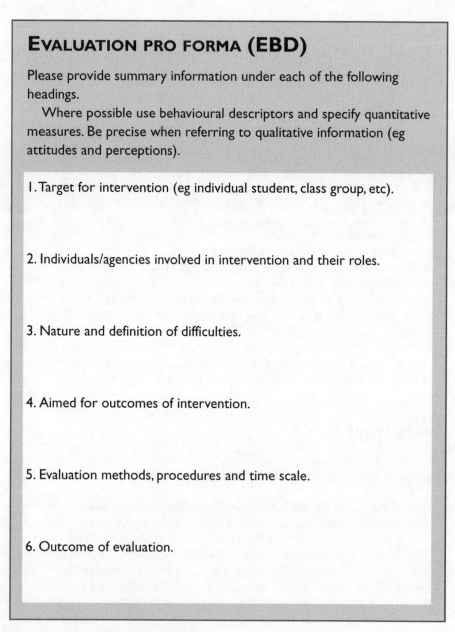

**EVALUATION PRO FORMA (EBD)**

Please provide summary information under each of the following headings.

Where possible use behavioural descriptors and specify quantitative measures. Be precise when referring to qualitative information (eg attitudes and perceptions).

1. Target for intervention (eg individual student, class group, etc).

2. Individuals/agencies involved in intervention and their roles.

3. Nature and definition of difficulties.

4. Aimed for outcomes of intervention.

5. Evaluation methods, procedures and time scale.

6. Outcome of evaluation.

Figure 13.1 Evaluation pro forma (EBD)

approximately three to five minutes per child). It is designed primarily as a screening tool for large groups of children, but can also be used as diagnostic tool for individual students (Hill and Cameron, 1999).

This tool provides a snapshot of the nature and range of behaviour problems as well as perceptions of their severity. The 'pro-social' scale is particularly useful in that it enables the recording of positive behaviour.

## TOAD schedule

The TOAD schedule (Goldstein, 1995) is reproduced in Appendix 2 see page 241. This is a simple observation schedule that can be used in classrooms to assess the relative frequency of specific behaviour problems. The original schedule is concerned with:

- T = Talking out of turn;
- O = Out of seat;
- A = (not paying) Attention;
- D = Disrupting others.

Users could adapt the format, however, to include other behaviours.

The schedule is used on a time-sampling basis, using the following procedure:

1. The observer selects up to three students (the target student + a second student randomly selected + a third student perceived to have no problems).
2. The observer records the frequency of TOAD behaviours performed by all three students over the specified time (eg the teacher or LSA observes each of the three students once, for example, every three minutes) and generates a frequency score for each of the TOAD items.
3. The observer compares the performances of the three students and records this in graphical form.

There are two main purposes to this. First, it provides comparative, quantitative data on the target student's behaviour as related to other students and, therefore, creates an opportunity to test the perception that the target student has 'problems'. Secondly, it enables quantitative comparison over time, so that improvement or decline can be recorded. The comparative element provides some indication of the effect of the situation (ie if all three students' behaviour deteriorates this is likely to be because of situational rather than individual factors).

The TOAD schedule can also be used in conjunction with an intervention record, whereby the observer records the timing of specific interventions and plots this against the TOAD score for individual students. If the TOAD score repeatedly declines during periods of intervention it may be hypothesized that the intervention is working.

## Interviews (with child; parents; other teachers)

The aim of the interview is to gauge perceptions of progress and beliefs about factors influencing progress. This should include accessing attributions and self-efficacy. That is do the students, teachers and parents believe that they have any control over or influence on behaviour? If so, what is the nature of that influence? If not, who or what is influential?

## Structured observation

Where specific behaviours are identified as problematic an observational schedule should be designed (see TOAD above) to assess frequency of these behaviours performed by the target student and other students (eg one perceived to have problems; one perceived not to have problems).

## Reflective diary

The maintenance of a diary, by the teacher, LSA, parent or student, can be used to record personal reflections about the nature of the target child's progress and the influences on it. It is valuable for subjective, emotive accounts to be included in such diaries. It may also be appropriate to guarantee confidentiality of the diary itself, given that its main purpose is to encourage the diarist to reflect on situations and their own involvement in them. Diarists should be encouraged to talk with confidants about the content of the diary, though they should not be required to hand the diary over to a third party, though they may be requested to provide generalized summary points, such as an account of whether or not there appears to have been any improvement in the student's behaviour, or whether they have developed any new insights about how to proceed with the intervention programme.

## Measures of educational progress

Educational progress can be measured against mainstream norms, national curriculum attainment targets and Standard Assessment Tasks (SATs) scores.

## Sociogram

All students in class are asked to nominate one student with whom they like to play/socialize and/or work, allowing a social 'map' of the class group to be generated.

# An evaluation strategy

## Assumptions

For the construction of an effective strategy, the following assumptions must be made:

- Effective intervention should target the integration and inclusion of the student into a mainstream classroom.
- Evaluation strategies must be manageable by and relevant to mainstream classroom teachers.
- Evaluation must be based on different data sources to enable triangulation (ie the use of different data sources, such as observation, interview and self-report diaries, to measure and describe a particular phenomenon, for example the incidence and nature of behavioural problems).
- Evaluation must be comparative.
- Evaluation must be quantitative as well as qualitative.

## Method

Identify at least 20 students defined as being disruptive, who have been targeted for intervention, and compare the progress of each target student with a second and third student (identified by mainstream class teacher in consultation with specialist teacher if appropriate).

- Student 1: target student undergoing intervention;
- Student 2: student with similar problems to 1 undergoing different intervention or no intervention;
- Student 3: student exhibiting no problems.

## Measurements

### Pre-intervention (baseline) measures

- parent, child and mainstream teacher fill out SDQs;
- TOAD observation carried out for all three students;
- attainment data (based on National Curriculum Attainment Targets);
- mainstream class sociogram.

### Post-intervention measures
After one term:

- parent, child and mainstream teacher fill out SDQs;
- TOAD observation carried out for all three students;
- attainment data (based on National Curriculum Attainment Targets);
- mainstream class sociogram.

After two terms:

- parent, child and mainstream teacher fill out SDQs;
- TOAD observation carried out for all three students;
- attainment data (based on National Curriculum Attainment Targets);
- mainstream class sociogram.

After three terms:

- parent, child and mainstream teacher fill out SDQs;
- TOAD observation carried out for all three students;
- attainment data (based on National Curriculum Attainment Targets);
- mainstream class sociogram.

Annual follow up:

- parent, child and mainstream teacher fill out SDQs;
- TOAD observation carried out for all three students;
- attainment data (based on National Curriculum Attainment Targets);
- mainstream class sociogram.

# Using the data

The numerical data generated by some of these instruments (eg the Goodman questionnaire) lends themselves to some highly sophisticated forms of statistical analysis. Having said this, most schools will find the raw data useful in itself. The Goodman data, for example can be presented in graphical form, as a single global score, or as an individual score for each sub-item. The TOAD schedule, similarly, generates numerical data that can be presented in graphical form. These two measures alone will enable staff to monitor individual student's behavioural progress over time and in relation to the wider student group.

A particular advantage of the range of evaluation tools suggested here is that they provide data not only about progress but also about possible targets for intervention. In this way the evaluation process is made formative, because it feeds directly back into the intervention plan. So, if in the course of interviews with parents it is discovered that a particular problem has arisen in the family (eg the bereavement of a close relative), steps can be taken at school to protect the student from situations where this may make the student vulnerable. The qualitative data, in this situation, is of value not only because it generates information, but because the process of gathering the data involves the school taking an active interest in the views and concerns of students and their families. In this way evaluation can contribute to the need for schools to show acceptance to their students and their families.

# Conclusion

Evaluation strategies such as these provide a systematic and transparent means of assessing progress of various kinds. They provide the basis for changing and improving teachers' practice and they can provide a visual representation of an individual student's or groups of students' progress. In this way positive evaluation results can in themselves become a kind of reward and a source of encouragement. In the same way an effective evaluation will enable us to know for sure: that the relevant subsystems are supporting appropriate behaviour; that the staff and students have access, in the form of knowledge and ownership, to positive behaviour; that behavioural limits are being observed; that there is a climate of acceptance; and appropriate direction is being given to students. These are ideas at the very heart of this book.

# 14

# Systems approaches in action: cross-sector educational liaison programmes

In this chapter (based on an extract from P. Cooper (2001) *What Works in Alternatives to Mainstream Educational Provision for Children with Social, Emotional and Behavioural Difficulties*, London: Barnardos) consideration is given to a number of UK programmes which deal with cross-sector and cross-agency liaison. The intention is to illustrate some of the ways in which knowledge and expertise from different sources can be combined to meet the needs of students with serious social, emotional and behavioural problems.

## Special schools and mainstream schools

Lund (1995) describes a rare example of a liaison programme between day special schools for students with special educational needs, including social, emotional and behavioural difficulties, and mainstream comprehensive schools and a further education college in the late 1980s. He focuses particularly on the links forged between one of the special schools and various departments in the mainstream schools. Interestingly, he describes these links as 'informal', being motivated by the 'like mindedness' of the special school head (Lund himself) and the various department heads. He describes the motivation for creating the links in the following terms:

- for the special school:
  - access to the latest developments in the teaching of particular subjects;
  - an opportunity to develop and maintain professional links with other

    like-minded specialists;
- – a chance to develop courses that suited pupils with EBD;
- for the mainstream departments:
  - – a fresh insight into securing curriculum relevance for students with EBD;
  - – help from specialist teachers in developing appropriate methods for pupils with EBD.

Lund also indicates that the developing relationship between the various institutions became 'mutually supportive' in relation to issues such as pastoral care, PSHE and behaviour management policies. Lund argues that by focusing the support on specific subject teachers, rather than students, the emphasis was placed on improving the accessibility of the curriculum rather than on behaviour management per se. Thus assessment was focused on the specific difficulties the teacher was encountering in attempting to engage particular students with their subject. Key themes in the adaptation of pedagogy were:

- planning learning experiences to give students experience of success;
- making a variety of teaching materials available to promote student attention;
- the use of a wide range of teaching approaches to reinforce and demonstrate learning;
- an emphasis on practical 'hands on' learning activities;
- an emphasis on 'child centred' approaches which engage the student as a person with regard to his or her own interests and preferences.

# Involving further education (FE) colleges

Lovey, Docking and Evans (1993) and, more recently, Cooper *et al* (2000) provide accounts of programmes for 14 to 19-year-old students excluded and at risk of exclusion from mainstream schools which involve liaison between the student's host institution (special schools, special units and mainstream schools) and FE colleges. The value of such programmes has received government endorsement (Dearing, 1996). Lovey, Docking and Evans, in their wide-ranging survey of 65 English LEAs, focus mainly on students who attended tailor-made vocational courses in FE colleges (including work-experience placements), whilst following basic skills programmes in off-site units. Cooper *et al* (2000) provide a single case study of students from a mainstream comprehensive school following a regular GCSE re-sit course in an FE college. Both studies present impressive findings, with the majority of students completing their courses successfully.

A very interesting aspect of the study by Lovey, Docking and Evans is the information they provide on the activities carried out in the special units to complement and support the FE programmes. These activities included 'club-type sessions', in which students engaged in social and leisure activities in the units. The activities echoed the purposes of 'activities' sessions in residential special schools, the effect of which is to facilitate interaction between staff and students in less formal and pressurized circumstances than often prevail in formal classrooms. These sessions were also sometimes used as rewards for positive engagement with the FE and work-experience programmes. Other unit activities included basic education classes in numeracy and literacy, personal and social education (PSE) classes and one-to-one counselling sessions. Cooper *et al* (2000) provide insight into a post-National Curriculum version of FE involvement. In accounting for the success of these initiatives Cooper *et al* point to important differences in the social ambience of the FE college as compared to the mainstream setting, with students describing their sense of being treated in ways more in-tune with their self images as young adults rather than children. This process was aided in the single case example by the fact that students were enrolled in a scheduled class with regular FE students who were re-sitting their GCSEs, and were, therefore, older than the mainstream school students. A key member of the college team in the Cooper *et al* study was the 'Home Tutor', whose role was to monitor student progress and attendance, and to act as a link person between college and school personnel as well as parents. She also played an important role in providing pastoral support for individual students.

In these studies a great deal of importance is attached to personal qualities of the staff involved. This is often reflected in students' references to the importance they attach to the willingness of staff to listen to them, and to treat difficulties they experience seriously. There is also evidence of responsiveness on the part of staff to student concerns and a willingness to make adaptations to programmes on the basis of these.

# Cross-agency outreach programmes

The challenge of students with EBDs has always been to be seen in terms that necessarily go beyond the scope of an education system that interprets 'education' in the narrow sense of school subjects and examination results. Such approaches have one key thing in common: a preoccupation with the idea that it is sometimes necessary for staff to take on roles that might be seen in terms of parenting or re-parenting children and young people. This idea may be offensive to some people. But this is only so if one has a restricted view of what parenting is, and whose responsibility it is. Children who enter the world via a family that is well resourced, attuned to the social, emotional and practical means of meeting the challenges of life in the 21st century are not only provided with important resources for meeting these challenges by the family, they are also the recipient of reinforcement from the agencies of social and personal reward in the broader society as they are progress beyond the family unit. Children who lack these advantages, for whatever reason, are left struggling in a wider social environment that is likely to punish their lack of preparedness. Their first experience of the education system is that of punishment.

This section considers some of the approaches that show an awareness of this situation, by seeking ways of offering direct support for families of children with EBD. Far from reflecting a deficit model of parenting, the examples chosen in this section represent attempts to rectify deficits in the social support mechanisms that serve some families but fail others.

With this view in mind Edwards and Jones-Young (1992), writing from the US perspective, argue that: 'schools must do more than merely refer students to social services and health departments. They must become multiple-service brokers for children'. They go on to make five recommendations:

1. Home/school strategies should be founded on the strengths of families and their understandings of their children.
2. Efforts should be organized around preventative strategies. The school personnel must understand the children and families they serve – including the wide range of social, personal, economic and psychological stresses that families may be encountering. They will need to assess how this information will facilitate closer relationships with families to support children's in-school and out-of-school development.
3. Schools should explore multiple models for reaching out to families and to agencies involved with the families that they serve.
4. Drawing on community services should become part of the school's daily routine, enabling speedy responses to children's immediate needs.
5. Prospective educators should encounter these issues in their professional preparation programmes (ibid: 80).

Blau and Brumer (1996: 289), in reviewing the effects of such coordinated systems of educational, social, health and other services in the United States, identify four programmes that have produced the following outcomes:

- Students receiving such coordinated services are less likely to be placed in restrictive environments such as hospitals or residential facilities.
- If the student is placed in such an environment the length of stay is reduced as compared to a youngster not receiving such coordinated intervention.
- Students receiving such care receive less contacts with the juvenile justice system than others, and they demonstrate improvements in related variables such as school attendance and academic performance.
- Parents of these students express more satisfaction with the services and support they receive.
- The approach is cost effective compared to alternative less coordinated forms of intervention.

## Barnardo's Blackford Brae project

Evaluation studies carried out by the children's charity Barnardos in Scotland point to the value of coordinated cross-agency approaches that are community based. The Blackford Brae project (Shachdev, 1996) is a joint project set up by a social services department and education authority which focuses on children in the primary school range 'whose home or school stability is threatened'. The aims of the project are to promote improvement in the children's social, emotional and educational functioning through the use of a range of settings in the form of:

● a day special school catering for 24 children who are underachieving in educational terms. A key aim of this provision is to improve children's educational functioning and to return the children to mainstream schools;
● a residential unit for children experiencing difficulties in functioning within the family setting. The aim of this provision is to prepare children for school placements or new foster or adoptive families;
● a short-term residential unit offering intensive intervention aimed at children who are being prepared for a return to their homes;
● a family Social Work service providing direct support for families and children in the form of individual and group work strategies.

(NB. Recent developments in this project have led to a decreased emphasis on the use of residential facilities.)

The evaluation highlights the efficacy of a coordinated service with clear aims for each component of provision that enable individual needs to be identified and met. Quantitative and qualitative data are presented indicating the effectiveness of the project, concluding that there was evidence 'of a major improvement in children's functioning in each setting. Children unable to function successfully in foster homes, home or school have been enabled to function successfully in the project' (ibid: 41).

In particular 22 out of 30 students attending the day school had been successfully reintegrated into mainstream schools, some with the support of the residential facilities. Specific gains were observed in all but four of the children's classroom functioning, in the form of their performance in such activities as following school rules, completing work tasks and their ability to play cooperatively with other children. The residential provisions were used to support children whose severe social and or behavioural problems rendered them out of the control of their parents, who were experiencing abusive relationships in the home situation, or for whom the home situation was deemed unsuitable for other reasons. The Family Social Work Service offered a range of interventions to children and their families, including: activities designed to encourage parental participation in their children's schooling; meetings with parents to discuss progress and resolve crises; information sharing regarding referral processes and placements; group meetings for parents where issues of concern are explored and discussed; and individual, parent-child and family counselling. Qualitative data highlighted the high value parents attached to the group work sessions.

## Barnardo's Linksfield project

A second Barnardo's evaluation describes the Linksfield project in Aberdeen, for children and young people between the ages of 9 and 14 and their families (Shachdev, 1999). This project centred around the coordinated work of personnel from Social Work and Education Services represented by: a residential team, an education team, and an outreach team. The aim of the project was:

> to develop and provide a multi-disciplinary service to support children and young people exhibiting complex and challenging behaviours at home and school in order to maintain or reintegrate them in their families and mainstream schools. If there has been a breakdown in the child/young person's placements at home or at school, the project aims to reintegrate the child in mainstream schooling and/or in the family, or in a suitable alternative placement.
>
> (Shachdev, 1999: 2)

The project adopted an ecosystemic orientation which considers children's/ young people's EBDs in terms of the contexts in which they occur. A major component of this was the use of systemic family therapy, conducted by members of the outreach team, which focuses on patterns of interaction and communication within families and between families and other subsystems (including schools and other community facilities). The aim is to identify patterns that promote or maintain presenting problems and to facilitate positive changes in these patterns (Hoffman, 1981). In the Linksfield project educational and residential interventions were employed in order to support these positive changes as and when needed. This work involved individually tailored programmes for the children focusing on educational, social, emotional and behavioural functioning.

The evaluation involved case studies of 10 children, nine boys and one girl aged 9 to 13 (mean age 11). The boys had all been referred to the project for severely disruptive behaviour in school and family settings, and the girl for self-injurious behaviour. Outcomes of the project for this group were generally positive, with six of them being maintained in mainstream schools and two placed in local behaviour support schools. Eight of the youngsters were maintained in their families, whilst the remaining two were maintained in families at weekends and boarding during the week in the residential school.

Parents were helped by the project to develop improved parenting skills, particularly in relation to the management of their children's behaviour. The duration of the children and their families participation in the project was between 8 and 23 months, with only two cases requiring support for 19 months or more.

These two Barnardo's projects echo many of the qualities of the multi systemic therapy model (Henggeler and Borduin, 1990) which is characterized by highly flexible community based and multidisciplinary intervention strategies. An example of a similar initiative adopted by an English LEA is described by Hayden (2000). And although caution must be taken in assessing the effectiveness of such interventions on the basis of small-scale case studies, such case-study data can be seen to combine powerfully with the wider evidence base (see Chapter 1) and therefore to support the conclusion that this kind of approach is highly effective. Furthermore, the means by which the efficacy of such approaches is measured needs to be carefully considered. Hayden's (2000) evaluation of a Joint School and Family Support Team working with primary-aged children had little short-term impact on permanent exclusion figures, but was successful in laying the foundations for a community-based, multi-service, integrated approach to school and family problems, which highlighted the need for the within-school and educational policy developments that would be necessary to complement gains made in family functioning. This study showed that whilst contextual/community factors needed to be addressed, within-school factors required at least equal attention, and that some of these in-school factors were the product of pressures created by unhelpful national and local educational policies (see Chapter 2).

# Factors associated with effective multidisciplinary cooperation

Hammill and Boyd (2001), also writing from the Scottish perspective, add further to our understanding of the factors associated with effective multidisciplinary cooperation in their account of an evaluation study of one Scottish Region's provision for young people with EBD carried out at Strathclyde University (Scottish Regions are the major institutions of local government, equivalent to the Local Authorities in England and Wales). The study was prompted by an inter-agency seminar, set up in 1997, which sought to examine the effectiveness of the Region's services in: 1) promoting an inclusive school ethos and reducing the number of young people with EBD being excluded from school; and 2) raising the educational attainment of all young people.

A major educational initiative associated with these aims was the establishment of a number of Pupil Support Bases, located in mainstream schools. The purposes of these bases was to provide within-school support for students whose behaviour was such that they could not be maintained in subject classrooms' (ibid: 3). It was widely felt that hitherto too many students with EBD had been referred to residential facilities outside the Region, and that, as a result, contact was being lost between the students and their home communities. Concerns were raised by participants in this seminar, that historically its provision for this group 'lacked co ordination, cohesion and a sense of direction' (ibid: 2). The aim of the study was to gain insight into the factors that would support the development of effective within-Region resources for students with EBD within the context of a coordinated Regional Youth Strategy. This multi-agency approach reflected the fact that from the outset it was realized that although the educational and other school-based outcomes were a key focus of the endeavour, such outcomes are dependent on the quality of the collaboration between providers of within-school support and a variety of agencies within the community served by the schools. Such Youth Strategies have been adopted by a number of Scottish Regional Councils.

The study was qualitative in design, within an action-research framework. It drew on client perceptions, as well as those of representatives from the following professions and agencies:

● education welfare officers;
● children's reporter and members of the children's panel;
● juvenile liaison police officers;
● youth strategy community education workers;
● youth strategy social workers;
● family services social workers;
● educational psychologist;
● teachers.

The action-research orientation meant that its findings were framed in terms of cues for service development. The following sections illustrate the key findings from the study included.

## Importance of a shared philosophy
In this instance a common commitment to educational inclusion was felt to be essential, with difficulties emerging where different professionals departed from this commitment. In order that common aims be pursued, a need was identified for all participating professionals to explore the concept of inclusion in order to establish a consensus on its meaning and implications for practice.

## Need for professionals to value one another
Negative effects were associated with situations in which certain professionals felt marginalized or placed in low positions with inter-professional

hierarchies. For example, non-educational professionals felt-occasions that their input was devalued by within-school staff, with the result that in-school support systems sometimes failed to take appropriate account of out-of-school factors. Where this happened the work of the in-school services was felt to be less effective in meeting the aims of the project. A related issue was the need for professionals to acknowledge and address negative stereotypes that they sometimes held of other professionals.

### Need for the full range of professional skills to be utilized
The complexity of EBDs is often such that no single profession has a sufficient skill base or set of functions to address the needs of clients. The principle of complementary professional knowledge and expertise was seen as a vital component of effective multi disciplinary working. This was felt to require clear shared understandings about different professionals' roles and responsibilities, the sharing of skills and expertise, and the development of a common language. Related to this was a need for a single professional to take on the role of coordinator for the multi-professional process within the educational setting.

## Summary

The findings and recommendations accord well with other work on multidisciplinary and inter-professional collaboration (Blau and Brummer, 1996; BPS, 2000; Munn, 1994). They illustrate the enormous challenges that the multidisciplinary agenda poses. There is a long-held view that is gaining increasingly wide acceptance, however, that it is this agenda that offers the most promising way forward in the search for effective provision for children and young people with EBD. It is essential, therefore, that those engaged in this process be given maximum support in their efforts to overcome these difficulties.

Scotland, as is evident from the above review, has been a particularly fertile ground for the development of multi-agency collaboration in relation to EBD. A project jointly funded by the Scottish Office and the Social Work Services Inspectorate identified five major issues perceived by professionals and experts to underpin effective practice in this area (Munn, 1994). The following sections provide a brief summary of these issues and serve to illustrate the complexity of factors that interact at local and national levels across the domains of policy and practice.

### Policy framework and policy planning (Barr, 1994)
It is essential that underlying practice is a clear policy which explicitly states the aims and guiding principles for policy in this area. At the national and local levels policy in this area needs to establish a clear set of rights for clients

and the responsibilities of service providers, along with appropriate mechanisms and resources for delivering and meeting these rights and responsibilities. It is essential that core elements of policy are the product of
multidisciplinary consensus, and that multi-agency cooperation is a consistent feature of planning and practice at all levels, with structures in place to
facilitate this. This requires a commitment to multidisciplinary cooperation at
the level of corporate planning within authorities, so that funds, resources and
inter-agency mechanisms (eg cross-disciplinary committees) are established
to support the process to ensure that relevant groups within an authority share
a sense of ownership of the policy and are able to make a full contribution.
Clarity in terms of rights, responsibilities and procedures enables evaluation,
and this should be a central feature of policy provision and form a basis for
development.

## Principles of inter-agency cooperation (based on Mckay, 1994)

As has already been noted, the *raison d'être* of inter-agency work is that no single agency can be expected to deal effectively with the complexity of EBD. It
is not an easy task to identify all of the statutory and voluntary agencies that
might be considered to have a role in this area. Almost any list of such agencies can be criticized as being exclusionary, often depending on who has com-
piled the list. There is no simple solution to this problem, other than to ensure
that mechanisms are in place to allow agencies to be self-selecting, and encourage opportunities for new agencies to join existing inter-agency groups. This
point extends to client groups also. It is uncontroversial to suggest that clients
should be seen as members of such groups, being both recipients of their services as well as active participants in the planning and implementation of the
group's work. However, the identification of who the clients actually are can
be problematic.

Publications on this topic often refer to the children and young people as
key clients, and their 'parents'. It is often recognized that 'parent' is not always
the correct term owing to widespread changes in family structure that have
occurred. Efforts need to be made, therefore, to think in terms of the young
person's 'primary network' (BPS, 2000), which may include significant others
in the young person's life who do not easily fit into categories of 'parent' or
'carer'. Furthermore, having identified a range of persons and agencies who
ought to be included, eliciting their involvement and cooperation is not
always straightforward. This point was illustrated in the Blackford Brae project (Shachdev, 1996 – see above) which experienced difficulty in eliciting the
involvement of the Health Service. It is difficult to legislate for these kinds of
problems because of the complexity and idiosyncracies of local conditions.
However, it is essential that the establishment and management of inter-
agency groups pays close attention to problems of identifying and securing
the involvement of potential participants and is willing to identify and tackle

structural, social and interpersonal barriers that may arise. Once established, issues of communication and other potential barriers to the development of shared values, purposes and cooperative practices have to be addressed (see Hammill and Boyd, 2001), and supported by, among other things, a programme of staff training and development.

# Conclusion

This chapter has shown the power of cross-agency and collaboration and systemic approaches. It has been shown how the power of individual agencies and settings can be enhanced when they forge cooperative relationships with other agencies and key stakeholders. Such an holistic approach reflects the complexity of EBD and addresses this with impressive results.

# 15

# Conclusion

As co-authors we started this project because of a strong joint interest in class-room management and a strong overlapping set of convictions about what helps in difficult school and classroom circumstances. The overlap in convictions wasn't perfect and the parts hanging over the edges, the bits that didn't match very well, provided us with many hours of discussion and debate, at the University of Cambridge, via e-mail between Australia and the UK, even at the Freud Museum in Hampstead. This, we believe, helped to inform our understanding of what the research tells us and what is practical or impractical for teachers, education managers and other staff to undertake in modern schools. We are optimistic because we also visited a number of schools in the United Kingdom and elsewhere and saw these schools looking at outcomes evidence in their own work, making decisions about what helps and what doesn't and combining approaches in ways that enabled them to help students who some educators may have considered impossible to help.

Less-successful teachers and schools tended to manage problem situations, including gambits, by reacting to them instead of setting goals for students to master, developing skills in teachers and planning for and preventing such problems before they occurred. In contrast, many of the successful schools fol-lowed the principles laid down in SALAD. These schools understand the importance of SYSTEMS interventions. Good communication enables an alliance to exist between stakeholders – the parents, teachers, principals, school counsellors, etc and, of course, the students in their care. The school has clearly defined the roles for these stakeholders and these are in place in a for-mal document. What follows from this systems approach is that common goals are in place for all these stakeholders.

The study mentioned in Chapter 5 (Daniels *et al*, 1999) listed five common features associated with good practice in UK mainstream schools that were particularly effective in supporting students with social, emotional and behavioural difficulties. These features represent some of the elements that we believe are important when Systems principles are embraced in schools:

- Leadership: heads and other members of Senior Management Teams (SMTs) provided effective leadership, particularly in communicating appropriate values, ethos and aspirations for the school as a whole.
- Shared values: a core of staff worked cooperatively and reflectively with one another and pupils to ensure the active participation of all students.
- Behaviour policy and practice: a common, consistent and well monitored behaviour policy for all pupils and staff was in place. A particular feature of this policy was that there was consistency between approaches to dealing with pupils with EBD and those who were not deemed to have EBD.
- Understanding EBD: there was a key member of staff who understood the nature of emotional and behavioural difficulties.
- Teaching skills and the curriculum: the curriculum was appropriately challenging for all students and approaches to its delivery were marked by opportunities for children to learn from their own actions, through purposeful involvement in learning tasks.

Students in successful schools we have visited have clear ACCESS to behavioural and academic skills that will help them in the school and community. Students own the behavioural policy and they own problems thrown up by the students' behaviour. Where possible, students own aspects of the curriculum. Teachers use the student's strengths and interests to formulate goals; the students are motivated to pursue these short- and long-term goals and other stakeholders – parents, other family members and so on – share ownership of these goals. To achieve these goals the students know and understand expectations of appropriate behaviour; students have been taught the necessary skills to achieve their behavioural and academic goals and teachers have rehearsed these skills with students.

When visitors, such as us, enter these schools, the LIMITS are apparent but never oppressive. Rules are clear, sometimes in prominent places in classrooms or common areas and quite often these rules and consequences attached to them, have been memorized by students. For example, students can tell a visitor what happens when someone is caught fighting in the playground, or in the school. In the same vein, consequences for rule infringement are clear and the routines used to help students work, get along with each other and maintain the rules, are known and owned by these students; always these routines, as well as appropriate behaviours, have been rehearsed. Other stakeholders, especially parents and staff members, understand the school rules, consequences and routines and these stakeholders agree with them and support the school.

In these successful schools there is an unmistakable milieu of ACCEPTANCE. Teachers accept their students and show this acceptance in tangible ways, often through interpersonal skills like active listening, or through smiles and a caring warm manner and through concern for the welfare of students in their care. Because of this milieu, the students accept their teachers and, with their pursuit of common personal and group goals, their knowledge of appropriate social skills and so on, these students accept each other. The other stakeholders mentioned above are aware of their roles in communicating and providing acceptance to students and each other.

It is worth revisiting here the five bases of power outlined by French and Raven (1960) because, they, especially reward and referent power, help teachers and school administrators achieve acceptance in the school and classroom:

1. Coercive power – based on threat of punishment. Teachers and students can frighten and humiliate each other.
2. Reward power – based on the use of rewards. Teachers and students can reward each other through the use of praise and the showing of approval.
3. Legitimate power – based on social position that is identified with a specific realm of authority.
4. Referent power – based on personal liking and respect. This can apply equally to teachers and students.
5. Expert power – based on the possession of special knowledge that is respected and valued by others.

In Chapter 8 we summarized from Tauber (1995) some ways that teachers can increase their referent power:

- use more self-disclosure;
- associate with students in non-teaching situations, for example in sports or with special interests;
- spend time in face-to-face interactions with all students;
- be accepting, yet not patronizing; recognize students' interests;
- discipline in a calm, businesslike manner. Avoid the personalization of discipline problems by not taking misbehaviour personally and by condemning negative behaviour rather than the perpetrator. Discipline should be administered with dignity so both teacher and student save face;
- teachers should make themselves aware of any tendencies to react differently to different students. Fairness is essential;
- use active listening;
- be a good role model.

Students in successful schools have a clear sense of DIRECTION. That is, after group and individual goals have been set collaboratively, the students can actually see growth, see how their mastery of sub-goals is rewarded – and by 'see' we mean they are often rewarded visually. Students see completion. They eventually reach their long-term goals and these important events are rewarded, sometimes with a class or school ceremony. The classwork in these schools stimulates and progresses and the other stakeholders mentioned above are aware of the students' growth and progress.

With these principles in place, the problems that arise in the classroom and school, including gambits, are often prevented, or at least managed much more effectively than they would be if teachers tried to react to these problems after they occurred.

## Finally: now the real work begins...

We believe that the information in this book will be of practical value to teachers and schools where there are serious problems of indiscipline and disruptive behaviour. As far as possible, the book has been evidence based, drawing on research findings as well as practical experience. Having said this, what we offer here is not a panacea. Readers who use this book as a basis for critical reflection and discussion will get the most out of it. The ideas in this book are like a flashlight which can help teachers and schools to scrutinize their own situation and practice. Hopefully this process of scrutiny will help readers to make some sense out of the shadowy chaos of disruptive behaviour. It will help them to move the light to where the solutions are (unlike the drunk with whom we introduced the book). The emphasis here is on active reflection rather than implementation of 'off the shelf' ideas. If this book helps schools and teachers to begin to ask the right questions and find positive ways forward then it will have succeeded. Effective and positive responses to problems of indiscipline and disruption in schools will never be solved by books, however. Such responses are only achieved when the people concerned find their own ways of communicating and working together cooperatively.

# Appendix I

# Strengths and Difficulties Questionnaire (SDQ)

The authors thank Professor Robert Goodman of the Department of Child Psychiatry at the Maudsley Hospital, King's College London, for his kindness in granting permission to reproduce the Strengths and Difficulties Questionnaire.

## Copyright notice

# Strengths and Difficulties Questionnaire (SDQ):
## Information Sheet

### What is the SDQ?

The SDQ is a brief behavioural screening questionnaire about 3-16 year olds. It exists in several versions to meet the needs of researchers, clinicians and educationalists. Each version includes between one and three of the following components:

*A) 25 items on psychological attributes.*

All versions of the SDQ ask about 25 attributes, some positive and others negative. These 25 items are divided between 5 scales:

| | |
|---|---|
| 1) Emotional symptoms (5 items) | Added together to |
| 2) Conduct problems (5 items) | generate a Total |
| 3) Hyperactivity/Inattention (5 items) | Difficulties Score |
| 4) Peer relationship problems (5 items) | (based on 20 items) |
| 5) Prosocial behaviour (5 items) | |

Identically worded items are included in questionnaires for completion by parents or teachers (Goodman, 1997). Questionnaires for self-completion by young people ask about the same 25 traits, though the wording is slightly different (Goodman et al, 1998). The SDQ compares favourably with longer-established questionnaire measures (Goodman, 1997; Goodman & Scott, 1999).

*B) An impact supplement*

Extended versions of the SDQ ask whether the respondent thinks the young person has a problem, and if so, enquire further about chronicity, distress, social impairment, and burden to others. This provides useful additional information for clinicians and researchers with an interest in psychiatric caseness and the determinants of service use (Goodman, 1999).

*C) Follow-up questions*

After an intervention, respondents are asked 2 questions: whether the intervention has reduced problems, and whether the intervention has helped in other ways, e.g. making the problem more bearable.

### English Versions

*One-sided versions*

By themselves the 25 questions on strengths and difficulties take up just one side of paper. Versions in common use include:

a) An informant-rated version (included in this pack on white paper) that can be completed by either the parents or the teachers of 4-16 year olds. There is a slightly modified version available for the parents or teachers of 3 to 4 year olds: 22 items are identical, the item on reflectiveness is softened, and 2 items on antisocial behaviour are replaced by items on oppositionality;

b) a self-rated version (included in this pack on salmon paper) for young people aged between 11 (roughly) and 16, depending on their level of understanding and literacy.

*Two-sided versions with impact supplements*
Several two-sided versions of the SDQ are available with the 25 items on strengths and difficulties on the front of the page and the impact supplement on the back:

**P4-16** (included in this pack on green paper) for the parents of 4-16 year olds

**T4-16** (included in this pack on yellow paper) for teachers of 4-16 year olds

**S11-16** (included in this pack on blue paper) for self-completion by 11-16 year olds

**P3/4** (included in this pack on pink paper) for the parents of 3 (and 4) year olds. There is an equivalent teacher version.

*Follow-up versions*
When two-sided versions of the SDQ have been used prior to a clinic attendance or some other intervention, using the equivalent follow-up versions can monitor the outcome of treatment. This information pack includes the P4-16 follow-up (on lilac paper), the T4-16 follow-up (on gold paper) and the S11-16 follow-up (on grey paper); there are also P3/4 and T3/4 versions available. Apart from including the follow-up questions, these versions differ from the standard two-sided versions of the SDQ in the following ways. Firstly, they are marked "FOLLOW-UP" in the top right hand corner. Secondly, they ask not about "the last six months or this school year" but about "the last month". Thirdly, follow-up versions do not ask about the chronicity of problems.

**Translations**
At least one version of the SDQ has been translated into 40 languages. Sample copies are available on request.

**Scoring the SDQ**
This pack contains separate scoring instructions for informant-rated and self-report SDQs, as well as a transparent overlay to help with hand scoring, and a sample record sheet. A computerised scoring and report-writing program will soon be available.

**Uses of the SDQ**
The SDQ is being used as part of clinical assessment, outcome evaluation, screening, epidemiological surveys and a wide range of research studies.

**Some Relevant Publications**
Goodman, R. (1997) The Strengths and Difficulties Questionnaire: A Research Note. *Journal of Child Psychology and Psychiatry*, **38**, 581-586.
Goodman, R. Meltzer, H & Bailey, V. (1998) The Strengths and Difficulties Questionnaire: A pilot study on the validity of the self-report version. *European Child and Adolescent Psychiatry*, 7, 125-130.
Goodman, R. & Scott, S. (1999) Comparing the Strengths and Difficulties Questionnaire and the Child Behaviour Checklist: Is small beautiful? *Journal of Abnormal Child Psychology*, **27**, 17-24.
Goodman, R. (1999) The extended version of the Strengths and Difficulties Questionnaire as a guide to child psychiatric caseness and consequent burden. *Journal of Child Psychology and Psychiatry*, **40**, 791-9.
Smedje, H., Broman, J.-E., Hetta, J & von Knorring, A.-L. (1999) Psychometric properties of a Swedish version of the "Strengths and Difficulties Questionnaire". *European Child and Adolescent Psychiatry*, **8**, 63-70.
Goodman, R., Renfrew, D., Mullick, M. (2000) Predicting type of psychiatric disorder from Strengths and Difficulties Questionnaire (SDQ) scores in child mental health clinics in London and Dhaka. *European Child and Adolescent Psychiatry*, **9**, 129-134.

**For more information and downloadable copies of the SDQ in many languages, visit our web page:**

**http://www.sdqinfo.com**

# Strengths and Difficulties Questionnaire $\quad$ T[4-16]

For each item, please mark the box for Not True, Somewhat True or Certainly True. It would help us if you answered all items as best you can even if you are not absolutely certain or the item seems daft! Please give your answers on the basis of the child's behaviour over the last six months or this school year.

Child's Name ............................................................................................. $\qquad$ Male/Female

Date of Birth ...........................................................

| | Not True | Somewhat True | Certainly True |
|---|---|---|---|
| Considerate of other people's feelings | ☐ | ☐ | ☐ |
| Restless, overactive, cannot stay still for long | ☐ | ☐ | ☐ |
| Often complains of headaches, stomach-aches or sickness | ☐ | ☐ | ☐ |
| Shares readily with other children (treats, toys, pencils etc.) | ☐ | ☐ | ☐ |
| Often has temper tantrums or hot tempers | ☐ | ☐ | ☐ |
| Rather solitary, tends to play alone | ☐ | ☐ | ☐ |
| Generally obedient, usually does what adults request | ☐ | ☐ | ☐ |
| Many worries, often seems worried | ☐ | ☐ | ☐ |
| Helpful if someone is hurt, upset or feeling ill | ☐ | ☐ | ☐ |
| Constantly fidgeting or squirming | ☐ | ☐ | ☐ |
| Has at least one good friend | ☐ | ☐ | ☐ |
| Often fights with other children or bullies them | ☐ | ☐ | ☐ |
| Often unhappy, down-hearted or tearful | ☐ | ☐ | ☐ |
| Generally liked by other children | ☐ | ☐ | ☐ |
| Easily distracted, concentration wanders | ☐ | ☐ | ☐ |
| Nervous or clingy in new situations, easily loses confidence | ☐ | ☐ | ☐ |
| Kind to younger children | ☐ | ☐ | ☐ |
| Often lies or cheats | ☐ | ☐ | ☐ |
| Picked on or bullied by other children | ☐ | ☐ | ☐ |
| Often volunteers to help others (parents, teachers, other children) | ☐ | ☐ | ☐ |
| Thinks things out before acting | ☐ | ☐ | ☐ |
| Steals from home, school or elsewhere | ☐ | ☐ | ☐ |
| Gets on better with adults than with other children | ☐ | ☐ | ☐ |
| Many fears, easily scared | ☐ | ☐ | ☐ |
| Sees tasks through to the end, good attention span | ☐ | ☐ | ☐ |

Do you have any other comments or concerns?

Overall, do you think that this child has difficulties in one or more of the following areas:
emotions, concentration, behaviour or being able to get on with other people?

|  | No | Yes - minor difficulties | Yes - definite difficulties | Yes - severe difficulties |
|---|---|---|---|---|
|  | ☐ | ☐ | ☐ | ☐ |

If you have answered "Yes", please answer the following questions about these difficulties:

● How long have these difficulties been present?

|  | Less than a month | 1-5 months | 6-12 months | Over a year |
|---|---|---|---|---|
|  | ☐ | ☐ | ☐ | ☐ |

● Do the difficulties upset or distress the child?

|  | Not at all | Only a little | Quite a lot | A great deal |
|---|---|---|---|---|
|  | ☐ | ☐ | ☐ | ☐ |

● Do the difficulties interfere with the child's everyday life in the following areas?

|  | Not at all | Only a little | Quite a lot | A great deal |
|---|---|---|---|---|
| PEER RELATIONSHIPS | ☐ | ☐ | ☐ | ☐ |
| CLASSROOM LEARNING | ☐ | ☐ | ☐ | ☐ |

● Do the difficulties put a burden on you or the class as a whole?

|  | Not at all | Only a little | Quite a lot | A great deal |
|---|---|---|---|---|
|  | ☐ | ☐ | ☐ | ☐ |

Signature ................................................................. Date .......................................

Class Teacher/Form Tutor/Head of Year/Other (please specify:)

**Thank you very much for your help**

## Scoring the Informant-Rated Strengths and Difficulties Questionnaire

The 25 items in the SDQ comprise 5 scales of 5 items each. It is usually easiest to score all 5 scales first before working out the total difficulties score. Somewhat True is always scored as 1, but the scoring of Not True and Certainly True varies with the item, as shown below scale by scale. For each of the 5 scales the score can range from 0 to 10 if all 5 items were completed. Scale score can be prorated if at least 3 items were completed.

| __Emotional Symptoms Scale__ | Not True | Somewhat True | Certainly True |
| --- | --- | --- | --- |
| Often complains of headaches, stomach-aches ... | 0 | 1 | 2 |
| Many worries, often seems worried | 0 | 1 | 2 |
| Often unhappy, downhearted or tearful | 0 | 1 | 2 |
| Nervous or clingy in new situations ... | 0 | 1 | 2 |
| Many fears, easily scared | 0 | 1 | 2 |

| __Conduct Problems Scale__ | Not True | Somewhat True | Certainly True |
| --- | --- | --- | --- |
| Often has temper tantrums or hot tempers | 0 | 1 | 2 |
| Generally obedient, usually does what ... | 2 | 1 | 0 |
| Often fights with other children or bullies them | 0 | 1 | 2 |
| Often lies or cheats | 0 | 1 | 2 |
| Steals from home, school or elsewhere | 0 | 1 | 2 |

| __Hyperactivity Scale__ | Not True | Somewhat True | Certainly True |
| --- | --- | --- | --- |
| Restless, overactive, cannot stay still for long | 0 | 1 | 2 |
| Constantly fidgeting or squirming | 0 | 1 | 2 |
| Easily distracted, concentration wanders | 0 | 1 | 2 |
| Thinks things out before acting | 2 | 1 | 0 |
| Sees tasks through to the end, good attention span | 2 | 1 | 0 |

| __Peer Problems Scale__ | Not True | Somewhat True | Certainly True |
| --- | --- | --- | --- |
| Rather solitary, tends to play alone | 0 | 1 | 2 |
| Has at least one good friend | 2 | 1 | 0 |
| Generally liked by other children | 2 | 1 | 0 |
| Picked on or bullied by other children | 0 | 1 | 2 |
| Gets on better with adults than with other children | 0 | 1 | 2 |

| __Prosocial Scale__ | Not True | Somewhat True | Certainly True |
| --- | --- | --- | --- |
| Considerate of other people's feelings | 0 | 1 | 2 |
| Shares readily with other children | 0 | 1 | 2 |
| Helpful if someone is hurt, upset of feeling ill | 0 | 1 | 2 |
| Kind to younger children | 0 | 1 | 2 |
| Often volunteers to help others | 0 | 1 | 2 |

__The Total Difficulties Score__:

is generated by summing the scores from all the scales except the prosocial scale. The resultant score can range from 0 to 40 (and is counted as missing if one of the component scores is missing).

## Interpreting Symptom Scores and Defining "Caseness" from Symptom Scores

Although SDQ scores can often be used as continuous variables, it is sometimes convenient to classify scores as normal, borderline and abnormal. Using the bandings shown below, an abnormal score on one or both of the total difficulties scores can be used to identify likely "cases" with mental health disorders. This is clearly only a rough-and ready method for detecting disorders – combining information from SDQ symptom and impact scores from multiple informants is better, but still far from perfect. Approximately 10% of a community sample scores in the abnormal band on any given score, with a further 10% scoring in the borderline band. The exact proportions vary according to country, age and gender – normative SDQ data are available from the web site. You may want to adjust banding and caseness criteria for these characteristics, setting the threshold higher when avoiding false positives is of paramount importance, and setting the threshold lower when avoiding false negatives is more important.

|  | Normal | Borderline | Abnormal |
|---|---|---|---|
| **Parent Completed** | | | |
| Total Difficulties Score | 0 - 13 | 14 - 16 | 17 - 40 |
| Emotional Symptoms Score | 0 - 3 | 4 | 5 - 10 |
| Conduct Problems Score | 0 - 2 | 3 | 4 - 10 |
| Hyperactivity Score | 0 - 5 | 6 | 7 - 10 |
| Peer Problems Score | 0 - 2 | 3 | 4 - 10 |
| Prosocial Behaviour Score | 6 - 10 | 5 | 0 - 4 |
| **Teacher Completed** | | | |
| Total Difficulties Score | 0 - 11 | 12 - 15 | 16 - 40 |
| Emotional Symptoms Score | 0 - 4 | 5 | 6 - 10 |
| Conduct Problems Score | 0 - 2 | 3 | 4 - 10 |
| Hyperactivity Score | 0 - 5 | 6 | 7 - 10 |
| Peer Problems Score | 0 - 3 | 4 | 5 - 10 |
| Prosocial Behaviour Score | 6 - 10 | 5 | 0 - 4 |

## Generating and Interpreting Impact Scores

When using a version of the SDQ that includes an "Impact Supplement", the items on overall distress and social impairment can be summed to generate an impact score that ranges from 0 to 10 for the parent-completed version and from 0-6 for the teacher-completed version.

|  | Not at all | Only a little | Quite a lot | A great deal |
|---|---|---|---|---|
| **Parent report** | | | | |
| Difficulties upset or distress child | 0 | 0 | 1 | 2 |
| Interfere with HOME LIFE | 0 | 0 | 1 | 2 |
| Interfere with FRIENDSHIPS | 0 | 0 | 1 | 2 |
| Interfere with CLASSROOM LEARNING | 0 | 0 | 1 | 2 |
| Interfere with LEISURE ACTIVITIES | 0 | 0 | 1 | 2 |
| **Teacher report** | | | | |
| Difficulties upset or distress child | 0 | 0 | 1 | 2 |
| Interfere with PEER RELATIONSHIPS | 0 | 0 | 1 | 2 |
| Interfere with CLASSROOM LEARNING | 0 | 0 | 1 | 2 |

Responses to the questions on chronicity and burden to others are not included in the impact score. When respondents have answered "no" to the first question on the impact supplement (i.e. when they do not perceive the child as having any emotional or behavioural difficulties), they are not asked to complete the questions on resultant distress or impairment; the impact score is automatically scored zero in these circumstances.

Although the impact scores can be used as continuous variables, it is sometimes convenient to classify them as normal, borderline or abnormal: a total impact score of 2 or more is abnormal; a score of 1 is borderline; and a score of 0 is normal.

## Strengths and Difficulties Questionnaire    S[11-16]

For each item, please mark the box for Not True, Somewhat True or Certainly True. It would help us if you answered all items as best you can even if you are not absolutely certain or the item seems daft! Please give your answers on the basis of how things have been for you over the last six months.

Your Name ..................................................................................    Male/Female

Date of Birth ...........................................................

| | Not True | Somewhat True | Certainly True |
|---|---|---|---|
| I try to be nice to other people. I care about their feelings | ☐ | ☐ | ☐ |
| I am restless, I cannot stay still for long | ☐ | ☐ | ☐ |
| I get a lot of headaches, stomach-aches or sickness | ☐ | ☐ | ☐ |
| I usually share with others (food, games, pens etc.) | ☐ | ☐ | ☐ |
| I get very angry and often lose my temper | ☐ | ☐ | ☐ |
| I am usually on my own. I generally play alone or keep to myself | ☐ | ☐ | ☐ |
| I usually do as I am told | ☐ | ☐ | ☐ |
| I worry a lot | ☐ | ☐ | ☐ |
| I am helpful if someone is hurt, upset or feeling ill | ☐ | ☐ | ☐ |
| I am constantly fidgeting or squirming | ☐ | ☐ | ☐ |
| I have one good friend or more | ☐ | ☐ | ☐ |
| I fight a lot. I can make other people do what I want | ☐ | ☐ | ☐ |
| I am often unhappy, down-hearted or tearful | ☐ | ☐ | ☐ |
| Other people my age generally like me | ☐ | ☐ | ☐ |
| I am easily distracted, I find it difficult to concentrate | ☐ | ☐ | ☐ |
| I am nervous in new situations. I easily lose confidence | ☐ | ☐ | ☐ |
| I am kind to younger children | ☐ | ☐ | ☐ |
| I am often accused of lying or cheating | ☐ | ☐ | ☐ |
| Other children or young people pick on me or bully me | ☐ | ☐ | ☐ |
| I often volunteer to help others (parents, teachers, children) | ☐ | ☐ | ☐ |
| I think before I do things | ☐ | ☐ | ☐ |
| I take things that are not mine from home, school or elsewhere | ☐ | ☐ | ☐ |
| I get on better with adults than with people my own age | ☐ | ☐ | ☐ |
| I have many fears, I am easily scared | ☐ | ☐ | ☐ |
| I finish the work I'm doing. My attention is good | ☐ | ☐ | ☐ |

Do you have any other comments or concerns?

Overall, do you think that you have difficulties in one or more of the following areas:
emotions, concentration, behaviour or being able to get on with other people?

|  | No | Yes - minor difficulties | Yes - definite difficulties | Yes - severe difficulties |
|---|---|---|---|---|
|  | ☐ | ☐ | ☐ | ☐ |

If you have answered "Yes", please answer the following questions about these difficulties:

● How long have these difficulties been present?

|  | Less than a month | 1-5 months | 6-12 months | Over a year |
|---|---|---|---|---|
|  | ☐ | ☐ | ☐ | ☐ |

● Do the difficulties upset or distress you?

|  | Not at all | Only a little | Quite a lot | A great deal |
|---|---|---|---|---|
|  | ☐ | ☐ | ☐ | ☐ |

● Do the difficulties interfere with your everyday life in the following areas?

|  | Not at all | Only a little | Quite a lot | A great deal |
|---|---|---|---|---|
| HOME LIFE | ☐ | ☐ | ☐ | ☐ |
| FRIENDSHIPS | ☐ | ☐ | ☐ | ☐ |
| CLASSROOM LEARNING | ☐ | ☐ | ☐ | ☐ |
| LEISURE ACTIVITIES | ☐ | ☐ | ☐ | ☐ |

● Do the difficulties make it harder for those around you (family, friends, teachers, etc.)?

|  | Not at all | Only a little | Quite a lot | A great deal |
|---|---|---|---|---|
|  | ☐ | ☐ | ☐ | ☐ |

Your Signature ..............................................................................

Today's Date .........................................

**Thank you very much for your help**

## Scoring the Self-Report Strengths and Difficulties Questionnaire

The 25 items in the SDQ comprise 5 scales of 5 items each. It is usually easiest to score all 5 scales first before working out the total difficulties score. Somewhat True is always scored as 1, but the scoring of Not True and Certainly True varies with the item, as shown below scale by scale. For each of the 5 scales the score can range from 0 to 10 if all 5 items were completed. Scale score can be prorated if at least 3 items were completed.

| **Emotional Symptoms Scale** | Not True | Somewhat True | Certainly True |
|---|---|---|---|
| I get a lot of headaches, stomach-aches or sickness | 0 | 1 | 2 |
| I worry a lot | 0 | 1 | 2 |
| I am often unhappy, downhearted or tearful | 0 | 1 | 2 |
| I am nervous in new situations | 0 | 1 | 2 |
| I have many fears, I am easily scared | 0 | 1 | 2 |

| **Conduct Problems Scale** | Not True | Somewhat True | Certainly True |
|---|---|---|---|
| I get very angry and often lose my temper | 0 | 1 | 2 |
| I usually do as I am told | 2 | 1 | 0 |
| I fight a lot | 0 | 1 | 2 |
| I am often accused of lying or cheating | 0 | 1 | 2 |
| I take things that are not mine | 0 | 1 | 2 |

| **Hyperactivity Scale** | Not True | Somewhat True | Certainly True |
|---|---|---|---|
| I am restless. I cannot stay still for long | 0 | 1 | 2 |
| I am constantly fidgeting or squirming | 0 | 1 | 2 |
| I am easily distracted | 0 | 1 | 2 |
| I think before I do things | 2 | 1 | 0 |
| I finish the work I am doing | 2 | 1 | 0 |

| **Peer Problems Scale** | Not True | Somewhat True | Certainly True |
|---|---|---|---|
| I am usually on my own | 0 | 1 | 2 |
| I have one good friend or more | 2 | 1 | 0 |
| Other people my age generally like me | 2 | 1 | 0 |
| Other children or young people pick on me | 0 | 1 | 2 |
| I get on better with adults than with people my age | 0 | 1 | 2 |

| **Prosocial Scale** | Not True | Somewhat True | Certainly True |
|---|---|---|---|
| I try to be nice to other people | 0 | 1 | 2 |
| I usually share with others | 0 | 1 | 2 |
| I am helpful if someone is hurt, upset of feeling ill | 0 | 1 | 2 |
| I am kind to younger children | 0 | 1 | 2 |
| I often volunteer to help others | 0 | 1 | 2 |

**The Total Difficulties Score:**
is generated by summing the scores from all the scales except the prosocial scale. The resultant score can range from 0 to 40 (and is counted as missing if one of the component scores is missing).

## Interpreting Symptom Scores and Defining "Caseness" from Symptom Scores

Although SDQ scores can often be used as continuous variables, it is sometimes convenient to classify scores as normal, borderline and abnormal. Using the bandings shown below, an abnormal score on the total difficulties score can be used to identify likely "cases" with mental health disorders. This is clearly only a rough-and-ready method for detecting disorders – combining information from SDQ symptom and impact scores from multiple informants is better, but still far from perfect. Approximately 10% of a community sample scores in the abnormal band on any given score, with a further 10% scoring in the borderline band. The exact proportions vary according to country, age and gender – normative SDQ data are available from the web site. You may want to adjust banding and caseness criteria for these characteristics, setting the threshold higher when avoiding false positives is of paramount importance, and setting the threshold lower when avoiding false negatives is more important.

### Self Completed

|  | Normal | Borderline | Abnormal |
|---|---|---|---|
| Total Difficulties Score | 0 - 15 | 16 - 19 | 20 - 40 |
| Emotional Symptoms Score | 0 - 5 | 6 | 7 - 10 |
| Conduct Problems Score | 0 - 3 | 4 | 5 - 10 |
| Hyperactivity Score | 0 - 5 | 6 | 7 - 10 |
| Peer Problems Score | 0 - 3 | 4 - 5 | 6 - 10 |
| Prosocial Behaviour Score | 6 - 10 | 5 | 0 - 4 |

### Generating and Interpreting Impact Scores

When using a version of the SDQ that includes an "Impact Supplement", the items on overall distress and social impairment can be summed to generate an impact score that ranges from 0 to 10.

|  | Not at all | Only a little | Quite a lot | A great deal |
|---|---|---|---|---|
| Difficulties upset or distress me | 0 | 0 | 1 | 2 |
| Interfere with HOME LIFE | 0 | 0 | 1 | 2 |
| Interfere with FRIENDSHIPS | 0 | 0 | 1 | 2 |
| Interfere with CLASSROOM LEARNING | 0 | 0 | 1 | 2 |
| Interfere with LEISURE ACTIVITIES | 0 | 0 | 1 | 2 |

Responses to the questions on chronicity and burden to others are not included in the impact score. When respondents have answered "no" to the first question on the impact supplement (i.e. when they do not perceive themselves as having any emotional or behavioural difficulties), they are not asked to complete the questions on resultant distress or impairment; the impact score is automatically scored zero in these circumstances.

Although the impact scores can be used as continuous variables, it is sometimes convenient to classify them as normal, borderline or abnormal: a total impact score of 2 or more is abnormal; a score of 1 is borderline; and a score of 0 is normal.

# SDQ Record Sheet

Name ..................................... Age ........... Male/Female    Clinic/Study Number ............

SDQ completed by: PARENT on ...........................

                            TEACHER on .......................

                            SELF on .................................

| Scale | | Normal | | | Borderline | Abnormal | | |
|---|---|---|---|---|---|---|---|---|
| **Total difficulties** | P | 0 1 2   4 5 6 7 8 9 10 11 12 13 | | | 14 15 16 | 17 18 19 20 21 22 23 24 25 ...... 40 | | |
| | T | 0 1 2 3 4 5 6 7 8 9 10 11 | | | 12 13 14 15 | 16 17 18 19 20 21 22 23 24 ..... 40 | | |
| | S | 0 2 4 6 8 10 11 12 13 14 15 | | | 16 17 18 19 | 20 21 22 23 24 25 ...... 40 | | |
| **Emotional sympt.** | P | 0       1       2       3 | | | 4 | 5    6    7    8    9    10 | | |
| | T | 0    1    2    3    4 | | | 5 | 6    7    8    9    10 | | |
| | S | 0    1    2    3    4    5 | | | 6 | 7    8    9    10 | | |
| **Conduct problems** | P | 0       1       2 | | | 3 | 4  5  6  7  8  9  10 | | |
| | T | 0       1       2 | | | 3 | 4  5  6  7  8  9  10 | | |
| | S | 0    1       2       3 | | | 4 | 5  6  7  8  9  10 | | |
| **Hyperactivity** | P | 0  1  2  3  4  5 | | | 6 | 7    8    9    10 | | |
| | T | 0  1  2  3  4  5 | | | 6 | 7    8    9    10 | | |
| | S | 0  1  2  3  4  5 | | | 6 | 7    8    9    10 | | |
| **Peer problems** | P | 0       1       2 | | | 3 | 4  5  6  7  8  9  10 | | |
| | T | 0    1    2    3 | | | 4 | 5  6  7  8  9  10 | | |
| | S | 0    1    2    3 | | 4    5 | 6  7    8    9    10 | | |
| **Prosocial behav.** | P | 10    9    8    7    6 | | | 5 | 4    3    2    1    0 | | |
| | T | 10    9    8    7    6 | | | 5 | 4    3    2    1    0 | | |
| | S | 10    9    8    7    6 | | | 5 | 4    3    2    1    0 | | |

# Appendix 2

# The TOAD system

See chapter 13 for further details.

Teacher: _____     Date: _____

Activity: _____     Time begin: _____ Time end: _____

Observer: _____     Location: _____

Interval: ____15 seconds ____30 seconds

____45 seconds ____60 seconds

____other

| INTERVAL | T | | | O | | | A | | | D | | |
|---|---|---|---|---|---|---|---|---|---|---|---|---|
| | Pupil 1 | Pupil 2 | Pupil 3 | Pupil 1 | Pupil 2 | Pupil 3 | Pupil 1 | Pupil 2 | Pupil 3 | Pupil 1 | Pupil 2 | Pupil 3 |
| | | | | | | | | | | | | |
| | | | | | | | | | | | | |
| | | | | | | | | | | | | |
| | | | | | | | | | | | | |
| | | | | | | | | | | | | |
| | | | | | | | | | | | | |
| | | | | | | | | | | | | |
| | | | | | | | | | | | | |
| | | | | | | | | | | | | |
| | | | | | | | | | | | | |
| | | | | | | | | | | | | |
| | | | | | | | | | | | | |
| | | | | | | | | | | | | |
| | | | | | | | | | | | | |

# OPERATIONAL DEFINITIONS OF BEHAVIOURS IN THE TOAD SYSTEM

1. Talking out: spoken words, either friendly, neutral, or negative in content, directed at either the teacher without first obtaining permissions to speak or unsolicited at classmates during inappropriate times or during work periods.
2. Out of seat: the child is not supporting his weight with the chair. Up on knees does not count as out of seat behaviour.
3. Attention problem: the child is not attending either to independent work or to a group activity. The child is therefore engaged in an activity other than that which has been directed and is clearly different from what the other children are doing at the time. This includes the child not following teacher directions.
4. Disruption: the child's actions result in consequences that appear to be interrupting other children's work. These behaviours might include noises or physical contact. They may be intentional or unintentional.

TOAD system. From Goldstein, S and Goldstein, M (1990), *Managing Attention Disorders in Children: A guide for practitioners*, John Wiley and Sons, Inc, New York. Used with permission.

# References

ACT Schools Authority (1983) *Working Party to Examine the Provision of Services for Emotionally Disturbed and Behaviourally Disturbed Pupils in the ACT School System*, unpublished report

Adler, A (1932) *What Life Should Mean to You*, Allen & Unwin, Sydney

Amatae, E (1988) Brief systemic interventions with school behavior problems: a case of temper tantrums, *Psychology in the Schools*, **25**, 174–83

Andersen, T (1990) *The Reflecting Team: Dialogues and dialogues about dialogues*, Borgman, Broadstairs, Kent

Aronson, E (1998) *The Social Animal*, Freeman, San Francisco

Balson, M (1987) *Understanding Classroom Behaviour* ACER, Melbourne

Barr, J (1994) Policy frameworks and planning, in P Munn *Schooling with Care*, SCRE, Edinburgh

Barkley, R (1990) *ADHD: A Handbook for assessment and treatment*, Guilford, New York

Bateson, G (1972) *Steps to an Ecology of Mind*, Chandler, New York

Bateson, G (1979) *Mind and Nature: A necessary unity*, Dutton, New York

Beard, R (1969) *An Outline of Piaget's Developmental Psychology*, Routledge and Kegan Paul, London

Bennathan, M and Boxall, M (1996) *Effective Intervention in Primary Schools: Nurture groups*, Fulton, London

Blagg, N (1987) *School Phobia and its Treatment*, Croom Helm, New York

Blau, G and Brumer, D (1996) Comments on adolescent behavior problems: developing coordinated systems of care, in G Blau and T Gullotta (eds) *Adolescent Dysfunctional Behavior*, Sage, London

Blau, G and Gullotta, T (eds) (1996) *Adolescent Dysfunctional Behavior*, Sage, London,

Bolton, R (1986) *People Skills*, Prentice Hall, Sydney

Bowlby, J (1975) *Attachment and Loss*, Penguin, London

BPS (2000) *ADHD: Guidelines and principles for successful multi-agency working*, BPS, Leicester

Bronfenbrenner, U (1979) *The Ecology of Human Development*, Harvard University Press, Cambridge, MS

Brophy, J and Evertson, C (1976) *Learning from Teaching: A developmental perspective*, Allyn and Bacon, Boston

Brown, JE (1986) The pretend technique: an intervention in the teacher–student system, *Family Therapy Case Studies*, **1**, 13–15

Brown, S and McIntyre, D (1993) *Making Sense of Teaching*, Open University, Buckingham

Bruner, J (1987) The transactional self, in J Bruner and H Haste (eds) *Making Sense: The child's construction of the world*, Methuen, London

Bruner, J and Haste, H (eds) (1987) *Making Sense: The child's construction of the world*, Methuen, London

Bull, SL and Solity, JE (1987) *Classroom Management: Principles to practice*, Croom Helm, North Ryde

Campion, J (1985) *The Child in Context: Family systems theory in educational psychology*, Methuen, London

Canter, L (1976) *Assertive Discipline: A take charge approach for today's educator*, Lee Canter and associates, Los Angeles

Charles, C M (1996) *Building Classroom Discipline: From models to practice*, 5th edn, Longman, New York

Charlton, T (1996) Where is control located? in K Jones and T Charlton (eds) *Overcoming Learning and Behaviour Difficulties*, Routledge, London

Charlton, T and David, K (1996) *Educating Pupils with Learning and Behavioural Difficulties*, Routledge, London

Clandinin, J (1986) *Classroom Practice: Teachers' images in action*, Falmer, Lewes

Cooper, P (1993a) Learning from the pupil perspective, *British Journal of Special Education*, **20** (4), 129–33

Cooper, P (1993b) *Effective Schools for Disaffected Students*, Routledge, London

Cooper, P (1996) Giving it a name: the value of descriptive categories in educational approaches to emotional and behavioural difficulties, *Support for Learning*, **11**, 146–50

Cooper, P (1999) Educating children with emotional and behavioural difficulties: the evolution of current thinking and provision, in P Cooper (ed) *Understanding and Supporting Children with Emotional and Behavioural Difficulties*, Jessica Kingsley, London

Cooper, P, Drummond, M, Hart, S, Lovey, J and McLaughlin, C (2000) *Positive Alternatives to Exclusion*, Routledge, London

Cooper, P and Ideus, K (1996) *ADHD: A practical guide for teachers*, Fulton, London

Cooper, P and McIntyre, D (1996) *Effective Teaching and Learning: Teachers' and students' perceptions*, Open University, Buckingham

Cooper, P and Upton, G (1991) An ecosystemic approach to emotional and behavioural difficulties, *Educational Psychology*, **8** (4), 301–21

Coopersmith, S (1967) *The Antecedents of Self Esteem*, WH Freeman, San Francisco

Daniels, H, Visser, J, Cole, T and Reykebill, N (1999) *Emotional and Behavioural Difficulties in Mainstream Schools*, DFEE, London

Dare, C (1985) The psychodynamic theory of children with emotional and behavioural difficulties, in V Varma (ed) *The Management of Children with Emotional and Behavioural Difficulties*, Routledge, London

Davie, R, Upton, G and Varma, V (1996) *The Voice of the Child*, Falmer, London

de Shazer, S (1982) *Patterns of Brief Family Therapy: An ecosystemic approach*, Guilford, New York

de Shazer, S (1985) *Keys to Solution*, Norton, New York

de Waal, F (1982) *Chimpanzee Politics: Power and sex among apes*, Unwin, London

de Waal, F (1989) *Peacemaking Among Primates*, Penguin, London

Dearing, R (1996) *Review of the National Curriculum*, NCC, York

DES, (1989) *Discipline in Schools (The Elton Report)*, HMSO, London

DfEE (1999) *Draft Guideline on Social Inclusion*, DFEE, London

Dowling, E and Osborne, E (eds) (1995) *The Family and the School*, 2nd edn, Routledge, London

Dreikurs, R, Grunwald, B and Pepper, F (1982) *Maintaining Sanity in the Classroom*, 2nd edn, Harper and Row, New York

Druian, G and Butler, J (1987) *Effective Schooling and At-risk Youth: What the record shows*, Northwest Regional Educational Laboratory, Portland, Ore

Edgar, D (1989) *Seen But Not Heard*, Collins Dove, Blackburn, Vic

Edwards, J and Jones-Young, K (1992) The importance of families, *Phi Delta Kappan*, **73**, 65–70

Epston, D (1988) It is frightening for a five-year-old to overpower his parents, *Australia and New Zealand Journal of Family Therapy*, **9**, 116

Evertson, C and Emmer, E (1982) Effective management at the beginning of the school year in junior high classes, *Journal of Educational Psychology*, **74**, 485–98

Eysenck, H and Eysenck, M (1981) *Mindwatching*, Michael Joseph, London

French, J Jr and Raven, B (1960) The bases for social power, in D Cartwright and A Zander (eds) *Group Dynamics: Research and theory*, Harper and Row, New York

Frith, U (1992) Cognitive development and cognitive deficit, *The Psychologist*, **5**, 13–19

Fullan, M (1998) *Successful School Improvement*, Open University, Buckingham

Garner, P (1996) Involving pupils in policy development, in K Jones and T Charlton (eds) *Overcoming Learning and Behaviour Difficulties*, Routledge, London

Garner, P (1999) *Pupils with Problems: Rational fears, radical solutions*, Trentham, Stoke-on-Trent

Glasser, W (1986) *Control Theory in the Classroom*, Perennial Library, New York

Glasser, W (1993) *Control Theory: A new explanation of how we control our lives*, Perennial Library, New York

Goldstein, AP, Sprafkin, RP, Gershaw, NJ and Klein, P (1980) *Skill Streaming the Adolescent: A structured learning approach to teaching pro-social skills*, Research Press, Illinois

Goldstein, SD (1995) *Understanding and Managing Children's Classroom Behaviour*, John Wiley and Sons, Chichester

Good, T and Brophy, J (1973) *Looking at Classrooms*, Harper and Row, New York

Goodman, J (1997) The strengths and difficulties questionnaire: a research note, *Journal of Child Psychiatry and Psychology*, **38** (8), 581–85

Goodman, R (1999) The extended version of the strengths and difficulties questionnaire as a guide to psychiatric caseness and consequent burden, *Journal of Child Psychology and Psychiatry*, **40** (5), 791–800

Graham, P (1991) *Child Psychiatry*, Oxford University Press, Oxford

Grundy and Blandford (1999) Developing a culture for positive behaviour management, *Emotional and Behavioural Difficulties*, **4** (3), 5–9

Guerin, Katz and Hsai (1984) The theory in therapy of families with school related problems: triangles and hypothesis testing, in B Okun (ed) *Family Therapy with School-related Problems*, Rockville, Aspen, CA

Haley, J (1979) *Leaving Home: Therapy with disturbed young people*, McGraw-Hill, New York

Haley, J (1987) *Problem-solving Therapy*, 2nd edn, Jossey-Bass, San Francisco

Hammill, P and Boyd, B (2001) in press

Happé, F (1994) *Autism*, Routledge, London

Hawkes, R (1982) Treatment of school refusal by strategic-based family therapy, *Australian Journal of Family Therapy*, **3**, 129–34

Hayden, C (1997) Exclusion from primary school: children in need and children with special educational need, *Emotional and Behavioural Difficulties*, **2** (3), 36–44

Hayden, C (2000) *Evaluation of a School and Family Support Team*, NFER, Slough

Heins, T (1996) Presenting rules to young children at school, *Australian Journal of Early Childhood*, **21** (7), 7–11

Henggeler, S (1999) Multisystemic therapy: an overview of clinical procedures, outcomes and policy implications, *Child Psychology and Psychiatry Review*, **4** (1), 2–10

Henggeler, SW and Borduin, CM (1990) *Family Therapy and Beyond: A systemic approach to teaching the behaviour problems of children and adolescents*, Brooks/Cole, Pacific Grove, CA

Hill, P and Cameron, M (1999) Recognising hyperactivity: a guide for the cautious clinician, *Child Psychology and Psychiatry Review*, **4** (1), 50–60

Hoffman, L (1981) *The Foundations of Family Therapy*, Basic Books, New York

Hooper, D and Whyld, K (1992) *The Oxford Companion to Chess*, Oxford University Press, Oxford

Horney, K (1972) *Our Inner Conflicts: A constructive theory of neurosis*, Norton, New York

Howell, K, Fox, SL and Morehead, MK (1993) *Curriculum-based Evaluation: Teaching and decision making* 2nd edn, Brooks/Cole, Pacific Grove, CA

Johnson, D, Johnson, R, Holubec, E and Roy, D (1984) *Circles of Learning: Co-operation in the classroom*, Association for Supervision and Curriculum Development, Alexandria, VA

Jones, F (1987) *Positive Classroom Discipline*, McGraw-Hill, New York

Jones, V and Jones, L (1990) *Comprehensive Classroom Management: Motivating and managing students*, 3rd edn, Allyn and Bacon, Boston

Kazdin, A (1998) Psychosocial treatments for conduct disorder in children, in P Nathan and J Gorman (eds) *A Guide to Treatments that Work*, Oxford University Press, Oxford

Kendall, PC and Braswell, L (1993) *Cognitive-behavioural Therapy for Impulsive Children* 2nd edn, Guilford, New York

Keys, W and Ferandes, N (1993) *What do Students Really Think about School?* NFER, Slough

Kounin, J (1970) *Discipline and Group Management in Classrooms*, Holt, Rinehart and Winston, New York

Krebs, JR and Davies, NB (1981) *An Introduction to Behavioural Ecology*, Blackwell Scientific, Oxford

Lazerson, DB, Foster, HL, Braun, SI, Hummel, JW (1988) The effectiveness of cross-age tutoring with truant, junior high school students with learning disabilities, *Journal of Learning Disabilities*, **4**, 253–55

Lea, SEG (1984) *Instinct, Environment and Behaviour*, Methuen, London

Lewis, R (1991) *The Discipline Dilemma*, ACER, Hawthorn, Vic

Lewis, R and Lovegrove, M (1984) Teachers' classroom control procedures: are students preferences being met? *Journal of Research for Teaching*, **10** (2), 97–105

Lindquist, B, Molnar, A and Brauchmann, L (1987) Working with school-related problems without going to school: considerations for systemic practice, *Journal of Strategic and Systemic Therapies*, **6** (4), 44–50

Lovey, J and Cooper, P (1997) Positive alternatives to exclusion from school, *Emotional and Behavioural Difficulties*, **2** (3), 17–23

Lovey, J, Docking, J and Evans, R (1993) *Exclusion from School: Provision for disaffection at Key Stage 4*, Fulton, London

Lucas, S (1999) The nurturing school: the impact of nurture group principles and practice in the whole school, *Emotional and Behavioural Difficulties*, 4 (3), 14–19

Lund, R (1995) Curriculum liaison between special and mainstream schools, in P Cooper (ed) *Helping them to Learn: Curriculum entitlement for children with EBD*, NASEN, Stafford

MacPherson, EM, Candee, BL and Hohman, J (1974) A comparison of three methods for eliminating disruptive lunchroom behavior, *Journal of Applied Behaviour Analysis*, **7**, 287–97

Madanes, C (1981) *Strategic Family Therapy*, Jossey-Bass, San Francisco

Maslow, A (1970) *Motivation and Personality*, Harper and Row, New York

McKay, J (1994) Policy framework and policy planning, in P Munn (ed) *Schooling with Care*, Scottish Office, Edinburgh

McManus, M (1989) *Troublesome Behaviour in the Classroom*, Routledge, London

McManus, M (1994) Classroom management, natural virtues and the education of children with emotional and behavioural difficulties, *Therapeutic Care and Education*, 3 (1), 49–62

Minuchin, S (1974) *Families and Family Therapy*, Harvard University Press, Cambridge, MA

Minuchin, S (1992) *Families and Family Therapy*, Harvard University Press, Cambridge, MA

Molnar, A and Lindquist, B (1989) *Changing Problem Behavior*, Jossey-Bass, San Francisco

Mortimore, P, Sammons, P, Stoll, L, Lewis, D and Ecob, R (1988) *School Matters*, Open Books, Wells

Munger, RL (1993) *Changing Children's Behaviour Quickly*, Madison, Lanham, MD

Munn, P (1994) The role of the learning support teacher in Scottish primary and secondary classrooms, in S Brown and S Riddell (eds) *Special Educational Needs in the 1990s*, Routledge, London

Okun, B (1984) Family therapy and the schools, in B Okun (ed) *Family Therapy with School Related Problems*, Rockville, Aspen, CA

Olsen J (1982) Duffield Place, unpublished report

Olsen, J (1989a) Duffield Place – The Duffield Place program – A framework for helping acting-out children, *Australian Journal of Remedial Education*, **21**, 12–17

Olsen, J (1989b) Red herrings and school refusal, *Australian Journal of Family Therapy*, **10**, 196

Olsen, J (1990) Bagging a case of school refusal, *Australian Journal of Family Therapy*, **11**, 183–84

Olsen, J (1992) Using O-LADS to structure a classroom discipline plan, in B Willis and J Izard (eds) *Student Behaviour Problems: Directions, perspectives, expectations*, ACER, Hawthorn, Victoria

Olsen, J (1993) The Power–Caring balance: can ecology help us understand the behaviour of troubled children? in D Evans, M Myhill and J Izard (eds) *Student Behaviour Problems: Positive initiatives and new frontiers*, ACER, Hawthorne, Vic

Olsen, J (1994) Responding to gambits that children use to disrupt classrooms, in M Tainsh and J Izard (eds) *Widening Horizons: New challenges, directions and achievements*, pp. 166–75 ACER, Camberwell, Victoria

Olsen, J (1997a) *Working with Troubled Students*, Author, Canberra

Olsen, J (1997b) *Managing Classroom Gambits: Working with difficult classes in schools* Author, Canberra

Olsen, J and Nathan, G (1987) On breaking the Chernobyl habit: school-based family counselling for aggressive children, *Family Therapy Case Studies*, **2**, 41–49

Parsons, C (1999) *Education, Exclusion and Citizenship*, Routledge, London

Patterson, G, Reid, J and Dishion, T (1992) *Antisocial Boys vol 4*, Casralia, Eugene, OR

Pringle, M (1975) *The Needs of Children*, Hutchinson, London

Provis, M (1994) *Dealing with Difficulty*, Hodder and Stoughton, London

Purkey, S and Smith, M (1983) Effective schools: a review, *Elementary School Journal*, **83** (4), 427–52

Reiber, R and Carton, A (1987) *The Collected Works of LS Vygotsky*, Plenum, London

Rose, S (1997) *Lifelines: Biology, freedom, determinism*, Penguin, London

Rosser, P and Harré, R (1976) The meaning of trouble, in M Hammersley and P Woods (eds) *The Process of Schooling*, Open University, Buckingham

Rutter, M, Maughan, B, Mortimore, P and Ouston, J (1979) *Fifteen Thousand Hours*, Open, London

Rutter, M and Smith, D (eds) (1995) *Psychosocial Disorders in Young People*, John Wiley and Sons, Chichester

Satir, V (1972) *Conjoint Family Therapy*, 3rd edn, Science and Behaviour Books, Palo Alto, CA

Sattin, R (1999) Effective EBD schooling: a view from the inside, *Emotional and Behavioural Difficulties*, **4** (3), 10–13

Schostak, J (1982) *Maladjusted Schooling*, Falmer, Lewes

Seligman, M (1990) *Learned Optimism*, Random House, Sydney

Seligman, M (1995) *The Optimistic Child*, Random House, Sydney

Selvini-Palazzoli, M, Boscolo, L, Cecchin, G and Prata, G (1973) *Paradox and Counter-Paradox*, Aronson, New York

Shachdev, D (1996) *The Blackford Brae Project*, Barnardo's, London

Shachdev, D (1999) *The Linksfield Project*, Barnardo's, London

Shavelson, R, Webb, N and Burstein, L (1986) *Measurement of teaching*, in M Wittrock (ed) *Handbook of Research on Teaching*, Macmillan, London

Sherif, M (1956) Experiments in group conflict, *Scientific American*, **195**, 54–58

Slee, P (1992) Peer victimisation at school: you can run but you can't hide, paper presented at the 1992 National Conference on Student Behaviour Problems, Canberra

Slee, R (1998) The politics of special education, in C Clark, A Dyson and A Millward (eds) *Theorising Special Education*, Routledge, London

Smith, CJ and Laslett, R (1993) *Effective Classroom Management: A teacher's guide*, Routledge, London

Stevens, A and Price, J (1996) *Evolutionary Psychiatry: A new beginning*, Routledge, London

Stokes, T and Baer, D (1977) The implicit technology of generalisation, *Journal of Applied Behavioral Analysis*, **10**, 349–67

Sulzer-Azaroff, B and Mayer, RG (1977) *Applying Behavior Analysis Procedures with Children and Youth*, Holt, Rinehart and Winston, Sydney

Swenson, CC, Henggeler, SW, Schoenwald, SK, Kaufman, KL and Randall, J (1998) Changing the social ecologies of adolescent sexual offenders: implications of the success of Multisystemic Therapy in treating serious antisocial behaviour in adolescents, *Child Maltreatment*, **3**, 330–38

Tattum, D (1982) *Disruptive Pupils in Schools and Units*, John Wiley and Sons, Chichester

Tauber, RT (1986) French and Raven's power bases: a focus for educational researchers and practitioners, *The Australian Journal of Education*, **30** (3), 256–65

Tauber, RT (1995) *Classroom Management: Theory and practice*, Harcourt Brace, Fort Worth, TX

Tom, A (1984) *Teaching as a Moral Craft*, Methuen, London

von Bertalanffy, L (1950) The theory of open systems in physics and biology, *Science*, **3**, 25–29

von Bertalanffy, L (1968) *General System Theory*, Brazillier, New York

Walker, H, Colvin, G and Ramsey, E (1995) *Antisocial Behavior in School: Strategies and best practices*, Brooks/Cole, London

Wheldall, K (ed) 1987) *The Behaviourist in the Classroom*, London, Allen and Unwin

White, M (1986) Negative explanation, restraint, and double description: a template for family therapy, *Family Process*, **25**, 109–83

Williams, J and Weeks, G (1984) The use of paradoxical techniques in a school setting, *American Journal of Family Therapy*, **12** (3), 47–57

Willis, P (1977) *Learning to Labour*, Saxon House, London

Wilson, E (1975) *Sociobiology: A new synthesis*, Belknap Press, Cambridge, MS and London

Worden, M (1981) Classroom behavior as a function of the family system, *School Counsellor*, **8** (3), 178–88

Yell, M, Drasgow, E and Rosalski, M (1999) Violence in America's schools: legal and disciplinary options, *Emotional and Behavioural Difficulties*, **4** (1), 19–27

Young Minds (1999) *Fact Sheet No. 1*, Young Minds

# Index